STUDIES IN EVANGELICAL HISTORY AND THOUGHT

Apostles of the Spirit and Fire

American Revivalists and Victorian Britain

STUDIES IN EVANGELICAL HISTORY AND THOUGHT

Apostles of the Spirit and Fire

American Revivalists and Victorian Britain

Nigel Scotland

WIPF & STOCK · Eugene, Oregon

Wipf and Stock Publishers
199 W 8th Ave, Suite 3
Eugene, OR 97401

Apostles of the Spirit and Fire
American Revivalists and Victorian Britain
By Scotland, Nigel
Copyright©2009 Paternoster
ISBN 13: 978-1-60899-166-2
Publication date 10/15/2009
Previously published by Paternoster, 2009

This Edition published by Wipf and Stock Publishers by arrangement with Paternoster

STUDIES IN EVANGELICAL HISTORY AND THOUGHT

Series Preface

The Evangelical movement has been marked by its union of four emphases: on the Bible, on the cross of Christ, on conversion as the entry to the Christian life and on the responsibility of the believer to be active. The present series is designed to publish scholarly studies of any aspect of this movement in Britain or overseas. Its volumes include social analysis as well as exploration of Evangelical ideas. The books in the series consider aspects of the movement shaped by the Evangelical Revival of the eighteenth century, when the impetus to mission began to turn the popular Protestantism of the British Isles and North America into a global phenomenon. The series aims to reap some of the rich harvest of academic research about those who, over the centuries, have believed that they had a gospel to tell to the nations.

Series Editors

David Bebbington, Professor of History, University of Stirling, Stirling, Scotland, UK

John H.Y. Briggs, Senior Research Fellow in Ecclesiastical History and Director of the Centre for Baptist History and Heritage, Regent's Park College, Oxford, UK

Timothy Larsen, McManis Professor Christian Thought, Wheaton College, Illinois, USA

Mark A. Noll, McAnaney Professor of History, University of Notre Dame, Notre Dame, Indiana, USA

Ian M. Randall, Senior Research Fellow, International Baptist Theological Seminary, Prague, Czech Republic

To my wife, Liz,
for her loving support and patience

Contents

List of Illustrations	xv
Preface	xvii
Acknowledgements	xxi
Chapter 1 Revivalist Religion	1
The Beginnings of American Revivalism	2
Revivalism as a Category	8
Literalism	8
Supernaturalism	10
Emotionalism	11
Conversionism	13
Laicism	14
Radicalism	15
The Raised Status of Women	15
Labour Movements	16
Anti-Slavery	16
Temperance	17
Adventism	17
The Continuing Appeal of American Revivalism	19
The Churches Needed Reviving	19
Doubts Needed Counteracting	22
Christian Influence Needed Recovering	23
Chapter 2 Lorenzo Dow and Camp Meeting Revivalism	27
Ireland and His Break with Methodism	29
Camp Meetings	31
Dow's Marriage to Peggy Holcomb	32
Dow's Later Travels and Literary Endeavours	35
'Crazy Dow': A Reputation Deserved	36
Dow's Understanding of Revival and His Impact in England	39
Camp Meetings	40
Gatherings for Mourners	43
Blunt Preaching	44
Revival Songs	45

Religious Exercises	45
Publicity and House-to-House Visiting	46
Postscript	47

Chapter 3 Zilpha Elaw and Reformist Revivalism — 49
Sanctified and Called to Minister	50
Ministry in England	56
Zilpha Elaw and Revival	60
The Holy Spirit	60
Preaching	60
Follow Up	61
House to House	61
Holiness	62
Justice and Slavery	62
Impacting the Culture	63
Conclusion	64
Zilpha's Last Years	65

Chapter 4 Charles Finney and the Beginnings of Professional Revivalism — 67
Campaigns in the North-Eastern States 1824–32	69
The Importance of Prayer	70
In-Your-Face Preaching	71
The Practice of Identifying Converts	72
The Remarkable Presence of God	73
Pastorate in New York City	74
Oberlin College 1835–75 and a Place for Women	75
Visits to England	77
Finney's Preaching and Writing	80
Finney's Final Days	80
Finney's Understanding of Revival	81
A Human Endeavour	81
Revivals Can Be Promoted	82
Concern for Social Justice	83
Finney's Preaching	84
The 'Protracted Meeting' and the 'Anxious Seat'	85
Publicity and Music	86
The Use of Independent Meeting Places	87
A New Understanding of Revival	87

Chapter 5 James Caughey and Holiness and Temperance Revivalism — 91
Early Days	91
Early Labours in America and the British Isles 1840–7	92
Campaigning in Britain	95

Caughey and the Meaning of Revival	99
Sanctification	101
Revival Methods	104
Preaching	104
Direct Words to Particular Individuals	107
Immediate Decisions and After Meetings	108
Prayer Gatherings	110
Answering His Critics Openly	111
Publicity	111
Follow Up	112
Caughley's Significance as a Revivalist	113
Chapter 6 Walter and Phoebe Palmer (1807–74) and Holiness Revivalism	**117**
The Context of Holiness	117
Marriage and Early Christian Experience	117
Phoebe's Publications	118
The Palmers' Influence	119
Phoebe Palmer, Sarah Lankford and Sanctification	120
Phoebe Palmer's Theology	122
Revival Campaigns in North America and Britain	124
Phoebe Palmer's Understanding of Revival	127
Revival as Sanctification	127
Revival Methods	129
Drink and Dealing with Evil	130
The Role of Women in the Church	132
Visiting Prisoners, the Poor and the Sick	134
Anti-Slavery	134
Benevolent and Mission Societies	135
The Impact of the Palmers	135
Chapter 7 Dwight L. Moody and Urban Revivalism	**139**
Christian Work in Chicago	139
Moody and the Civil War	141
Marriage to Emma Revell	142
Trial by Fire	142
Baptism in the Holy Spirit	143
Moody Joins Forces with Ira Sankey	143
Moody's Campaigns in the British Isles	144
Moody's Appeal	147
Later Years	150
Revival and Revivalism	151
Revival Methods	152
Preaching	152

Confidence in the Bible 154
Music and Song 154
Prayer 156
The Inquiry Room 157
All Day Meetings 159
Publicity 159
His Interdenominational Sympathies 160
The Poor 161
Style and Lifestyle 162
Moody's Impact 162

Chapter 8 Edward Payson Hammond and Children's Revivalism **165**
Early Years 165
London and the Children's Special Service Mission 170
Work in America 173
Hammond's Revival Methods 175
   Union Meetings 175
   Pressure for Decisions 177
   The Work with Children 179
   The Personal Question 181
   The Use of Hymns and Songs 181
   The Covenant 182
   Hammond's Tracts and Books 184
An Assessment of Hammond's Labours 185

Chapter 9 Amanda Berry Smith and Holiness and Singing Revivalism **187**
Early Years 187
Marriage and Conversion 188
Sanctification 190
Call to Public Preaching 191
Camp Meetings 192
Call to England 192
India, Africa and a Return to England 195
Revival Methodology 195
   Full Salvation 196
   Singing 197

Chapter 10 Robert and Hannah Pearsall Smith and 'Higher Life' Revivalism **199**
Early Years to 1865 199
Their Quaker Upbringing 199
Discovering the 'Higher Christian Life' 202
   Personal Faith and Baptism 202

Holiness Camp Meetings	203
The Essence of 'Higher Christian Life' Teaching	205
Revival Years 1865–75	207
Meetings in America	207
Robert's Breakdown	208
Ministry in England and Europe 1873–5	209
The Broadlands Conference July 1874	209
The Oxford Conference 29 August – 7 September 1874	210
Robert Preaches in Europe	211
The Brighton Convention 28 May – 7 June 1875	212
The First Keswick Convention and Robert's Fall from Grace June 1875	213
Robert and Hannah in America 1875–89	214
Last Years in England 1888–1911	215

Chapter 11 The Impact of American Revivalism — 217

Individual Contributions	217
Moody and Sankey: A Watershed in American Revivalism	220
A Stimulus to British Revivalism	221
Greater Parochial Concern	223
Encouragement to Foreign Missions	224
Stimulus to Radicalism	225
Enduring Legacy	226

Bibliography — 227

Index — 233

List of Illustrations

Lorenzo Dow	29
Zilpha Elaw	51
Charles Finney	70
James Caughey	93
Phoebe Palmer	119
Dwight L. Moody	144
Revd Edward Payson Hammond	167
Amanda Berry Smith	193
Hannah Pearsall Smith about the time of her marriage	201
Robert Pearsall Smith	211

Preface

This is a book about American revivalist religion and the ways in which it impacted British Christianity in nineteenth-century England. The term 'revivalist' seems to have first been used in the period after the 'Second Great Awakening' in the United States. It designated those individuals and churches who sought to manufacture or create revival by human endeavour rather than, as in former times, pray and wait for a sovereign move of God's Spirit. Revivalism had a number of marked features which are charted in detail in chapter 1. It was invariably characterized by emotion, excitement and religious exercises.

In both America and Britain at the beginning of the nineteenth century revival was still, for the most part, seen as a gracious sovereign outpouring of the Spirit of God in response to earnest prayer and seeking after God. That said however, the evangelical movement that had been inspired by John and Charles Wesley had done two things. First, it had set in motion a forceful antidote to Calvin's predestinarian theology which had strongly impacted British Protestantism since the Reformation, although it should perhaps be noted that the Church of England Article 17 had studiously sought to avoid the pitfalls of the double decree. Second, not only had the Methodist Arminian gospel impacted the established church, it had also begun to persuade many Baptists and Congregationalists to put energy into evangelising, in some cases with a new vigour.

In 1770 Dan Taylor (1738–1816) had formed a New Connexion General Baptist group. They reported a membership of 5,471 with 58 churches and 339 baptisms for the year 1810. By the time of their centenary they numbered 20,488 with 153 churches.[1] In 1792 William Carey (1761–1834) had preached to Baptists in Nottingham on the theme: 'Expect great things from God; attempt great things for God'. It was soon after this that the Baptist Missionary Society was formed marking the beginning of the modern foreign missionary movement in the English-speaking world. Carey, who became the society's first missionary, was a remarkable man and one of the first fruits of his zeal for study was his treatise entitled *An Inquiry into the obligations of Christians to use Means for the Conversion of the Heathen* (1792). The title was indicative of the fact that Carey and others like him were beginning to break free from the hyper-Calvinism of the day that had convinced many that the conversion of the

---

1 A.C. Underwood, *A History of the English Baptists* (Kingsgate Press, 1947), p. 214.

heathen was the Lord's own sovereign work and that no human endeavour could do anything to hasten it into being. Ernest Payne pointed out that though most Dissenters in the later eighteenth century were Calvinists they were not uninfluenced by the revival of evangelical interest and activity.[2] He noted that George Whitefield, though an ordained clergyman of the Church of England, was often welcomed by the Dissenters and that the chapels which he established with the Countess of Huntingdon became closely associated with the older dissenting bodies.[3]

More recently Richard Carwardine suggested that English theology rejected 'high Calvinism' largely as a result of the influence of the Wesleyan revivals.[4] One practical consequence of this was that it led to the Congregationalists establishing 500 new chapels between 1800–30.[5]

The influence of the Wesleys had prepared and made British Christians more open to receive the revivalism which was emerging in the wake of the 'Second Great Awakening' in the southern states of America, particularly from the great camp meetings at Gasper River in 1800 and Red River.[6] Whilst it was the case that these gatherings appeared to be a sovereign move of God, the leaders had begun to use human means to stimulate and assist the revival. These included action sermons,[7] the use of exhorters[8] and more particularly the emphasis on camp meetings.[9] Iain Murray noted that by 1812 it was estimated that at least four hundred Methodist camp meetings, large and small, were held annually in the United States.[10] Primitive Methodism which was largely a rural movement was perhaps the first significant expression of nineteenth-century English revivalism. It had a spontaneous aspect but its founders Hugh Bourne and William Clowes both studied the ways in which revivals 'could be got up'. Indeed it was the case that Primitive Methodism was developed in large measure as a result of visits from Lorenzo Dow who had himself participated in the activities of the frontier and was a great promoter of camp meetings.[11]

---

2   E.A. Payne, 'Toleration and Establishment: A Historical Outline', in G.F. Nutall and O. Chadwick (eds.), *From Uniformity to Unity 1662–1962* (SPCK, 1962), pp. 267–8.
3   Payne, 'Toleration and Establishment', p. 268.
4   R. Carwardine, *Transatlantic Revivalism: Popular Evangelicalism in Britain and America 1790–1865* (Greenwood Press, 1978), p. 60.
5   Carwardine, *Tranatlantic Revivalism*, p. 60.
6   See, for example, C.C. Cleveland, *The Great Revival in the West 1797–1805* (University of Chicago, 1916), p. 56.
7   Cleeveland, *The Great Revival in the West*, p. 184.
8   Cleeveland, *The Great Revival in the West*, p. 183.
9   Cleeveland, *The Great Revival in the West*, p. 58.
10 I.H. Murray, *Revival and Revivalism: The Making and Marring of American Evangelicalism* (The Banner of Trust Trust, 1994), p. 183.
11 See L. Dow, *The Dealings of God, Man, and the Devil: as exemplified in the Life, Experience, and Travels of Lorenzo Dow* (1860).

Preface

Reflecting on the Wesleyan Conference's pronouncement against camp meetings H.B. Kendall in his history of Primitive Methodism noted that 'it is not camp meetings in themselves that are objected to' but the fact that they 'had come to be associated with Revivalism'.[12] In England other similar revivalist groups included 'Tent Methodists',[13] the 'Magic Methodists' of the Delamere Forest, the 'Bible Christians' of Cornwall and the 'Revivalist Methodists' of Derbyshire, Shropshire, Staffordshire and Leicestershire.[14] The Cornish group was much in the public eye thanks to the exploits of the legendary Billy Bray who built chapels and even started revival singing in the parish church of Baldu when the rector, William Haslam, was converted in the middle of his own sermon.

Professor John Kent contended that the publication of the Revd C.G. Colton's *History and Character of American Revivals of Religion* in 1832 marked a turning point for revivalism in Britain. In this book Colton advocated the new style revivalism which he stated was characterised by 'human instrumentality', 'systematic effort' and 'human calculation by the arithmetic of faith in God's arrangements'.[15] Richard Carwardine made more or less the same point but also underlined the fact that the book's publication coincided with the advent of cholera in London thus boosting its sales.[16] In light of the above, it seems to me that the date at which revivalism (as opposed to revival) became a feature of the British religious landscape was well before the 1830s. Whether or not that is the case, the fact is revivalist religion was a marked feature of nineteenth-century religious life and worship. Certainly from the 1840s onwards revivals were being organized in advance with publicity being sent out, and halls and theatres booked as venues. In Britain American revivalism probably reached its peak in 1875 with the campaigns of Moody and Sankey. This is a book which examines the impact of ten prominent American revivalists who held extended campaigns in nineteenth-century Britain. It considers what they understood by the term 'revival', the methods by which they sought to achieve it, and assesses their impact on British Christianity.

---

12 H.B. Kendall, *The Origin and History of the Primitive Methodist Church*, Vol. 1 (Dalton, 1907), p. 77.
13 See J.K. Lander, *Itinerant Temples: Tent Methodism 1814–1832* (Paternoster Press, 2003).
14 For the Revivalist Methodists, see Lander, *Itinerant Temples*, p. 222.
15 J.H.S. Kent, 'American Revivalism and England in the Nineteenth Century' (Past and Present Conference Papers, 1966), cited in I. Sellers, *Nineteenth-Century Nonconformity* (Edward Arnold, 1977), p. 31.
16 Carwardine, *Transatlantic Revivalism*, p. 82.

Acknowledgements

My debts are many and various, but I would like to express my grateful thanks to a number of people who have helped me at different points during this project. I am particularly grateful to the University of Gloucestershire who gave me a term's sabbatical leave which I was able to spend at Wheaton College, Illinois. There my wife and I were given a gracious and hospitable welcome by Professor Edith Blumhofer, Professor of History at Wheaton College, and Director of the Institute for the Study of American Evangelicalism. I also received much help from Lon Allison the Director, and members of his staff, at the Billy Graham Center which is on the Wheaton campus. They readily made the private papers and collections of a number of American revivalists available to me. The Center is also rich in relevant journals and biographies which have formed the basis of much of this study. Robert Lewis of Manchester University Library and Information Service, helped me to uncover details concerning the last years in England of the American revivalist, Zilpha Elaw. Dr Michael Breeley kindly opened up the Methodist collections at Wesley College, Bristol, on a number of occasions. I benefited considerably from interaction with a number of students in my course on Revival and Revivalism at Trinity College, Bristol. Their questionings helped to sharpen my focus on a number of the issues that are raised in this book.

Dr Ian Randall, Senior Research Fellow at the International Baptist Theological Seminary in Prague, Dr Lisa Nolland and Frank Booth very kindly read the manuscript and offered much helpful advice. Errors or wrong emphases are of course solely my own.

I am very grateful to Accompli for compiling the index and preparing the camera ready copy.

Finally and most importantly, I thank my wife, Liz, for her loving support and patience while I have spent many hours on this project.

Nigel Scotland
Honorary Research Fellow,
University of Gloucestershire
and Tutor, Trinity College, Bristol

CHAPTER 1

Revivalist Religion

Seventeenth-century United States of America had seen a 'Great Awakening' under Jonathan Edwards (1703–58) in 1735 in the town of Northampton, Massachusetts and in other parts of New England. Following on almost immediately[1] there had been a momentous move of God's Spirit under the preaching of George Whitefield (1714–70). These 'outpourings' Edwards and others who shared his views regarded as 'revivals'. For Edwards who wrote a classic piece entitled *The Distinguishing Marks of a Work of The Spirit of God* (1741), such revivals were so designated because they were sovereign works of God's Spirit in which men and women played only an insignificant part. Such revivals could not be predicted. They were 'surprising works of God' which could not be anticipated. As he put it in *The Distinguishing Marks*, 'The prophecies of Scripture give us reason to think that God has things to accomplish, which have never yet been seen …. The Holy Spirit is sovereign in his operation; and we know he uses a great variety.'[2]

After the Great Awakening died down there was a period of decline in American Christianity which lasted until the 1790s. At this point there emerged what became known as the 'Second Great Awakening' which has been seen as perhaps the most significant event in American religious history. Mark Noll wrote that 'The Second Great Awakening was the most influential revival of Christianity in the history of the United States' and again, 'From 1795 to about 1810 there was a broad and general rekindling of interest in Christianity throughout the country.'[3] It was in the wake of this that what has become known as revivalism first emerged.

---

1 Edwards reported in 1735 that 'We have about six hundred and twenty communicants, which include almost all our adult persons' and 'The church was very large before; but persons never thronged into it as they did in the late extraordinary time.' In the same year he reported, 'I hope that more than 300 souls were savingly brought home to Christ, in this town, in the space of half a year.' See J. Edwards, *A Narrative of Many Surprising Conversions,* 1737 (Banner of Truth Trust, 1991), pp. 18–19.
2 J. Edwards, *The Distinguishing Marks of a Work of the Spirit of God*, 1741 (Banner of Truth Trust), p. 89.
3 See M. Noll, *A History of Christianity in the United States and Canada* (Eerdmans, 1992), p. 166.

The Beginnings of American Revivalism

The 'Second Great Awakening' had its beginnings in Kentucky and Tennessee in 1795. Although Noll suggested that its impact lasted until at least 1810,[4] other scholars have urged that its influence was much longer and extended to as late as 1830. Certainly its impact was felt up to that time on other continents of the world. Andrew Reed and James Matheson wrote in 1835,[5] 'One of the most remarkable and extensive revivals ever known has passed over this people.'[6] This was a vigorous and vibrant revival which impacted all sections of the people and particularly those on the margins of frontier society. It began through large-scale camp and sacramental meetings but spilled over to impact many hundreds of local communities. It was at its strongest among the Baptists and Methodists and less well received by the Presbyterian and Congregationalists with their largely Calvinist convictions which made them suspicious of anything that appeared to be contrived by human endeavour.

This was a revival of the old time religion. There were awesome scenes never to be forgotten at Cane Ridge in August 1801, where a crowd estimated at between twenty and thirty thousand[7] gathered together for six or seven days. They would have continued longer but for lack of food. This revival was marked by what Barton Stone (1772–1844), who was the host minister, termed 'uncommon agitations'.[8] These included 'the falling exercise – the jerks – the dancing exercise – the barking exercise & co'.[9] Stone's understanding of these phenomena was that religion had sunk 'so low' and that 'carelessness so universally had prevailed' that 'nothing else could have arrested the attention of the world'.[10] Many of those who came to Cane Ridge lived in isolated places and experienced life in the raw surrounded by perilous circumstances, and it may well be that the religious exercises can be interpreted as Noll intimates as 'a powerful psychological release'.[11] Stone noted in his *Autobiography* that the soldiers returning from the War of Independence brought back with them 'many vices almost unknown to us before; as profane swearing, debauchery, drunkenness, gambling, quarrelling and fighting'.[12] 'Their influence in demoralising society', he wrote, 'was very great. These vices soon became general, and almost honourable.' However, it was not long before published

---

4 Noll, *A History of Christianity*.
5 See J. Kent, *Holding the Fort* (Epworth, 1978), p. 13.
6 A. Reed and J. Matheson, *A Narrative of the Visits to the American Churches by Deputies of the Congregational Union of England and Wales* (1835), Vol. 2, pp. 273–7, cited in Murray, *Revival and Revivalism*, p. 117.
7 See B.W. Stone, *A Short History of the Life of Barton Stone Written by Himself* (J.A. and U.P. Jones, 1847), p. 37.
8 Stone, *A Short History of the Life of Barton Stone*, p. 38.
9 Stone, *A Short History of the Life of Barton Stone*, p. 39.
10 Stone, *A Short History of the Life of Barton Stone*, p. 38.
11 Noll, *A History of Christianity*, p. 167.
12 Stone, *A Short History of the Life of Barton Stone*, p. 2.

accounts of their transformed lives began to reach British shores. People in the Old Country began to reason that if the American military and their unwholesome influence could be transformed through such meetings why not the British soldiers and the demoralising after-effects of the Napoleonic wars?

It wasn't only the ordinary citizens of the Southern States who were impacted by the Second Great Awakening. Its influence spread among the elite and Yale in particular was lastingly impacted with one third of the entire student body being converted in 1802 under the ministry of President Revd Timothy Dwight (1752–1817) who was the grandson of Jonathan Edwards. Away from the places of learning, others who had become sceptical through the influence of Deist thinking or perhaps by reading Paine's *Age of Reason* were captivated by the new moves in which there appeared to be direct divine intervention. In consequence many threw in their lot with the revivalists and endorsed and supported the social improvement campaigns for temperance, anti-slavery and educational reforms.

Regardless of how we interpret the phenomena of American frontier revivalism, the fact is that all the Protestant denominations witnessed a remarkable expansion in their membership between 1800 and 1810. The Presbyterian Church grew from 70,000 to 100,000. The denomination's General Assembly of 1803 remarked, 'There is scarcely a Presbytery under the care of the Assembly from which some pleasing intelligence has not been announced.'[13] Baptist membership rose more dramatically in the same period from 95,000 in 1800 to 160,000 in 1810.[14] Half their number was in the states of Virginia, North and South Carolina, Georgia and Kentucky.[15] The membership of the Methodist Episcopal Church totalled 104,070 in 1803[16] and by 1809 it had reached 163,038.[17] Inevitably accounts of the Cane Ridge and the Gaspar River sacramental meetings soon began to appear in the Methodist magazines in England. These together with accounts of the travels and ministry of men such as Francis Asbury and Thomas Coke prepared the way for American preachers to transport the revival to British shores. Indeed such writings helped to generate a high degree of expectancy in various towns, circuits and communities.

In the early part of the nineteenth century some clergy of a Calvinistic persuasion tried to drive a wedge between what had happened on the frontiers and elsewhere in the early nineteenth century, and the earlier awakenings that had occurred under the ministries of Edwards and Whitefield. Those in earlier times, they claimed, were a sovereign work of God, or to use Edwards' own words 'a surprising work of God'. In fact Jonathan Edwards believed implicitly

---

13 Murray, *Revival and Revivalism*, pp. 123–4.
14 Murray, *Revival and Revivalism*, p. 124.
15 Noll, *A History of Christianity*, p. 178.
16 See F.W. Briggs, *Bishop Asbury: A Biographical Study* (Wesleyan Conference Office, 1879), p. 341.
17 Murray, *Revival and Revivalism*, p. 125.

that human agency 'had no more ability to produce revival than it had in producing thunder or a storm of hail'.[18]

William Sprague, an American Presbyterian minister, published in 1832 his major study entitled, *Lectures on Revivals of Religion*,[19] in which he stated that 'in all ordinary cases in which revival takes place, it would be no difficult thing to mark a distinct providential agency preparatory to it'.[20] Again trailing his Calvinistic coat tails, he stated, 'In every revival we are distinctly to recognize the sovereignty of God.'[21] More recently J.H. Armstrong made the same point in an article entitled 'Revival What and Why?',

> Revivals are God-given and cannot be staged. Humans, who long for revival to come, cannot bring them through their own energy or wills. We cannot bring revival any more than we can breathe life into a dead sinner. We can, and we must, pray to God to work, but we cannot bring life! The author of life is God.[22]

One further point is seen in these men's endorsement of Edward's view that God only moved in sovereign revival power in response to scriptural means, which they took to be the faithful preaching of the word of God, private and corporate prayer, especially joined with fasting, and the faithful fulfilment of parental and Christian duties. In opposition to this position, many of the nineteenth-century revivalists were happy to utilise 'means' which, though not having explicit Scriptural endorsements, were nevertheless in their view in keeping with scriptural principles. Such practices, they believed, included exhortations to the anxious or inquirers to cry out to God for mercy, calls for public decisions or pledges to follow Christ at the end of meetings, and anxious benches at the front of meeting places where those convicted of their need for God could come for prayer and counsel.

As today, there were often sharp disagreements between those who were adamant that only explicitly biblical means must be employed if revival was to be genuine and those revivalists who took this slightly wider view of what was permissible practice. That said, both were adamant that no authentic revival could be born of methods which were clearly against the teaching and principles of Scripture. Representatives of the two groups both eschewed techniques such as rhetoric that was deliberately designed to stir up human emotions and excitement. Revivalists were however for the most part happy with 'religious

---

18 W.G. McLoughlin, *Modern Revivalism: Charles Grandison Finney to Billy Graham* (Ronald Press, 1959), p. 41.
19 W. Sprague, *Lectures on Revivals of Religion* (Banner of Truth, 1959).
20 Sprague, *Lectures*, p. 93.
21 Sprague, *Lectures*, p. 105.
22 J.H. Armstrong, *Reformation and Revival*, Vol. 1, No. 2 (Spring 1992), p. 11.

exercises' such as 'jerking', 'shaking' and 'barking' provided they hadn't been induced by irresponsible rhetoric.[23]

Gardiner Spring (1758–1873) who ministered at Brick Church, New York City, was among those who eschewed the new kind of revivalism that he witnessed growing up around him. He wrote, 'Revivals are always spurious when they are got up by man's device, and not brought down by the spirit of God.'[24] William Sprague (1795–1876) who also stood firmly in the Calvinist tradition forcefully echoed Spring's views in the following paragraph:

> Suppose that for the simple, and honest, and faithful use of the sword of the spirit, there should be substituted a mass of machinery designed to produce its effect on animal passions; – suppose the substance of religion, instead of being made to consist in repentance, and faith and holiness, should consist of falling, and groaning, and shouting; we should say unhesitatingly that that could not be a genuine work of divine grace; or if it were some pure wheat, there must be a vast amount of chaff.[25]

It was over this issue that what came to be regarded as 'revivalism', as opposed to 'revival', began to emerge on the North American continent in the early part of the nineteenth century. Both parties were agreed that there often was a human element in genuine revivals, such as concerted prayer or faithful preaching, but the revivalists were of the view that given the right conditions a revival could be made to happen. In other words, they did not subscribe to the view that the revival was always a sovereign work of God. It could, in their view, be planned and organized to happen at a particular place and at a particular time. J. Edwin Orr observed that from the 1820s there were those who distinguished between 'revival' and 'revivalism'. Indeed, he pointed out, that the term 'revivalism' was first used in 1815 and 'revivalist' in 1820 in the aftermath of the Second Great Awakening.[26] Iain Murray concurs with Orr's view stating the word 'revivalism' emerged in the Southern States during the Second Great Awakening.[27] Such men and women began to substitute 'a revival ritual' in place of what they regarded as 'real revival'.[28] They stressed the importance of the human will and human response. An individual, as they saw it, could of their own volition get up in a meeting, go to the front of a hall, sit on the penitent form and make a decision for Christ. Murray has suggested, on his own admission without absolute proof, that the term 'revivalist' was first

---

23 These phenomena are discussed in chapter 2 of this book.
24 G. Spring, *Personal Reminiscences of the Life and Times of Gardiner Spring*, Vol. 1 (1866), pp. 217–18, cited by Murray, *Revival and Revivalism*, p. xv.
25 Sprague, *Lectures*, pp. 17–18.
26 J.E. Orr, *The Re-study of Revival and Revivalism* (School of World Mission, 1981), p. iii.
27 Murray, *Revival and Revivalism*, p. 190.
28 Murray, *Revival and Revivalism*.

used by New England Unitarian opponents of revival and then unwisely adopted by those of Arminian persuasion.[29]

In 1832 Calvin Colton (1789–1857), a Presbyterian minister, published *The History and Character of American Revivals of Religion* in which he contended that genuine revivals could be placed in two categories, the old and the new. The former came mysteriously and unexpectedly 'directly from the presence of the Lord'.[30] In such revivals, he noted, 'the hand of God has always been undeniable. For nobody expected, nobody prayed, nobody tried for such a work – as appeared.' 'This', he continued, 'was the more ordinary character of revivals of religion in American churches, and Christians waited for them as men are wont to wait for showers of rain.'[31] This old understanding of revival, Colton contrasted with 'the promotion of revivals by human instrumentality' that had emerged 'in the past few years'.[32] Colton who was himself an advocate of this new style revival was of the view that simply waiting for a revival to happen was an 'expression of sloth'. As far as he was concerned, the date of a revival could be ascertained in advance with halls booked, music planned and handbills and other publicity printed in readiness. Colton's view was that revival is 'the divine blessing upon measures concerted by men and executed by men'.[33] Charles Finney went further, writing in his *Lectures on Revivals of Religion* that 'A revival is not a miracle, nor dependent on a miracle, in any sense. It is a purely philosophical result of the right use of the constituted means.'[34]

Reflecting on the opinions of Colton and others who shared his views, it becomes apparent that the distinction between the old style understanding of 'revival' and 'revivalism' is not perhaps as rigid and distinct as some have contended. For it is clear enough that Jonathan Edwards, as Kent and others have pointed out, laboured hard and long in his pastoral care of his Northampton flock. Perhaps of greater significance, he deliberately preached on doctrines such as hell, the judgment of God and everlasting punishment in such a way as to achieve a deep conviction of wretchedness on the part of his hearers that would cause them to cry out for divine mercy and forgiveness.[35] The same could be said of the 'old style' revivals under George Whitefield in which there was undoubtedly a strong human element. By the time 'the grand itinerant'

---

29 Murray, *Revival and Revivalism*, p. 201.
30 C. Colton, *History and Character of American Revivals of Religion* (1832), p. 6.
31 Colton, *History and Character of American Revivals*.
32 Colton, *History and Character of American Revivals*.
33 Colton, *History and Character of American Revivals*, p. 9.
34 C.G. Finney, *Revivals of Religion* (Marshall, Morgan and Scott, 1910), p. 5.
35 Kent, *Holding the Fort*, p. 18. Kent's views are a little stronger than my own at this point. He wrote, 'It is obvious that Jonathan Edwards set out to preach his congregation into a state of religious hysteria and that his merciless analysis of the nature of everlasting punishment was carefully calculated to achieve this end. If no one had thought of the result as less than the work of God himself, this was partly because of the Protestant reverence for preaching.'

arrived in America for the second time in October 1739 he was already a celebrity who everybody wanted to listen to. Indeed the actor David Garrick wished he could move audiences as much as Whitefield did just by uttering the word 'Mesopotamia'. Benjamin Franklin (1706–90), the celebrated author, statesman, diplomat, scientist and philanthropist, heard many of Whitefield's sermons and recorded his impressions in the following lines.

> By hearing him often I came to distinguish easily between sermons newly composed and those which he often preached in the course of his travels. His delivery of the latter was so improved by frequent repetition, that every accent, every emphasis, every modulation of voice, was so perfectly well-tuned, and well-placed, that without being interested in the subject, one could be pleased with the discourse; a pleasure of much the same kind with that received from an excellent piece of music.[36]

One of Whitefield's great gifts, as Harry Stout has shown, was his ability to dramatise the Scriptures. He was in short a 'Divine Dramatist' who took great delight and enjoyment in his preaching. Whitefield also utilised other 'means' in his revival ministry. He was well aware of his celebrity status and frequently travelled with an entourage of up to forty like-minded Protestant preachers. Shortly after landing at Cape Henlopen, near Delaware, in October 1739, he commenced the journals of his American experience which raised the profile of his ministry. He also printed other things he had written and accounts of his present meetings and sent them on ahead for printing and distribution at his next intended location. In this way he raised people's expectation levels in a manner which undoubtedly helped to engineer revival phenomena. He also used music 'to mobilise his audience, to transform them from passive viewers to participants'.[37] In the light of these facts, Harry Stout made a convincing case that Whitefield in fact moved revivals on to become a form of entertainment.[38]

Regardless of how we regard the human element in the revivals that occurred under Whitefield's preaching, it was a succession of men and women who favoured Colton and Finney's philosophy who came to promote and hold revivalist campaigns in the towns and cities of nineteenth-century England. They were men and women who, like Finney, unashamedly used human means to engineer and create what they took to be revival at specific times in designated places. Indeed, as John Kent has shown, Colton published his book on revivals with a London publisher with the clear intention of introducing their new methods to the British public. In particular, Colton was a strong advocate of the practice of putting pressure on people to make a public commitment of their lives to Christ.

---

36 Cited by H. Stout, *The Divine Dramatist George Whitefield and the Rise of Modern Evangelicalism* (Eerdmans, 1991), p. 104.
37 Stout, *The Divine Dramatist*, p. 79.
38 Stout, *The Divine Dramatist*, pp. 212 and 235.

In fact he regarded this as an indispensable aspect of a revival meeting. When there is 'a manifestly special degree of feeling in the congregation ... ordinarily towards of the end of the meeting', a challenge is issued to all who are willing 'to publicly signify their anxiety to secure an interest in the great salvation – to separate themselves from the congregation and come forward and be seated by themselves'.[39] By this act they are known as 'inquirers'. After they have come forward further appeals are made with warnings that tomorrow 'is the grave of souls' and may be too late. Eventually the offer comes to an end and fervent prayers are offered up for all those souls who kneel in tears before their maker. Following counselling they are dismissed, having it is believed, been converted in that moment. Colton noted that 'the same amazing power of the circumstances, instrumentally, seems to bring out their feelings, to enforce them to the crisis of submission to God'.[40] Kent observed that to come forward in this way and to sit on the anxious seat or its equivalent was to be subjected to wave after wave of emotional pressure impelling the individual in one direction. Such rhetoric and control made critics question whether such conversions were genuine or merely a form of social conformity to the pressure exerted by the assembled congregation. Although the preaching was still of vital importance in the new revivalism, it was the preacher's appeal to make a public commitment that brought about the conversion. This technique or variations of it was part of the armoury of all the significant American revivalists who came to hold campaigns in nineteenth-century England. Indeed it is on this crucial issue that the distinction between the old style revival and the new style revivalism is most sharply defined. For men such as Edwards, conversion was the hand of the sovereign Lord taking hold of the individual, while for men such as Finney, it was the individual by a deliberate act of the will taking hold of God.

Revivalism as a Category

Although revivalism is not easily defined, it has a number of common and readily recognizable features, a grasp of which facilitates a better understanding of the American campaigns in nineteenth-century England. Perhaps the most obvious of these was the revivalists' literal interpretation to the Bible.

Literalism

At the beginning of the nineteenth century almost all Christians on both sides of the Atlantic believed the Old and New Testaments to be inspired and accepted them at their face value in a largely uncritical manner. Lorenzo Dow for

---

39 Colton, *History and Character of American Revivals*, p. 106, cited Kent, *Holding the Fort*, p. 19.

40 Colton, *The History and Character of Revivals of Religion*, pp. 96–8, cited Kent, *Holding the Fort*, p. 20.

example justified the use of camp meetings on a number of biblical passages in which it is stated that God's people dwell in tents. Abraham, for instance, quit his house and lived in tents. Jacob dwelt in tabernacles. Dow also wrote of the Feast of Tabernacles as 'a camp meeting to be held annually for a period of seven days'.[41] However as the nineteenth century progressed Higher Criticism began to make its presence felt, and people's doubts about the inspiration and historicity of the Bible began to increase considerably, especially in England in the later Victorian years following the publication of *Essays and Reviews* in 1860. Whereas Liberal theologians had begun to have deep misgivings about the morality of doctrines such as penal substitution and the literal understanding of heaven, hell and everlasting punishment, revivalists entertained no such doubts. As one of Lorenzo Dow's hymns put it.

> A Heaven or Hell, and these alone,
> Beyond the present life are known,
> There is no middle state;
> Today attend the call divine,
> Tomorrow may be none of thine,
> Or it may be too late.

On the surface at least, theirs was a world of black-and-white certainties in which what the Bible said was literally true. It was without error in its historical details and totally reliable in all it moral prescriptions. To take any other view was simply a lack of trust in God and his word. Thus hell was a place where people were tormented in flames and heaven was as much a city as Boston or Chicago. This literalism was most apparent in their interpretations of prophecies, particularly those relating to the millennium and the end times. Charles Finney for example, stated in his *Lectures on Revival* that if the church would do its duty 'the millennium would come in this country in three years'.[42] D.L Moody taught pre-millennialism, the doctrine that asserted that the return of Christ would precede the millennium or end-time thousand-year period of bliss. He professed to be attracted to the doctrine because its pessimistic view of culture gave a strong impetus to evangelism. Moody expected that Christ's return was imminent. For these reasons George Marsden contended that 'Moody's contribution to emerging fundamentalism was both large and complex.' Indeed, he continued, 'it could be argued that he was its principal progenitor'.[43]

With the passing of time the American emphasis on literalism was subsumed by what became known in the 1880s as 'Fundamentalism' and which began to

---

41 Dow, 'On Camp Meeting', included in *Journal in the Dealings*, Vol. 2, p. 248.
42 C.G. Finney, *Revivals of Religion Lectures by Charles Grandison Finney* (Oliphants, 1928), p. 282.
43 G. Marsden, *Fundamentalism and American Culture* (Oxford University Press, 1980), p. 108.

stress the crucial importance of supernatural knowledge and power.[44] The Jesus of the revivalists was not merely an ethical teacher and role model, He was the author of forgiveness, the redeemer and healer who intervened in individual lives.

Supernaturalism

Fundamentalism came increasingly to stress the divine Christ over against the ethical teacher and social reforming Jesus of the liberals. Rivivalists in general tended to sit light on the rational. Theirs was the world of the supernatural Jesus who intervened powerfully on behalf of his people and of a God who brought judgement on those who perpetrated evil. Thus a man like James Caughey was always ready to announce that there were people in his congregation who were destined to die 'this very week' on account of their mocking his addresses or because of their unwillingness to repent and respond the message of salvation. Revivalists believed God intervened and spoke through events and natural disasters. In October 1817 there were a series of earthquakes in Tennessee which caused many in the area to believe that the return of Jesus was imminent. Peter Cartwright related that in consequence of the excitement brought on by these earthquakes 'hundreds joined the Methodist Episcopal Church'.[45]

As far as revivalists were concerned the supernatural power of Christ was probably nowhere more apparent than in their great camp and sacramental meetings. James McGready wrote in his 1803 *A Narrative of the Revival in Logan County* that 'Little children, young men and women, and old grey headed people of every description, white and black, were to be found in every part of the multitude .... Crying for mercy in the utmost distress.'[46] Perhaps more than any other it was the 'falling exercise' that seemed to be the most obvious sign of a powerful divine intervention. A report of a camp meeting in 1802 in the *New York Missionary Magazine* noted 'a very great number of people or every age from 10 to 70, were struck down. To risk a conjecture of the precise number would be idly uncertain because they fell in the camps, on their way home, and after they got there.'[47] Peter Cartwright (1785–1872), a Methodist preacher who was actively involved in the Second Great Awakening, recounted many instances of what were held to be typical of the supernaturalism of the revival. He noted in his *Autobiography* of 1856 that he had seen 'more than a hundred sinners fall like dead men under one powerful sermon'.[48] Sometime later he

---

44 It should be noted that some scholars set a later date for the rise of fundamentalism. See for example, M. Noll, *The Old Religion in a New World* (Eerdmans, 2002), pp. 144–5.
45 Cartwright, *The Backwoods Preacher*, p. 127.
46 J. McGready, 'Narrative of the Revival in Logan County', *New York Missionary Magazine* (1803), pp. 192–4, cited Cleeveland, *The Great Revival in the West*, p. 57.
47 Cleveland, *The Great Revival in the West*, p. 59.
48 Cartwright, *The Backwoods Preacher*, p. 15.

saw 'not less than three hundred fall like dead men in mighty battle' at the quarterly camp meeting of the Scioto Circuit in Ohio State.[49] He also related that he saw 'more than five hundred persons jerking at one time in my large congregation'[50] and witnessed 'a very large drinking man' fetch 'a very violent jerk' that 'snapped his neck' causing him to expire with his mouth still full of cursing and bitterness'.[51]

Emotionalism

Tightly locked in with the revivalist preoccupation with what they perceived as the supernatural was the raw expression of emotions that frequently pervaded their meetings and campaigns. Revivalist religion was experiential religion which touched the feelings. If nothing was felt in the emotions the individual clearly had not been 'revived'. Preaching, as John Wolffe observed, 'induced strongly emotional reactions from those who felt themselves convicted of sin, but the weeping and crying were merely the preliminary to true conversion'.[52] Overwhelmed also by the intensity of the fervent singing, the exultant cries of the exhorters or the ecstatic release of accepting that the past was forgiven, new converts would often cry out aloud or sometimes sink to the ground while still screaming. At the end of meetings people who were anxious about their state before God would be invited to make their way to the front of the meeting place to kneel at the altar rail or sit on a penitent form. It frequently happened that in the moment of their pledging allegiance to Christ they would experience a sudden release and cry out or shout 'Glory to God!'. At a Tennessee camp meeting in the autumn of 1814 Peter Cartwright observed a man who came up to and leant on the railing outside the altar. 'Suddenly he leaped over into the altar, and fell at full length, and roared like a bull in a net, and cried aloud for mercy.'[53] A visitor at a revivalist gathering in an African American Methodist church at Brooklyn in 1819 was shocked by the proceedings and recorded, 'I cannot now describe for you the effect it had on me to see twenty or thirty Negresses, who thought they were full of the Holy Ghost, behave like regular furies. Their bellowing, dancing and jumping on benches was hideous and extremely barbaric.'[54] The anxious inquirer who came forward to sit on the penitent form or kneel at the altar rail, felt under such immense pressure to submit to a preacher's rhetoric, and conform to the expectations of the assembled congregation and the friends and relatives who had brought

---

49 Cartwright, *The Backwoods Preacher*, p. 72.
50 Cartwright, *The Backwoods Preacher*, p. 45.
51 Cartwright, *The Backwoods Preacher*, p. 46.
52 J. Wolffe, *The Expansion of Evangelicalism* (Inter-Varsity Press, 2006), p. 45.
53 Cartwright, *The Backwoods Preacher*, p. 102.
54 J.H. Wigger, 'Taking Heaven by Storm: Enthusiasm and Early American Methodism, 1770–1820s', *Journal of the Early Republic*, 14, 1994, cited Wolffe, *The Expansion of Early Evangelicalism*, p. 64.

them, that they cried out in an ecstasy of release as they finally surrendered. Phoebe Palmer recounted that at the meetings she and her husband had been holding at Sunderland in October 1859 that 'people are weeping all over the house [Sans Street Chapel], and that there are hundreds of sinners here'.[55] William McLouglin summarised this point succinctly: '"Experience religion" or "heart religion" as opposed to "head religion" was the essence of revivalism from its outset despite Finney's (and Beecher's) Lockean claims regarding the reasonableness of Christianity.'[56]

Singing was a prominent aspect of revivalist emotionalism. Fresh outbursts of song seem to have been a recurring feature of their campaigns. It was so under the Wesleys with Charles reputed to have written some six thousand five hundred hymns and songs, many with short verses that those who were unable to read could memorise and sing fervently. 'The Second Great Awakening' was also marked by vibrant and powerful singing with Isaac Watts' *Hymns and Spiritual Songs* selling in huge numbers. The Methodist revivalist, Lorenzo Dow, who arrived in England in the first decade of the nineteenth century made great use of songs at his meetings. In 1806 he published *A Collection of Spiritual Songs used at Camp Meetings in the Great Revival in the United States of America*. It was printed in Liverpool and sold for sixpence. It was the first specifically revivalist songbook to be produced in England and it was by no means the last. The singing which Dow promoted was blunt, vigorous and intense. Of greater significance than any other hymnody was Ira Sankey's collection, *Sacred Songs and Solos*, which by 1900 had sold 80 million copies worldwide. William Booth who had on one occasion famously exclaimed, 'Why should the devil have all the best tunes?', published a *Revival Hymnbook* in 1875.

What enabled those who attended revivalist gatherings to feel and experience the overwhelming presence of God in their lives was the witness of the Holy Spirit. In this respect many of the American revivalists were drawing on the Methodist tradition and in particular John Wesley's doctrine of the 'witness of the Spirit' in the life of the believer. This teaching emerged from his own experience in the Moravian Chapel at Aldersgate Street when his heart was strangely warmed while he listened to someone reading Luther's preface to the Epistle to the Romans. Wesley later wrote: '… the testimony of the Spirit is an inward impression on the soul whereby the Spirit witnesses with my spirit that I am a child of God; that Jesus hath loved me and given himself for me; that all my sins are blotted out and I, even I, am reconciled to God'.[57]

---

55 P. Palmer, *Four Years in the Old World* (Walter C. Palmer, 1869), p. 120.
56 McLouglin, *Modern Revivalism*, p. 67.
57 J.E. Rattenbury, *Wesley's Legacy to the World* (Epworth, 1928), p. 97.

Conversionism

Conversionism refers to practices or techniques which were designed and developed to 'convert' or bring the uncommitted to a position of faith. John Kent in his seminal study, *Holding the Fort* analysed a number of different conversion types: *conversions to teetotalism*; *family conversions* in which whole families were converted often as a result of one child first coming to a meeting; *conversions from Roman Catholicism* and *Conversions to Sabbatarianism*.[58] These differing types, he suggested, enabled the observer to see what satisfaction the audience found in revival meetings and to discern their hopes. That said, Kent notwithstanding, it must be emphasized that the key task of the revivalist was always his or her ability to achieve conversion above all bringing their hearers to a point of decision and public commitment to Christ. More important than a powerful platform presence, or being able to preach a stirring message that held people captive, was the ability bring the 'unsaved' to a point of pledging their lives to Jesus. If revivalists were not successful at this crucial point, they were not likely to be in high demand, least of all by churches that needed reviving. For this reason most nineteenth-century revivalists were always keen to count the numbers who came forward at the close of their campaigns. This was part of the reason why they asked people to register their names. They could then publish lists of the numbers who had been justified, sanctified or taken the pledge. These statistics were then published by them, and sometimes sent on ahead to the next place to which the revivalist was travelling, with the anticipation that the statistics would raise people's expectancy levels.

A great deal of nineteenth-century American revivalism, and indeed revivalism in general, was therefore about searching for improved and better methods of bringing the unconverted hearers to this point of personal commitment to Jesus. In a manner not dissimilar to that of contemporary Charismatics, nineteenth-century American revivalists were constantly searching for 'the next new thing', or latest technique, that would enable them to get better results. Throughout the nineteenth century the conversion techniques employed during campaigns were developed and extended with the later revivalists often building on the strategies of their predecessors. At the turn of the century Methodists such as Lorenzo Dow simply asked penitents to come forward to the front of the building or to the penitent's pen at camp meetings. Sometimes when Dow was in the open air he formed the people into a circle and invited those who wanted to make a commitment to Christ to step inside. Those who came after Dow made use of the penitent form or anxious bench as it was sometimes called. This was seating at the front of the meeting on which at the end of the service those who were convicted of sin were invited to come and sit. Towards the close of the century some revivalist who felt this technique created too much emotional pressure or was too intrusive, began to make use of the inquiry room. This was a separate room or church vestry where those who

---

58 See Kent, *Holding the Fort*, pp. 87–100.

were concerned at their spiritual state could have the chance to share their feelings and make a pledge of commitment if they felt inclined to do so.

Revivalists presented Jesus in intimate and personal terms. He was the compassionate, forgiving friend to all who shed his life-blood to save the sinner from guilt and condemnation. The revivalist would invariably end his or her address by emphasizing the sacrificial nature of the cross and the great extent of the love of Christ for everyone. The unconverted would then be challenged to respond being reminded by the preacher that God gave his all for them. Increasingly as the century progressed, it became customary at the crucial point when people were invited to give their lives to Christ to make use of singing. The congregation would be invited to sing a song such as Charlotte Elliott's 'Just as I am without one plea but that Thy blood was shed for me', each verse ending with the line, 'O Lamb of God I come'. Sometimes in the later Victorian years a soloist such as Ira Sankey, D.L. Moody's music director, would sing a sacred solo such as 'Come home, come home! Ye who are weary at heart' each verse ending with the line, 'O prodigal child! Come home; oh, come home!'.

Laicism

Typically revivalists avoided the guise and the manner of the denominational clergyman. Even those who were recognized preachers or were themselves ordained, sat light when it came to things ecclesiastical. For the most part theirs was an outside- of-the-box Christianity. The unpredictable Lorenzo Dow could hardly have been more unconventional when it came to conforming to his denominational ethos, practice and rulings, and both he and his fellow Methodist, James Caughey, had little truck with society rulings or Conference pronouncements. Charles Finney, as Kent noted, knew more about the law in which he had early been trained, than he did theology. His image was also decidedly unclerical.

Significantly the American revivalists who set foot in Britain in the middle and later Victorian years, Walter and Phoebe Palmer, D.L. Moody and Ira Sankey, Amanda Berry Smith and the Pearsall Smiths, were all lay men and women. This was part of their appeal. These were anti-clerical years in which a resurgent grassroots Protestantism surfaced in the face of the restoration of the Roman Catholic hierarchy and emergence of ritualistic extremes in the Church of England. Moody in particular was able to present himself to the British public in the image of a straightforward efficient and pleasant man. Against the background of ecclesiastical doctrinal disputation and biblical higher criticism Moody's unsophisticated no nonsense plain Christian faith endeared him to his very large audiences. Neither Moody nor any of the other American revivalists deliberately set out to be anti-clerical. The truth was the reverse. They all sought to bring local clergy together and persuade them to work in concert. Indeed it was in this fact that much of their success lay as they were able to reach into all parts of the community.

Radicalism

By their nature, as has just been observed, revivalists tended not to conform to denominational norms. Indeed their religion was most often a reaction to the coldness and decline of establishment Christianity. Their concern was to breathe new life into dying stereotyped formalism. Their expression of the faith therefore had an inbuilt radical element. The very presence of a fundamentalist revival preacher from America drawing in the crowds at an independent or Primitive Methodist chapel in the same town presented a challenge to the more staid and ecclesiastical churches. Jabez Bunting, the dominant Wesleyan leader during the first part of the nineteenth century, constantly complained that the pastoral role and leadership of circuit ministers was being undermined by revivalists such as James Caughey.

The Raised Status of Women

L.S. and D.W. Dayton have argued that revivalism, especially the forms practised by Charles G. Finney, tended to raise the status of women by employing their services in putting out publicity, visiting and organizing prayer groups.[59] They point out that Finney's famous convert and assistant, Theodore Weld, encouraged women to testify with the almost immediate result that seven females confessed their sin in being restricted by their sex.[60] Such practice was one of the 'new measures' for which Finney was severely criticised. Oberlin College, where Finney later served as Professor of Theology, was one of the first co-educational colleges in the world and was committed to 'female reform'. Finney insisted that the scripture did not prohibit women from praying and speaking in mixed assemblies and he encouraged them to participate in class discussions. The Daytons point out that a number of Oberlin graduates went on to become the most important feminists of the period, among them Lucy Stone who championed equal marriage contracts and Sallie Holly a prominent anti-slavery lecturer.

A number of the American revivalists who campaigned in Victorian England were women. Some such as Phoebe Palmer[61] and Amanda Berry Smith gave or wrote competent and forceful justifications of women's rights to preach and minister in churches and hold revival campaigns.[62] But more than their writings it was the success of their meetings which challenged the establishment. During the 1840s the English Wesleyans were seeking to enhance the status of their

---

59 L.S. Dayton, '"Your Daughters Shall Prophesy": Feminism in the Holiness Movement', *Methodist History*, Vol. XIV, No. 2, January 1876, pp. 70–4.
60 Dayton, '"Your Daughters Shall Prophesy"', pp. 70–1.
61 See P. Palmer, *Promise of the Father or A Neglected Speciality of the Last Days Addressed to the Clergy and Laity of all Christian Communities* (Henry V. Degen, 1859).
62 The Daytons point out that while Mrs Palmer insisted on women's rights to preach she never pressed ordination. This was because she believed the whole system of ordination to be unscriptural.

travelling preachers and had begun to turn away from allowing women to preach which they deemed to be an aspect of radicalism. Zilpha Elaw, Phoebe Palmer and Amanda Smith, who were Methodists, all encountered opposition from Wesleyan Circuit ministers during their time in England, but it blunted neither their enthusiasm nor the level of popular demand for their services. Zilpha and Amanda were in frequent demand on account of their powerful singing voices and this often led to their being invited to testify, pray or exhort at meetings to which they hadn't specifically been invited to give an address.

Labour Movements

Revivalists generated other forms of radicalism. Often a challenge to the religious establishment developed into a challenge to the political status quo. Such, for example, was the case with Primitive Methodism. Lorenzo Dow's presence among them and his advocacy of American frontier style camp meetings to enable the people to come together for a day's praying and religious exercises later became the model for trade union camp meetings which were organized to add religious fervour and solidarity to the fight for better wages and improved conditions of labour. This was particularly visible in the campaigns of the agricultural workers' unions in East Anglia where union camp meetings were reported to 'have been productive of much good'.[63] Mine workers in parts of Derbyshire and of Nottinghamshire also found camp meetings were an effective means of raising morale and generating extra funds. There is little evidence that the revivalists taught the poor to be content with their station in life or that poverty was their God-ordained lot. In general revivalists stood firmly on the side of the disadvantaged and liminal elements of society.

Anti-Slavery

American revivalists were also strong in their support for the anti-slavery campaigns. Charles Finney championed the cause from pen and pulpit. The parents of Amanda Smith, the Black African American revivalist, bought their way out of slavery and during her childhood years she remembered that 'our house was one of the main stations on the Under Ground Railroad'.[64] Together with Zilpha Elaw, another Black revivalist, Amanda played a vital role in awakening the churches to their prejudice and discrimination against the black communities.[65] Elder Barton Stone, who was an active leader in the great revival

---

63 *English Labourers' Chronicle*, 1 September 1877. See also N.A.D. Scotland, *Methodism and the Revolt of the Field in East Anglia 1872–96* (Alan Sutton, 1981), pp. 77–80.

64 See A. Smith, *Amanda Smith* (J.H. Books, 1977), pp. 18–21. The Under Ground Rail Road was a network of safe houses and staging posts set up across the southern states to enable black slaves to escape to freedom in the north.

65 See Wolffe, *The Expansion of Evangelicalism*, p. 58.

in the southern states, 'was decidedly opposed to slavery'. In 1828 he published *An Humble Address to Christians on the Colonization of Free People of Colour* in which he wrote, 'All who know me, well know that for more than thirty years I have advocated the cause of liberty.'[66] He also wrote, 'The question is no longer now as thirty years ago – is slavery of Africans right or wrong, both politically and morally? The light of truth and intelligence has removed our doubts. No man of intelligence now presumes to justify it, whether he be politician, moralist or Christian.'[67] Bishop Francis Asbury (1745–1816), who was at the centre of southern revival, wrote, 'If the gospel will tolerate slavery, what will it not authorise?'[68] Peter Cartwright wrote in his *Autobiography*, 'I was opposed to slavery, though I did not meddle with it politically, yet I felt it my duty to bear my testimony against it.'[69]

Temperance

The revivalists of the Second Great Awakening were strong advocates of temperance. In the wake of their influence *The American Education Society for the Promotion of Temperance* was founded in 1826. James Caughey, the Methodist revivalist who arrived in England in the 1840s, was a staunch advocate of temperance, and in addition to his revival meetings he often spoke at temperance society tea meetings and other gatherings urging people to take the pledge. Brian Harrison in his study of temperance noted that temperance pledges sometimes prompted revivalist activities.[70] At her holiness meetings Phoebe Palmer made temperance almost a condition of achieving sanctification and on some occasions declared that God's blessing had been withheld because some of those present were in the grip of strong drink.

Adventism

Adventism, the belief that the second return or advent of Christ was imminent, was perhaps not so immediately visible as some of the features that have been noted above. That said, it was never very far below the surface in the thinking of many revivalists. Adventism was simply the doctrine of the personal, powerful and bodily return of Jesus with the attendant consequence of separate destinies of heaven for the righteous and hell for those who had failed to take up the gospel invitation. This was a powerful ingredient in the revivalist's armoury. First of all the fact that Jesus could return suddenly at any particular moment added a note of urgency to the preaching. In consequence, revivalists such as Moody felt compelled to bring as many as possible to the Master before

---

66 Stone, *A Short History of the Life of Barton Stone*, p. 288.
67 Stone, *A Short History of the Life of Barton Stone*, p. 288.
68 F. Asbury, *Journal*, Vol. 3, February 1801.
69 Cartwright, *The Backwoods Preacher*, p. 119.
70 B. Harrison, *Drink and the Victorians 1815–1872* (Faber, 1972), p. 104.

he returned. Moody, who was strongly impacted by Darby's Dispensationalism, summed the matter up in the following lines:

> The word of God nowhere tells me to watch and wait for the coming of the millennium, but for the coming of the Lord. I don't find any place where God says the world is to grow better and better, and that Christ is to have a spiritual reign on earth a thousand years. I find that the earth is to grow worse and worse and at length there is going to be a separation (of the saved from the unsaved).[71]

Moody's reference to the millennium draws attention to this further aspect of revivalist religion, the expectation of a thousand year period of earthly bliss which would either follow or precede the return of Christ. For most of the earlier American revivalists the utopian vision was a post-millennial one[72] with the earth being transformed by the impact of revival. However, later nineteenth-century revivalists for the most part came to share Moody's view that the millennium would be preceded by Christ's return.

Then there was the question of those who were 'anxious' about their sinful state but failed to come forward to the inquiry room to make their peace with God when the appeal was given. Added pressure could be applied in their case by reminding them that Christ might come again finally and decisively as a thief during the following night, and it would then be too late. As the last verse of 'The Lord is Coming', Song No. 182 in Sankey's *Sacred Songs and Solos* put it.

> To judgement called at His Command,
> From every clime, from every land,
> Before His throne we all must stand;
> Be ready when He comes!

The song carried a refrain repeated after each verse.

> Will you be ready when the Bridegroom comes?
> Will you be ready when the Bridegroom comes?
> Will your lamps be trimmed and bright,
> Be it morning, noon or night?
> Will you be ready when the Bridegroom comes?

Sankey's collection contains a substantial section entitled 'His Second Coming'. Almost half of the 26 songs in it stress the importance of being ready and prepared for the Lord's return. Revivalists such as James Caughey did not

---

71 R.E. Lovelace, *Dynamics of Spiritual Life* (Paternoster Press, 1979), p. 377, citing Curtis, *They Called Him Mr Moody*, p. 266.
72 Wolffe, *The Expansion of Evangelicalism*, p. 78.

spare their hearers the graphic details of what hell might hold out for them if they failed to respond to the call. Indeed, Moody himself occasionally preached pointedly on the subject of hell.

The whole concept of the imminent return of Christ was also linked with revivalism on account of those biblical texts which appeared to teach that in the last days there would be powerful and special outpourings of the Holy Spirit. D.L. Moody often said that it was his belief in the imminence of Christ's return that caused him to be urgent in his preaching. That said, the doctrine did on occasion produce dysfunctional outcomes when preachers reckoned they had discerned the exact date of the advent. Such was the case when William Miller (1782–1849), a New York State farmer and Bible student, announced that the Second Coming would happen between 21 March 1843 and 21 March 1844. In 1838 Miller published his views in a book entitled *Evidence from Scripture and History of the Second Coming of Christ, About the Year 1843*. At the zenith of Millerite fever there were more than fifty thousand convinced believers and 'as many as a million others who were sceptically expectant'.[73] As expectation mounted meetings took place in Albany, Utica and in the Mohawk Valley while in Rochester there was a huge boom in the textile trade with a massive demand for ascension robes. When 21 March passed Miller declared that he had miscalculated and that 22 October was the certain date. When this also passed without incident Miller was discredited and a period which became known as 'the Great Disappointment' followed.[74]

The Continuing Appeal of American Revivalism

There were a variety of reasons that caused sections of the nineteenth-century British public to continue to be receptive to the campaigns of the American revivalists who set foot on English soil, each with their differing perceptions of revival and their accompanying messages and techniques. Some of these factors, such as a general dissatisfaction with mainstream denominational religion and a desire for something new, were a constant and ongoing factor. Others were more specific to particular times and places.

The Churches Needed Reviving

In contrast to America, Christianity in Britain during the first two decades of the nineteenth century in particular was in a state of decline and in desperate need of reviving. For much of the first 15 years of the nineteenth-century England had been in a state of more or less continuous war in Europe. Indeed it wasn't until 1815 when Napoleon was finally defeated at Waterloo that England was at last able to take stock the situation. It then emerged that the churches were in a

---

73 W.S. Hudson, *Religion in America* (Charles Scribner's Sons, 1965), pp. 194–6.
74 See M. Ruthven, *The Divine Supermarket* (Chatto and Windus, 1989), pp. 51–2.

state of serious decline and nowhere more so than in the great towns and cities which had expanded during the Industrial Revolution.

The organizational structure of the established church required that the clergy administer the Poor Law, conduct baptisms and marriages, bury the dead and also collect church rates as well as care the spiritual needs of the parishioners. In the countryside where the parson and the squire worked alongside one another the system was just about able to provide for the needs of the poor. But even in rural counties many clergy were either non-resident or pluralists and did little to get to know their flocks or communicate the Christian faith to them.[75] In areas of sprawling urban development where 15,000 to 20,000 souls pressed into a single parish, one lone incumbent, even with the help of several curates, could barely scratch the surface as he struggled to fulfil his duties. The Seventh Earl of Shaftesbury described the parochial system as 'a beautiful thing in history and ... of great value in the small rural districts but in large towns it is a mere shadow and a name'.[76] If testimony were needed regarding the inadequacy of the parish structure the comments made in 1811 by the Evangelical Prime Minister, Spencer Perceval, would suffice. In a speech he highlighted the fact that in the parish of St Marylebone, there was only church seating for barely one ninth of the population. In 1814 Dr William Howley was appointed Bishop of London and soon came to the same conclusion recognizing that in many of parts of his diocese there were seats in church for less than one tenth of the population. The following year, the Revd Richard Yates published a famous pamphlet entitled, *The Church in Danger,* in which he stated that in London 953,000 souls were left without the possibility of parochial worship.[77] The situation was little better elsewhere. In his charge of 1832 Henry Ryder, the Bishop of Lichfield, noted that Wolverhampton had church accommodation for only one fifth of its population. He spoke of those who drifted from church as straying 'from compulsion in the wilderness of this evil world'.[78] In 1841 the parish of Sheffield contained 112,492 persons for whom the Church of England provided a total of 15,000 seats of which only 6,000 were free.[79]

---

75 As late as 1857 Bishop of Gloucester was begging his diocesan clergy to use simple illustrations in their sermons that ordinary people in their pews could readily understand. See C. Baring, *A Charge Delivered to the Clergy of the Diocese of Gloucester and Bristol at His Primary Visitation of the Diocese in October 1857* (Seeley, Jackson and Halliday, 1857), pp. 29–32.

76 Cited K.S. Inglis, *Churches and the Working Classes in Victorian England* (Routledge & Kegan Paul, 1962), p. 24.

77 See R. Yates, *The Church in Danger*, cited by G.F.A. Best, *Temporal Pillars* (Cambridge University Press, 1964), pp. 147–51.

78 H. Ryder, *Charge Addressed to the Clergy and People of Lichfield and Coventry at His Third Visitation* (A. Morgan, 1832).

79 E.R. Wickham, *Church and People in an Industrial City* (Lutterworth Press, 1969), p. 71.

At the beginning of the nineteenth century the Establishment was dominated by the High Churchmen, who were intent on preserving the privileged position of the Church of England as the National Church, and the Latitudinarians who distrusted religious enthusiasm and regarded Christianity as chiefly useful for preserving morals and supporting venerable institutions. One of their most prominent representatives was Archdeacon William Paley (1743–1805) who published his celebrated *Natural Theology* in 1802 in which he set out rational arguments for the existence of God. The problem was that most ordinary men and women were not attracted by these dry and arid expressions of Christianity

At this point in time the Evangelicals were still only a relatively small group within the Church of England. Most of their number had strong sympathies with Methodism although since Wesley's death in 1791 his organization had begun to take on an altogether different stance. During his lifetime the Methodist societies had been happy to follow in the steps of their founder who called himself 'God's steward of the poor' but already by the turn of the new century things were beginning to change. Many Wesleyans were beginning to prosper and to see themselves on the other side of the social hierarchy. During the war years there was a growing fear that the radicalism of the French Revolution might take root among England's lower orders. In consequence the Wesleyan Conference and many of the circuit authorities began to side with government and the establishment, and to make pronouncements against anything that smacked of socialism or the rights and betterment of the working-classes. For almost thirty years after 1820 Wesleyan Methodism fell under the influence of Jabez Bunting (1779–1859). Elected as President of Conference on four separate occasions[80] the Wesleyan body under him became theologically and politically conservative seeking status for its clergy and eschewing revivalism.

At the same time the Older Dissenters who were largely made up of Presbyterians, Congregationalists, Unitarians, Quakers and Baptists were, generally speaking, in a state of decline with the possible exception of some Baptists who had been revived through Wesley's preaching.[81] Alec Vidler suggested that during the course of the eighteenth century the dissenting bodies had for the most part fallen into the same condition as the established church and were 'dry, commonsensical, averse to enthusiasm and acclimatised to the age of reason'[82]. This surfeit of rationalism led many dissenters to drift into weak views of Jesus' divinity and deist philosophy. After 1830 the Quakers began to lose a number of their adherents to the newly formed Plymouth Brethren. The stage was therefore set for fresh and vibrant expressions of the Christian faith and the revivalists who came from America were ready and willing to offer it.

In 1905 Hodder and Stoughton published a volume entitled *Do We Believe?* Based on 9,000 letters sent in to the *Daily Telegraph* it showed that church

---

80 1820, 1828, 1836 and 1844.
81 The New Connexion of General Baptists had been formed by Dan Taylor.
82 A.R. Vidler, *The Church in an Age of Revolution* (Penguin, 1971), p. 40.

attendance had clearly been on a downward spiral for some time. In one section of the book an ex-MP put forward the view that only 16 per cent of the population of Liverpool attended Sunday church in 1901 leaving 33,000 empty pews in the city's churches. In 1903 *The Daily News* published a census of London church attendance. It showed that attendance had fallen from 535,715 in 1886 to 396,196.[83] Among more recent writers who have focused on the later Victorian years, Hugh McLeod demonstrated that Anglican attendances declined slightly between 1851 and 1881 and much more rapidly between 1881 and 1901.[84] Robin Gill also showed that Anglican church attendance was in 'noticeable decline' in most large towns and cities in the1880s. Gill surveyed a number of large towns and cities, including Birmingham, Sheffield, London and Gloucester, to make his point that the traditional view that churches and chapels continued to thrive into the early twentieth century is incorrect.[85] If the fact needed illustration perhaps the comment of the Vicar of Leeds in 1846 would suffice. He wrote, 'Not one in a hundred attends any place of worship, but the usual practice is for men to lie in bed on Sunday morning, while the women cook the dinner, and for an adjournment in the evening to take place to a public house.'[86] Frederick Engells summed up the matter when he wrote some three years later, 'All the writers of the bourgeoisie are unanimous on this point that the workers are not religious and do not attend church.'[87]

Doubts Needed Counteracting

Another factor that caused an interest in revivalism was the fact that Britain witnessed a steady and growing secularisation throughout the nineteenth century. Historians such as Alan Gilbert and John Kent have underlined the fact that, although this secularising process began before the Victorian era, it accelerated rapidly during the later nineteenth century.[88] Whilst it was the case that outwardly

---

83 R.C.K. Ensor, *England 1870–1914* (Oxford University Press, 1936), p. 308.
84 H. McLeod, *Religion and Society in England 1850–1914* (MacMillan, 1996), p. 172.
85 R. Gill, *The Myth of the Empty Church* (SPCK, 1993), p. 182.
86 E. Royle, *Radical Politics, Religion and Unbelief 1700–1900* (Longman, 1971), p. 6.
87 F. Engells, *Condition of the Working Classes in England* (1892 edition), p. 125.
88 See A.D. Gilbert, *Religion and Society in Industrial England: Church, Chapel and Social Change 1740–1914* (Longman, 1976), p. 55: 'Paine gave the working classes a reason for throwing religion overboard or to put it in the sociological jargonese of one writer, "he offered ideological legitimation to those members of the working classes for whom traditional religiosity ... became incongruous as the nineteenth century proceeded."' Kent, *Holding the Fort*, p. 9: 'More important, however, was the overall process of secularisation which had been affecting Western culture before the Victorian era, but which developed rapidly in the nineteenth century.'

speaking religious attendance was relatively high, at least until the time of the 1851 Religious Census,[89] the fact was that below the surface there was much uncertainty about some of the creedal doctrines and the authority of the Bible in particular. Of major concern was the fact that the census demonstrated that it was the working poor of the large towns and cities who were absent from any place of worship. After reviewing the statistics of religious attendance, Horace Mann, the government appointed enumerator, concluded of the English working classes that 'they are habitual neglecters of the public ordinances of religion'. He continued that such people are 'unconscious secularists engrossed by the demands and trials or pleasures of the passing hour'.[90] This growing sense of doubt even on the part of the poor was well-charted in the novels of Elizabeth Gaskell, Mrs Humphry Ward and others. Mr Hale, the Rector of Helston in Mrs Gaskell's *North and South*, had such doubts that he resigned his living. His observation was that the labourers in the north 'don't believe the Bible, – not they. They may say they do, for form's sake.'[91]

Christian Influence Needed Recovering

By the close of the nineteenth-century Britain was no longer a Christendom but, along with most other European nations, Church and State which once had overlapped were fast separating, resulting in the loss of Christian influence in the public arena. At the same time at the local level the State was fast taking over from the Church in running education, administering the Poor Law and Public Health. Indeed the parish clergyman of 1800, who had been the 'Parson' or chief person of the parish, found himself a century later with little more public authority than any layman in his cure. This loss of church influence in public life was viewed by the sociologist, Bryan Wilson,[92] as being key reason for secularisation. Owen Chadwick in his book *The Secularisation of the European Mind* highlighted the significant period of secularisation as extending from the publication of *Origin of Species* in 1859 until the downward turn in English churchgoing statistics in the 1880s. This period, he contended, has the merit of being the period in which the word 'secularisation' came to mean the loss of religious influence.[93] Secularisation began as 'an intellectual fact' and ended as a 'social fact'.[94] John Kent made the point that the churches felt

---

89 Horace Mann who computed the statistical returns of the 1851 Census of Religion calculated that on census Sunday, the last Sunday in March, 58 per cent of the population worshipped God in a place of worship.
90 G. Parsons, *Religion in Victorian Britain* (Manchester University Press, 1988), p. 64.
91 E. Gaskell, *North and South* (Penguin, 1970), p. 289.
92 B. Wilson, *Religion in Secular Society* (Watts, 1966), p. xiv ff.
93 O. Chadwick, *The Secularisation of the European Mind in the 19th Century* (Canto, 1990; original Cambridge University Press, 1975), p. 18.
94 Chadwick, *The Secularisation of the European Mind*, p. 18.

increasingly 'pushed to the margin of society' and that 'the hostility of a secular world was tightening its grip on them'.[95]

Secularisation spread among the poorer sections of society in consequence of the increased literacy among them. Indeed it has been demonstrated that between 1830 and 1870 there was a steady growth in the number of working men and women who could read and write. Much of this was due to the rapid growth in the number of Sunday schools that provided a rudimentary education of reading, writing and arithmetic. T.W. Laqueur pointed out that many of the Sunday schools, far from imposing a regime and ethos of social control, created an atmosphere that encouraged free thought and instilled ideals of equality and social justice.[96] As these former pupils entered adult life many of them became readers of the penny papers. According to Chadwick, the power of the press lay in its 'ability to expose ecclesiastical abuse' and 'to make fanaticism more foolish by printing it' and 'they also made intolerance more disreputable'.[97] Some of the secularists such as Charles Bradlaugh and George Jacob Holyoake[98] denounced the churches' condemnation of working class movements and their upholding of the social hierarchy which demanded that the poor be content with their lot.[99]

The factor that boosted intellectual secularism was the expansion of the sciences in the mid-Victorian years with the publication of Charles Darwin's *Origin of Species* in 1859 undoubtedly being a major event in this development. Although Darwin's theory of evolution was not new, his grandfather, Erasmus Darwin, having published very similar ideas as early as 1794 in *Zoonomia or the Laws of Organic Life*, it appeared at a critical moment in time. Something of the threat that was felt by the Church was seen in Bishop Samuel Wilberforce's ill-judged confrontation with Huxley at a meeting of the British Association for the Advancement of Science in 1860. Interestingly the sociologist, Bryan Wilson, made the point that the threat was the growing general perception of the superiority of science over religion. He wrote: 'The real danger of science to religion, however, was rather in the increased prestige of science and the decline of religion …. As governments became less concerned with the promotion of religion, so they became increasingly disposed to sponsor science.'[100]

Darwin's *Origin of Species* which was described as 'the first complete statement of the theory of evolution', immediately began to cause many

---

95 Kent, *Holding the Fort*, p. 10.
96 See T.W. Laqueur, *Religion and Respectability: Sunday Schools and Working Class Culture 1780–1850* (Yale University Press, 1976). See also N.A.D. Scotland, *Evangelicals in a Revolutionary Age* (Paternoster Press, 2004), pp. 230–4.
97 Chadwick, *The Secularisation of the European Mind*, pp. 38–40.
98 George Jacob Holyoake (1817–1906) was advised to call himself a secularist to escape the charges of atheism and infidelity.
99 Royle, *Radical Politics*, p. 93.
100 Wilson, *Religion in Secular Society*, p. 49.

Victorian Christians to question some of the fundamental tenets of the creedal Christian faith. Doubts were expressed about the early chapters of Genesis, in particular the days of creation and order of events with land animals seemingly coming before marine life. Later the publication of Darwin's second book, *The Descent of Man* in 1871, raised fundamental questions about the status of the human race. If mankind gradually evolved from some common ancestry of the great ape and human race was it possible to speak of the fall of man from perfection? Further questions presented themselves in the wake of Darwin's findings. His theory of natural selection and the survival of the fittest had raised the whole question of suffering in a new light. How could a good and just God have set in motion a created order that proceeded on the basis of bloodshed and death? The poet Tennyson highlighted the problem in his poem *In Memoriam* when he spoke of nature 'red in tooth and claw'. Christians who had formerly been impressed by William Paley's teleological argument began to ask was there really evidence of a divine designer in such a system? And what sort of design was it that created species for gradual extinction?

Inevitably it wasn't long before the secularists began to pick up on these arguments and circulate them in books and journals. Whilst it was the case that most of their ideas probably only reached a small minority in the later years of the century, the views of Karl Marx became increasingly influential. Although he was the son of Christian Jewish parents, Marx came to doubt the traditional Christian faith through imbibing the theories of Bruno Bauer who maintained that the gospels were so encrusted with legend that is was impossible to distil any history from within them. Later Marx picked up on Feuerback's phrase 'God is illusion'[101] and utilised Charles Kingsley's words that 'religion is an opium'. For Marx it was clear that faith in a God was a 'construct' that enabled the working poor in particular to cope with the harsher realities of an unjust social order. By the middle 1840s Marx was clear that 'religion lives from the earth, and men must dispose of it by attending to earthly needs'.[102]

Undoubtedly the intellectual ferment and the social secularisation of the nineteenth century caused many men and women to doubt the existence of a personal God who could intervene in their lives and in the events of the world in which they were living. The one thing that could bring them renewed assurance on this score was a fresh, immediate, spiritual experience that could touch the very core of their beings. It was here that the revivalists from America had a particular appeal and a role to play. They were men and women who themselves possessed a strong sense of the presence of God in their own lives. They were experienced in conveying it through fervent song, emotional rhetoric, exhortations and religious exercises at holiness gatherings and protracted and camp meetings out on the frontiers as well as in the new industrial heartlands of America. As John Kent put it, '... one reason for the

---

101 Cited Chadwick, *The Secularisation of the European Mind*, p. 55.
102 Cited Chadwick, *The Secularisation of the European Mind*, p. 55.

popularity of the American revivalist was that he claimed to be able to lead people into what might be called, in modern terms, an existential awareness of the realities underlying the classical Protestant pattern of religious behaviour'.[103] Put another way, 'he claimed to be able to produce the circumstances in which men would be open to an invading sense of self-despair and the divine intervention which brought them the assurance that their sins were forgiven'.[104]

Professionals such as James Caughey could bring their hearers to feel an overwhelming sense of God's presence at the altar. Walter and Phoebe Palmer could offer a mighty baptism in the Holy Spirit and D.L. Moody could show those who doubted the veracity of the Bible that it was nevertheless a very practical handbook for living. Revivalists such as these men and women came with their proven track records including fulsome statistics of those justified, sanctified and helped at their meetings. Many British church leaders were also impressed at the ways in which American revivalism had elevated the intellectual, spiritual and social conditions of whole towns and cities encouraging industry, improving morality and resulting in good habits. Indeed William Sprague in his celebrated *Lectures on Revivals of Religion* underlined the fact that revivals 'lend an important influence to the support of our benevolent institutions' and went to point out that 'all our great benevolent institutions – our Missionary, and Bible, and Tract, and Education, and Temperance, and all kindred societies have flourished as a result of revivals'.[105]

The chapters of this book which follow are an examination of the religion, theology and practice of prominent American men and women revivalists who came to the British Isles in the nineteenth century to revive the flagging religious life and worship of the nation's declining churches. Attention has been paid to their understandings of revival, their strategies for achieving it, and their impact on church and society.

---

103 Kent, *Holding the Fort*, p. 12.
104 Kent, *Holding the Fort*, p. 12.
105 See Sprague, *Lectures*, pp. 272–4.

CHAPTER 2

Lorenzo Dow and Camp Meeting Revivalism

Lorenzo Dow came to England in 1806 and again in 1818. The main focus of his missionary endeavours was in Staffordshire and Cheshire, where he worked with a group of the somewhat disgruntled Wesleyan Methodists led by Hugh Bourne (1772–1852) who were attracted to revivalist ideas, particularly those of the frontiers of the Southern American states of Kentucky and Tennessee. The area around Tunstall where Dow came on his first visit was one in which a crumbling Anglicanism had for the moment lost its influence on the working classes in the countryside.[1] Dow's influence proved to be a major catalyst in the founding of the Primitive Methodist Connexion, a Methodist body that came to be of major significance in the development of Victorian working religion and politics.

Lorenzo Dow was born in Coventry, Connecticut, on 16 October 1777, the fifth of six children of Humphrey Dean and Tabitha Dow.[2] They provided an education for their children which Lorenzo later recalled was frugal 'both in religion and in common learning'. About the time he was thirteen, Hope Hull, a Methodist preacher came to his town[3] and Lorenzo, after hearing him one day, was brought under deep conviction as to 'the damnable nature' of his sins and felt 'I was unable to die.' Shortly afterwards he came to experience the pardoning love of God as he pleaded for mercy.[4] He cried out in his room, 'Lord, I give up: I submit; I yield; if there be any mercy in heaven for me, let me know it.' Then he felt the words of Scripture were powerfully impressed on his mind, 'Son thy sins which are many, are forgiven thee; thy faith has saved thee; go in peace.' Immediately 'the burden of sin and guilt and the fear of hell vanished from my mind, as perceptibly as an hundred pounds weight falling from a man's shoulder'.[5] His soul soon flowed out in love and concern for his people and all humankind.

It was not long after this experience that Lorenzo began to feel a call to preach the gospel. One day when he was alone in prayer 'the words were suddenly impressed on my mind; "Go ye into all the world and preach the

---

1 Kent, *Holding the Fort*, p. 11.
2 L. Dow, *Nuggets of Golden Truth: or Reflections on the Love of God, on Predestination, Deism and Atheism and on Christian Experience*, preface by William Antliff (R. Davies, 1863 edition), p. 7. See also L. Dow, *Travels and Providential Experience of Lorenzo Dow*, Vol. 1 (self published, 1806), p. 7.
3 Dow, *Journal in the Dealings*, p. 10.
4 Dow, *Journal in the Dealings*, p. 33.
5 Dow, *Journal in the Dealings*, p. 33.

gospel to every creature".[6] After some initial resistance, Lorenzo submitted to what he knew to have been God's voice and felt 'the sweet cords of love' drawing him forward. On Sunday 5 October 1794 he offered his first prayer at a public prayer meeting held in the town[7] and shortly afterwards on 14 November, he delivered his first public exhortation for which his parents afterwards gave him 'tender reproof'.[8] Although only a youth of seventeen he started to grapple with the doctrines of unconditional election and final perseverance.[9] On 7 January 1796 he was requested to visit Tolland in order to test out his gifts of preaching.[10] He also visited the New London Circuit, East Harford and other places during which time he rode with Mr Snethen, a Methodist travelling preacher. After a few days Snethen delivered a rebuke to his young aspirant telling him, 'You are but eighteen years of age; you are too important, and you must be more humble, and hear and not be heard so much.' He continued, 'You had better learn some easy trade, and be still for two or three years yet; for your bodily health will not admit of your becoming a travelling preacher at present.' This was a reference to his suffering from asthma. Despite Snethen's discouraging remarks, Dow soon recovered his initial determination and was further strengthened in his resolve when his uncle sold him a horse on a year's credit and his parents relented and provided him with clothing and money.[11] This was March 1796.

The following month on Sunday 3 April, Dow recorded in his journal, 'This day for the first time I gave out a text before a Methodist preacher.'[12] However, after three months preaching on the Warren Circuit he was dismissed as 'not likely to suitable'. In several places he was well-received but in others 'people were not happy with him'.[13] On 20 September he was examined by the bishop at the Methodist Conference at Thomson, Connecticut. There he was rejected on the ground that he had no written recommendation. Dow was so deeply affected by this rebuff that he was unable to take any food for 36 hours. To make matters worse, he was 'harassed by strong temptations' and on one occasion, he sought the river with the intention of committing suicide but the thought of eternity prevented him from doing so.

In September 1797 the Conference met at Wilbraham in Massachusetts and after much opposition from a Mr J. Lee and others, it was voted to permit Lorenzo to travel. However, it was thought best that his name should not be printed in the minutes, a decision which Dow found offensive and in consequence of which he renounced the name 'Methodist'. Nevertheless, he

---

6 Dow, *Journal in the Dealings*, p. 45.
7 Dow, *Journal in the Dealings*, p. 55.
8 Dow, *Journal in the Dealings*, p. 57.
9 Dow, *Journal in the Dealings*, p. 64.
10 Dow, *Journal in the Dealings*, p. 74.
11 Dow, *Journal in the Dealings*, p. 83.
12 Dow, *Journal in the Dealings*, p. 90.
13 Dow, *Journal in the Dealings*, p. 90.

Lorenzo Dow

began his ministry at Pittstown, New York on the Cambridge Circuit where 'great excitement' soon attended his preaching. Many were converted under his forthright messages but 'the unrepentant, wicked and lukewarm mocked him as "Crazy Dow"'. In January 1799 Lorenzo was stationed in the Pittsfield Circuit, 'the most despised of any in New England'. He noted in his journal, 'I began to pursue the Circuit regularly after my own irregular manner, preaching to sinners, lukewarm professors and back-sliders.' Always on the move and responding to the inner promptings of his mind, it was not long before he began to set his sights in another direction. He developed a strong mental impression that he should visit Ireland but when he shared this with his fellow Methodists they opposed the idea with 'much earnestness'. It was of no avail however and, as was to be the case on many subsequent occasions, Lorenzo was quick to follow his initial impression.

Ireland and His Break with Methodism

Going on to Ireland at this point meant breaking with Methodist discipline and from this point the majority of Wesleyan preachers in both Britain and the United States gave him short shrift. On his arrival in Dublin, Mr Tobias, a Methodist preacher, advised him to return to America at once. Later when he returned to Dublin after a spell of rural preaching, the Methodist bishop, Dr Coke, who had just returned from America urged him to go to Canada as a missionary. By this time, however, Dow had prompted a revival as a result of his preaching at a military barracks, and was continuing to attract significant congregations at Mount Mellick and the surrounding neighbourhood.[14] He then sailed to Belfast and made several trips inland. This proved a harsh experience and he recorded on 6 March, 'My soul is much pained on Zion's account. The sores upon my feet grow worse, and I have no one, who can sympathise with me in my singular state.' After a period of serious illness with smallpox in August 1800 and some further preaching which included 'a shaking time' at Pill-town, Dow sailed for America on 2 April 1801.

Inevitably a man of Dow's disposition and character was going to find Methodist Connexional discipline a burden too hard to bear. After managing to labour in his appointed charge until the end of the same year, 'his mind was powerfully exercised on the subject of quitting his circuit'. Having once made the break Dow quit the circuit and sailed to Savannah arriving there on 8 January 1802. For the next three years he lived rough, travelling either on horseback or on foot, sleeping in the open and preaching wherever the opportunity arose. This was the time of the Second Great Awakening and he journeyed 800 miles through Tennessee and Kentucky. At many places he was well received, as for example in Charlestown, where in January 1804 he preached in both the Episcopal and Methodist churches.[15] From there he crossed the Alleghany mountains and came to Seversville and Knoxville where he observed the 'jerks' among those congregations. Significantly, he noted that in both towns that though they strove to keep as still as they could their emotions were 'involuntary and irresistible'.[16] At Marysville where Dow addressed about one thousand five hundred, many appeared 'to feel the word' and 'about fifty felt the jerks'.[17] From this relatively early point in his travels Dow appears to have taken a great interest in the phenomenon of the jerks and seems to have regarded them as an aspect of revival.

Early in 1804 he lodged with a family of Nicolite Quakers who felt it wrong to wear coloured clothing. While at tea Dow observed that one of the daughters of the house had the jerks and dropped the teacup in her hand as a result of her violent agitation. He inquired how long she had been taken with the exercise. She replied 'a few days, and that it had been the means of the awakening and conversion of her soul, by stirring her up to serious consideration about her careless state'.[18]

At Knoxville where Dow spoke on 19 February 1804 about one hundred and fifty appeared to have the jerking exercise. Among them was a circuit preacher by the name of Johnson, who had previously opposed them. After the meeting,

---

14 Dow, *Journal in the Dealings*, pp. 316–17.
15 Dow, *Journal in the Dealings*, p. 632.
16 Dow, *Journal in the Dealings*, p. 644.
17 Dow, *Journal in the Dealings*, p. 644.
18 Dow, *Journal in the Dealings*, p. 645.

Lorenzo rode 18 miles and preached in what was largely a Quaker area. The Friends there asserted that 'the Methodists and Presbyterians had the jerks because they prayed so much'. 'We are a peaceable people', they declared, 'and therefore do not have them.' About twenty of them attended Dow's meeting but found their usual stillness interrupted for, as Dow noted in his journal, 'about a dozen of them had the jerks so keen and powerful as to occasion a grunt or groan when they jerked'.[19]

Camp Meetings

Although people took to the jerks in a variety of different contexts, it seems to have been the case that they most often occurred in the camp meetings. These meetings were a marked feature of the Second Great Awakening in the Southern States. Their origin is perhaps to be found in the open-air preaching of George Whitefield and John Wesley. Certainly it was the Methodists who were the chief exponents of camp meetings in Kentucky and Tennessee where there was a camp meeting ground in every circuit. They were often located in a grove with a preaching stand and logs set out in front of it for seats. The stand would have an altar rail around it forming the 'altar' or 'glory pen' as critics preferred to call it. The preachers then exhorted the 'anxious', 'mourners' and 'seekers' to come forward into this enclosure where they were 'exhorted' to repent and to receive pardon for their sins or the sanctifying power of the Holy Spirit. People came in their hundreds, and indeed sometimes in their thousands, and camped in wagons and tents for several days around the preaching area, hence the term 'camp meeting'.

Dow makes frequent reference in his journal to camp meetings which he either attended, preached at or organized. A typical instance was the one that he organized on 31 August 1804 at Weston in Vermont. On his arrival he found three companies in the woods and stood on a log and preached to them. Several of their number, he recorded, 'then desired that I should pray for them and soon nine were sprawling on the ground, some apparently lifeless'.[20] Confusion soon set in and doctors who were present supposed that they had fainted and called for water and fans. Some suggested they were dying and others that it was the work of the devil. Dow however told the people that, 'if it was the devil's work, they will use the dialect of hell when they come to'. As things turned out they all were brought through 'happy' during the course of the night with the exception of one young woman who 'continued shrieking for mercy for eight hours'. Dow continued to exhort her until she testified to having found peace. He concluded the entry in his journal with the following line, 'About thirty found peace, and I appointed another camp meeting to commence in May.'[21]

---

19 Dow, *Journal in the Dealings*, p. 645.
20 Dow, *Journal in the Dealings*, p. 696.
21 Dow, *Journal in the Dealings*, p. 696.

A little later on 19 October, Dow reported on a camp meeting at Liberty. 'Here', he wrote, 'I saw the jerks, and some danced ... the people are taken irresistibly.' He observed that when they strove to resist the jerks, 'it worried them much' and that those who resisted their urge to dance felt 'a deadness and barrenness' taking hold of their minds. But as soon as they yielded to their impulse 'they feel happy, and there is a heavenly smile and solemnity on their countenances that carries conviction to the minds of the beholders'.[22] Dow's general feeling about the jerks was that they were most often a sign or encouragement to unbelievers that they needed to examine their state before God.

Many of Dow's preaching tours were particularly arduous. For example, he arrived at Tioga Point in Pennsylvania on 14 April 1805 having travelled 750 miles in 15 days, and spoken 26 times on the way, the appointments having been given out 13 months before. His anonymous Methodist biographer commented, 'No wonder Lorenzo frequently broke down his horses, as appears from his journal to have been the case. No horse could stand such incessant driving.'[23]

Dow's Marriage to Peggy Holcomb

Dow relates in his journal that when he was first in Ireland he 'saw the first pair that I thought were happy in marriage or showed a beauty in their connexion as a result of matrimony'.[24] The memory of this encounter remained with him and set his thoughts on the possibility of finding a spouse though he had resolved when he began to travel 'that no created object should be the means of rivalling my God'.[25]

While residing overnight in the home of Smith Miller of Western during the course of one of his preaching tours, Lorenzo inquired of his host if he had any children. He replied that he had a young woman whom he and his wife had brought up as their own daughter. Dow was unable even to catch a word with her before he left for his preaching appointment but did manage to do so on his return journey. He recorded his conversation with Smith in the following lines: 'I asked if he would object if I should talk to his daughter concerning matrimony? He replied. "I have nothing to say, only I have requested her, if she had any regard for me, not to marry so as to leave my house."'[26] Dow however was not easily deterred, particularly as he felt what he described as 'an uncommon exercise' run through his mind concerning the matter. On reaching the Millers' residence, he at once put the issue to Mrs Miller who replied that 'Peggy was resolved never to marry unless it were to a preacher who would continue travelling.' At that point

---

22 Dow, *Journal in the Dealings*, p. 701.
23 Anon., *The Eccentric Preacher: Or a Sketch of the Life of the Celebrated Lorenzo Dow* (E.A. Rice, 1841), p. 86.
24 Dow, *Journal in the Dealings*, p. 697.
25 Dow, *Journal in the Dealings*, p. 697.
26 Dow, *Journal in the Dealings*, p. 697.

Peggy came into the room and Dow took the opportunity to confirm that this was the case. When she answered in the affirmative he asked, 'do you think you could accept such an object as me?' 'This', he added, 'was the first time of my speaking to her.' Perhaps understandably, she left the room without making any reply. The next morning, still unabashed, Dow made a further proposal that he would return in 12 or 13 months time and that if she had found no one she liked better she would then consent to their being married. He also emphasized that she would have to 'be willing to give me up twelve months out of thirteen, or three years out of four to travel, and that in foreign lands, and never say, do not go to your appointments and co.'

On his return a year later, Dow found Peggy still single and 'they all willingly agreed to comply with my request'. Accordingly a preacher came in and 'we were married that night though only we five were present, this being the third of September, 1804'.[27] Early the very next morning Dow set off with Smith, Peggy's guardian, to his preaching appointment at Natchez, Westmorland and Augusta. He did not return to Western for a further eight months and when he did so he found that Peggy was not at home.[28] This set the pattern for the following 15 years of their marriage. Notwithstanding Peggy Holcomb, who was born at Granville, Massachusetts, in 1780, proved a resourceful and steadfast helpmeet despite the alternating hardships when she travelled with Lorenzo and the acute loneliness while he was away, often for many months at a time. Like her husband she kept a journal which provides some additional information about their travels. It also reveals her deep devotion to God and the sweet affection and regard that she had for her husband, whom she frequently refers to as 'my dear Lorenzo'. He, for his part, comes across as a rather more distant and unfeeling individual often referring to Peggy as 'his rib'!

Peggy graphically describes the rigours of their times on the revival circuit. For a period of four months they lived in a small cabin in the Mississippi swamp lands,[29] shortly after which Lorenzo made another preaching tour that lasted for a year and six days leaving her to fend for herself. On Lorenzo's return she decided to accompany him on his next tour through the wilderness of Georgia recording that 'my heart trembled at the thought of sleeping out in this desert place with no company but my husband'. They often slept under the stars with only the wild beasts for company. They cut cane for their horses and fed on hard biscuit and coffee which they cooked on an open fire.[30] Peggy gave the following description of their gruelling experience.

> I had got a fall from my horse and hurt myself considerably; and I was as much fatigued and worn out by travelling as ever I was in my life.

---

27 Dow, *Journal in the Dealings*, p. 697.
28 Anon., *The Eccentric Preacher*, p. 86.
29 Anon., *The Eccentric Preacher*, p. 118.
30 Dow, *Journal in the Dealings*, p. 221.

> I thought sometimes that I should never stand it, to get through the wilderness, but providence gave me strength of body beyond what I could have expected. We left the Indians' camp in the morning, and reached Col. Hawkings' that night. This was within thirty miles of the settlements of Georgia. I felt grateful to the God of all grace, for his tender care over us, while in this dreary part of the land – where our ears had been saluted by the hideous yells of the wolf – and had been surrounded by the savages, more wild and fierce than they; and yet we were preserved from all danger, and brought through in safety.[31]

Rather than endure an extended period of loneliness Peggy decided to accompany Lorenzo on his first trip to England. It was a journey of heartache and suffering that lasted from November 1805 to June 1807. There, Peggy gave birth to their daughter, Letitia, and then fell seriously ill with a fever at Warrington. At this critical juncture, as happened from time to time, Lorenzo felt strongly impressed that he must visit Ireland once more. Despite remonstrations from his friends he took a ship to Dublin leaving his wife acutely sick and an infant daughter in the care of friends. During his stay in Ireland he received the solemn news of the death of their only child and wrote that 'I felt as if part of myself were gone.' 'Yet', he continued, 'I could not murmur, but felt submission.' It was all but three months before he set foot on English soil once more and was somewhat consoled to find Peggy recovered. He later recorded that 'many condemned me for going to Ireland when and as I did, but had I tarried I could have done no good, as I obtained the nurse I wished for, and by going I answered a clear conscience'.[32]

After their return from England, Lorenzo resumed his punishing schedule of travel and preaching despite often being dogged by asthmatic attacks and other physical ailments. On some his subsequent tours Peggy went with him, going for example to Virginia in the autumn of 1807 and to Albany in June 1808. In 1814 she journeyed with Lorenzo to Petersburg, Richmond, Alexandria, Washington and Baltimore. In April 1816 he installed Peggy in his father's house until the spring of the following year while he spent most of his time journeying through Vermont, New Hampshire and Connecticut to Philadelphia.

Towards the end of the second decade when Lorenzo was again on the point of departing for England, it became clear that Peggy's health was in serious decline. Notwithstanding these circumstances Lorenzo set sail for the old country in May 1818. By the spring of the following year it appeared that some people in England had been made aware of the situation and Dow recorded in his journal that 'several strangers had told me in different parts of my travels, that if I did not return shortly, I would see my companion no more, which

---

31 Dow, *Journal in the Dealings*, p. 223.
32 Dow, *Journal in the Dealings*, p. 864.

testimony so corroborated my own feelings as to give rise to my return sooner than intended'.[33]

Dow arrived back in America in June 1819 and supposing Peggy not as frail as the reports had led him to believe, he encouraged her to travel with him to various meetings in Rhode Island. However while they lodged at Providence her consumption took a turn for the worst and it was clear that her end was near. They returned home in September and apart from two brief occasions they never parted until she died on 6 January 1820. Her funeral service was attended by 'a large concourse of people' and she was laid to rest in the Methodist Burial Ground in Hebron, Connecticut. Dow later wrote, 'My Peggy is gone to meet our infant in yonder world, where I trust to meet them both by and bye – which is a sweet and pleasing thought to me.'

In November of that year Dow resided in Washington for a brief period in order to launch 'Lorenzo Dow's Family Medicine'. The recipe for this came from his English friend and benefactor, Dr Paul Johnson. Sellers suggested that this was a sincere attempt on Lorenzo's part to relieve the sufferings of his fellow countrymen.[34] As someone who was prone to bouts of asthma Dow was probably deeply concerned for those who suffered severe bronchial infection.

Dow's Later Travels and Literary Endeavours

In the first year of his second marriage he introduced his new wife, Lucy, to the nation, first journeying through the six New England states and then going south as the cold weather began to set in. Other travels followed in the succeeding years. In 1823 for example, we find him visiting Niagra Falls and then being arrested in Troy. In1826 he passed through many places in Indiana and visited Indianapolis. In 1828 he preached in Boston and Rochester and then in a number of towns and villages in Ontario and 1831 was spent principally in New England.

Increasingly however in this latter period of his life Lorenzo preached less and wrote more. As his fame spread throughout the nation he seems to have become growingly obsessed with his own reputation and importance. He perhaps never fully recovered from having been convicted of libel and spent much time and energy collecting and publishing affidavits and testimony to his good character. During the last decade of his life Lorenzo began to read more widely but, as C.C. Sellers observed, 'his delvings into book learning were largely superficial'.[35] Much of his output was polemical as for example, *The Chain of Lorenzo*, which was an assault on Calvinism and *On Church Government* which was an attack on both Methodism and Roman Catholicism. Some of his other literary endeavours were more practical, such as his

---

33 Dow, *Journal in the Dealings*, p. 26.
34 C.C. Sellers, *Lorenzo Dow Bearer of the Word* (Minto, Balch, 1928), pp. 200–4.
35 Sellers, *Lorenzo Dow*, p. 216.

Reflections on Marriage, Rules for Holy Living and *Omnifarious Law Exemplified* in which 27 kinds of law are briefly examined, including 'Jockey Law' which represented his experience in the horse trade!

'Crazy Dow': A Reputation Deserved

Often described as 'an hairy man' there is no doubt that Dow was an unusual eccentric individual. His hair was always long and flowing and his beard unshorn, some said in imitation of the apostles! His dress was mean and his appearance unkempt. His voice was reported to be harsh and his gesticulation and delivery ungraceful. He witty retorts were occasionally crude and out of order and on some occasions he would smash chairs for effect or attract attention by arranging for a trumpet blow to be sounded at a strategic moment.[36] He seemed ever ready to engage in the unexpected and spontaneous, a trait made obvious when he took his leave from a Congregational church at Bethel by jumping out of the window beside the pulpit![37] From his earliest endeavours as a preacher, people began to call him 'Crazy Dow', a term which he accepted and indeed used of himself in his journal.

These characteristics became more apparent after his return from his trip to the British Isles in 1807. From that point on he began to refer to himself, often in the third person, as 'Cosmopolite'. He also speaks of having suffered an unusual physical ailment which may perhaps have been exacerbated by the sheer exhaustion of the punishing schedule he set for himself. He recounted his condition and its effects on his lifestyle in the following lines.

> Whilst in Europe, Cosmopolite was attacked with spasms of a most extraordinary kind, which baffled the skill of the most celebrated of the faculty, and reduced his nervous strength and shook his constitution to the centre, more than all his labours heretofore. Now his sun appeared declining and his career drawing to a close. But the idea of yielding and giving up the itinerant sphere, was trying to Cosmopolite, seeing it was his element and paradise to preach the gospel. Hence he got a stiff leather jacket, girted it with buckles, to serve as stays, to support his tottering frame and to enable him to ride on horseback. This the doctors remonstrated against. When it would answer no further, he took the gig and a little wagon: but was obliged to sit or lay down some part of the meeting to be able to finish his discourse; mostly for seven years.[38]

---

36 Wolffe, *The Expansion of Evangelicalism*, p. 111.
37 Anon., *Eccentric Preacher*, p. 89.
38 Dow, *Journal in the Dealings*, p. 882.

The strains and stresses of his time in England had clearly adversely affected his health and for some while Lorenzo appeared to be in a low condition. In 1809 he catalogued some of his major burdens.

> First, some heavy debts.
> Second, No money or flush loose property.
> Thirdly, A sick companion without house or home.
> Fourthly, Reputation on all sides, and in remote parts, through the States. Stories that Cosmopolite was revelling in riches and luxury, with a fine brick house, sugar and cotton plantations, flour and sawmills, slaves and money in the banks, like a nabob in the East.[39]

If there was one occurrence that encapsulated Dow's bizarre nature it was the events surrounding his second marriage to Lucy Dolbeare, the daughter of a well-to-do farmer of Montville, a few miles south from Hebron. Notwithstanding the many harsh demands that he had exacted on Peggy during his travels he found her loss a terrible blow. He wrote that the loneliness was too sensible to contemplate in his feelings. Thus, in an attempt to find comfort and consolation he married Lucy. Unlike Peggy she was described as 'a handsome, healthy woman, with a strong arm, a strong voice and an inexhaustible flow of language'. Dow's approach to Lucy differed little from his blunt and gauche first encounter with Peggy 15 years earlier. The most conservative version of what took place is that having felt attracted to her as she sat in front of him during a meeting, he went to her the moment it concluded and proposed and that she responded with an immediate acceptance. A quainter and more bizarre account cannot be altogether discounted. The setting was reportedly an open-air meeting under the great elm on Bean Hill, near Norwich. It was said that Lorenzo, after having preached a sermon in which he extolled Peggy's fidelity and purity, concluded by announcing: 'I am a candidate for matrimony; and if there is any woman in this audience who is willing to marry me, I would thank her to rise.' In response to this sudden and unexpected opportunity two women took to their feet, one near the pulpit, and one towards the back of the congregation. For a brief moment Lorenzo scrutinized them both, and then pronounced with great solemnity: 'There are two. I think this one near the front rose first; at any rate I will have her.'[40] Subsequently in the cold light of day Lucy tried to back out and it took Lorenzo until midnight on a later evening to secure her consent. Having done so, he at once escorted her to the Revd John Whittlesey and their marriage was solemnised.

The manner of Lorenzo's marriage to Lucy illustrates the way in which, in company with a number of other revivalist preachers, he seems to have operated his life on the basis of what he describes as 'religious impressions'. He

---

39 Anon, *Eccentric Preacher*, p. 117.
40 Sellers, *Lorenzo Dow*, pp. 197–8.

frequently acted on them in impulse without any reflection or consideration of the likely consequence of his sudden actions. In this respect he must be categorised as an 'enthusiast'. His journals abound with phrases such as the following: 'Sabbath morning, I heard one preach, and then by an impression on my mind took upwards of a hundred of my handbills ... and went through the town distributing them.'[41] Again in January 1801 he wrote, 'Having it impressed on my mind to give the people of Dublin a general warning ...'[42] He had sought the hand of Peggy in marriage after experiencing 'an uncommon exercise ... run through my mind'.[43] In his early days he had broken with Methodism after his mind had been 'powerfully exercised on the subject of quitting his circuit'.[44] On the matter of these promptings, Dow's anonymous biographer wrote: 'It seems that these impressions were the guides which directed his wanderings. If they proceeded from the Divine Spirit, he did right in following them: but of this there is much to doubt, since the desires and inclinations of our fickle hearts may easily be confounded with the teachings of a higher Monitor.'[45] Such was the case when Dow joined the Freemasons in 1824, a move which provoked much criticism from his contemporaries. He related the circumstances surrounding this decision in *Omnifarious Law*.

> When in Rhode Island, 1824, in my sleep, I thought myself in a Masonic Lodge, where I received a degree, after which I stood up to give an address, in doing which I worked myself up. A strange weighty exercise – sleep fled – early I crossed the ferry to Warren, where I related the circumstance at breakfast – noticed the countenance of some present, which appeared to be an index of the mind – concluded they were masons – on inquiring found it to be so.[46]

Arriving back in Bristol he found his dream to be a reality and so on Christmas Day he was initiated at St Alban's Lodge No. 6 of that town. Moreover on the following day the distinguished preacher initiate was raised to the degree of 'Fellow Craft' and made a Master Mason. When in 1826 a member who was publishing the order's secrets was murdered and the country was stricken with fear, Lorenzo stoutly defended his allegiance. In sermons and pamphlets he stressed the order's ancient roots and its benevolent activities in society. He also reminded anti-masons that 'his lordship, the Pope' was among their members. Dow himself justified guidance by feelings on the ground that this was a natural part of human experience. He gave the example of 'a man walking along, spies a wild beast of the forest, and feels his hair rise and his flesh creep upon his

---

41 Anon., *Eccentric Preacher*, p. 11.
42 Anon., *Eccentric Preacher*, p. 53.
43 Dow, *Journal in the Dealings*, p. 697.
44 Anon., *Eccentric Preacher*, p. 56.
45 Anon., *Eccentric Preacher*, p. 111.
46 L. Dow, *Omnifaroius Law* (Applegate, 1860), p. 185.

bones'. Why, he asked, should not God similarly guide us through our feelings? Dow felt that this was often much more reliable than biblically-based reason which frequently resulted in strong disagreements.

In February 1834, just a few months after having met with President Andrew Jackson for the second time, Lorenzo was seized with a fever in the house of his friend and fellow Mason, George W. Haller. He died shortly afterwards and was buried in Holmead's cemetery with the usual Masonic ceremonies being administered by the brethren of Potomac Lodge. The inscription on his tombstone suggests that his faith had departed from his early days as a Methodist preacher.

> A Repository
> of
> LORENZO DOW
> who was born in Coventry
> Connecticut
> Octr. 16, 1777 died Feb 2
> 1834 Age 56
> A Christian is the highest
> Style of man.
> He is
> A slave to no sect, takes
> no private road
> But looks through nature
> up to nature's God.

Dow's Understanding of Revival and His Impact in England

Dow was an active participant in many camp meetings of the Second Great Awakening which took place in the southern states in the early years of the nineteenth century. His understanding of revival was that of Peter Cartwright and other Methodist circuit preachers. His early links with the followers of Wesley doubtless helped to shape his strongly anti-Calvinist views which he expressed with rigour in his book, *Nuggets of Golden Truth*.[47] Thus, as Dow understood it, there was always a human element in 'revival'. For him revival was the coming together of a large number of preferably unchurched people to hear and respond to the claims of Christ. Revival also involved 'an outpouring of the Spirit of God'[48] which in turn was manifested in religious exercises such as 'jerking' and 'falling'. Dow had also experienced what he termed 'the

---

47 Dow, *Nuggets of Golden Truth*, p. 77. Dow wrote, ' Yet I adopt the idea, that a man can fall from grace, according to conscience, reason and scripture.'
48 Dow, *Journal in the Dealings*, p. 800.

blessing of sanctification' at some point while he was in Canada.[49] After falling to the floor and groaning out for God he was left with 'an inward, simple, sweet running peace from day to day, so that prosperity or adversity doth not produce ups and downs as formerly'.[50] There is no doubt that he sought to minister this experience to those he exhorted in the sinners pen at his camp meetings and at the conclusion of his preachings.

Camp Meetings

Dow focused on preaching and prayer as the biblical means of achieving revival although, because he was constantly on the move, it was often difficult for him to organize sustained times of corporate prayer. That said, Dow was above all a leading exponent of camp meetings and found them to be a vital and useful means of stimulating times of revival. Camp meetings, which were first observed in the closing years of the eighteenth century, became a dominant feature in the south as the revival spread. Dow attended them, appointed them and made frequent use of them.

Dow wrote a pamphlet entitled On *Camp Meetings* which was subsequently included in all the editions of his collected works. Dow began by discussing a number of biblical passages in which God's people dwell in tents. Abraham for example 'quit his house and lived in tents'. Jacob dwelt in tabernacles. Dow also wrote of the Feast of Tabernacles as 'a camp meeting to be held annually for a period of seven days'.[51] He then went on to consider how men such as George Fox, John Wesley and George Whitefield were made useful when they started to hold meetings in the open air. Dow concluded by relating that he had appointed the first of a series of regular camp meetings that were held in the centre of Virginia in 1804 and in the same year the first of many that were subsequently held in the states of Mississippi and New York.

Dow's strong commitment to camp meetings found a ready acceptance during his two visits to England in 1805–7 and 1818–19. In the early years of the nineteenth century there were a series of enthusiastic accounts of American camp meetings in the *Wesleyan Methodist Magazine* which attracted the attention of numbers of working-class revivalists whose activities were only loosely attached to official Wesleyanism and already causing them concern. It was among their number, particularly in the Potteries and North-West England around Warrington and Chester, that Dow found a ready welcome and indeed a warm acceptance of camp meetings. After a visit to Macclesfield on 20 July 1806 where he spoke in the street to 'about five thousand' and 'wrestled with mourners at night'[52] and some time in Congleton where he found 'more than a hundred had been taken

---

49 L. Dow, *History of Cosmopolite or the Writings of Lorenzo Dow* (Joshua Martin and Alex S. Robinson, 1849), p. 142.
50 Dow, *History of Cosmopolite*, p. 143.
51 Dow, *On Camp Meetings*, p. 248.
52 Dow, *Journal in the Dealings*, p. 827.

into society since my other visit',[53] Dow went on to visit 'the revivalistic societies' in the Burslem area which had risen up under the leadership of Hugh Bourne. Here he later recalled being at a meeting on Mow Hill where 'I was drawn to speak particularly on the origin of Camp Meetings in America, which affected the minds of the people who were in the spirit of a revival'.[54]

Dow printed and sold tracts on the great benefit of camp meetings and Bourne not only purchased a copy for himself but his followers embraced these meetings wholeheartedly. Indeed for a time, they were known as the 'Camp Meeting Methodists'.[55] Although camp meetings were warmly accepted by the Methodist Church in America, the English Conference pronounced against them at its annual conference at Liverpool in 1807 'as highly improper and likely to be of considerable mischief'.[56] Their judgement was subsequently printed in their magazine of 1807.

> What is the judgement of the CONFERENCE, concerning what are called 'CAMP MEETINGS'?
>
> It is our judgement that, that even if such meetings be allowable in America, they are highly improper in ENGLAND, and likely to be productive of considerable mischief. And WE disclaim all connexion with them.
>
> Have our people been sufficiently cautious respecting the permission of strangers to preach in OUR congregations?
>
> WE fear not; and we again DIRECT that no STRANGER FROM AMERICA, or elsewhere, be suffered to preach in any of OUR PLACES, unless he come fully accredited: if an Itinerant Preacher, by having his name entered on the Minutes of Conference of which he is a member: and if a Local Preacher, by a recommendatory note from his Superintendent.[57]

There were several reasons that combined to prompt the Wesleyan Conference to make this decision. In an era when the authorities feared unlawful gatherings and the *Conventicle* and *Five Mile Acts* prohibited unlicensed preachers, these were just the kind of gatherings that they most feared. Reports of some American camp meetings had included very large numbers of people coming together and violent emotionalism not unmixed with

---

53 Dow, *Journal in the Dealings*, p. 865.
54 Dow, *Journal in the Dealings*, p. 318.
55 See Kendall, *The Origin and History*, Vol. 1.
56 *Wesleyan Methodist Conference Minutes*, 1807.
57 Dow, *Journal in the Dealings*, p. 164 (no paragraphs are cited on this page). See also *Minutes of the Methodist Conferences, From the First, Held in London by the Late John Wesley A.M. in the year 1774* (Thomas Cordeux, 1813) Vol. 2, 1807, p. 403.

sexual license. Additionally, there was the fact that Dow had broken with Wesleyan Methodist discipline and failed to comply with the instructions of his American superiors. Be that as it may, it is clear from Bourne's *History of the Primitive Methodists* that Dow's advocacy of the camp meeting was a major factor in the origin of his organization which took the name of Primitive Methodism in 1811. Bourne wrote of Dow, 'This man spoke of camp meetings, both in public and private, and printed several tracts on the subject. These things ... filled the country with camp meeting conversations.'[58]

When Dow returned to England in 1818 he revisited the Potteries and Staffordshire and found the Primitives in good heart, recording in his journal that, 'this Society amounts to several thousand strong and I visited between thirty and forty chapels'. He was particularly gladdened to find that 'some of my spiritual children still stood fast'.[59] During that time he evidently took part in camp meetings, Hugh Bourne recording the following note in his diary: 'Sunday 19 (July) Camp Meeting at Tunstall. Lorenzo Dow was there. We had some rain and thunder and lightning. Monday 20 July was at Tunstall, we had a number of preachings. Lorenzo Dow spoke at five in the morning and five in the evening.'[60] He noted that 'They have three circuits – about 150 preachers, among whom are about thirty women.'[61] The *Primitive Methodist Magazine* of June 1820 reported that the whole Tunstall Circuit had been revived to 'its present prosperity' when the decision was taken to make the praying service the central aspect of the camp meetings.[62] Whilst it is true that camp meetings were a major factor in both the origin and development of Primitive Methodism they should not be overplayed. William Clowes, Bourne's co-worker, never took to them in the same way in which Hugh Bourne did. He held aloof from them for a period of 15 months following his expulsion from the Wesleyan body in 1807.[63] In January 1819 Clowes entered Hull and within six months it became the fourth Primitive Methodist circuit. Whilst it was the case that camp meetings were held within Clowes' Hull diaspora, they do not appear to have been quite such a prominent feature.[64] That said, it seems clear that Dow's return visits to Tunstall, Nottingham, Leicester and other places in the Midlands injected fresh life into the Primitives.[65]

---

58 H. Bourne, *History of the Primitive Methodists in Dealings* (1833 edition), p. 414.
59 Dow, *Journal in the Dealings*, p. 170.
60 Cited Kent, *Holding the Fort*, p. 56.
61 Dow, *Journal in the Dealings* (1833 edition), p. 320.
62 *Primitive Methodist Magazine*, June 1820, pp. 227–8, article entitled, 'On the Progress of Tunstall Circuit'. See also, 'Camp Meetings. On the mode of conducting the Worship at Camp Meetings in America', *Primitive Methodist Magazine*, July 1819, pp. 149–51.
63 Kendall, *The Origin and History*, Vol. 1, p. 87.
64 Kendall, *The Origin and History*, Vol. 1, p. 87.
65 Kent suggests that Dow's second visit which rejuvenated Primitive Methodism may have been somewhat played down by Bourne. See Kent, *Holding the Fort*, p. 57.

Lorenzo Dow and Camp Meeting Revivalism

Certainly in 1850 Thomas Church could write as follows of camp meetings in his *Popular Sketches of Primitive Methodism*.

> The subject of camp meetings, comes next in order. These meetings are so generally known in all parts of the kingdom, that we need say but little by way of explanation. Hundreds, and we may say thousands, have been savingly converted to God through the instrumentality of these meetings; and we are glad to find, that in our 'Consolidated Minutes' for 1849, 'Camp meetings are still regarded as beneficial to the spiritual interests of the breathing masses; and anxiety for their prudential management, and continued usefulness, is so far felt, as to call forth, a page of directory regulations. Testimonies to the grand effects of camp meetings, – in their promotion of social happiness, in their (instrumental) securance [sic] of ETERNAL LIFE the repenting humanity, may be gathered from nearly all parts of our Empire'.[66]

Gatherings for Mourners

Dow, like Charles Finney after him, believed it to be crucially important to invite 'mourners' or those who were anxious about their state before God, to come forward in some public way where he could minister to their needs and record their names in a more specific manner. Thus for example, when Dow held a meeting at Macclesfield at half past five in the morning on Monday 17 November 1806, he recalled, 'I invited mourners to meet me at twelve.'[67] On the following day after he had preached his final sermon, he invited mourners to come forward. About fifty did so and several 'professed to find deliverance'.[68] What this was like in practice is well illustrated by a passage in George Herod's *Biographical Sketches*. Herod, who was a Primitive Methodist itinerant and died in 1862, met Dow in 1818 and heard him when he held an open-air service in the market place on 14 September.

> He commenced by singing one of his American hymns, which the people had been accustomed to sing for some months past; thus hundreds joined the grand chorus of hallelujahs. After delivering a very pointed and pithy discourse (for it was full of Jesus Christ) he saw that a great many were deeply wrought upon by the spirit and the word; he therefore immediately went into the centre of the congregation and requested the people to draw back and form a circle; he then stood and invited the penitents to come forward and receive a blessing of pardon; and in a few minutes the whole

---

66 T. Church, *Popular Sketches of Primitive Methodism being a Link in the chain of British Ecclesiastical History* (Thomas Church, 1850).
67 Dow, *Journal in the Dealings*, p. 131, paragraph 835.
68 Dow, *Journal in the Dealings*, p. 131, paragraph 835.

space was filled; he then enlarged the space by requesting the congregation to go further back; but this was also soon taken up – we should judge that not less than two hundred were on their knees seeking pardon. He then commenced prayer and very soon his voice was lost among the groans and cries for mercy; and in less than half an hour we should suppose one hundred souls were brought into gospel liberty.[69]

Dow's techniques were clearly effective and to the point. The practice of praying for mourners became prominent feature of early Primitive Methodist revivalism as H.B. Kendall makes clear in his history of the movement.

Blunt Preaching

Preaching was clearly the major means by which Dow sought to foster revival among the people. His journal gives only passing hints as to the content of his sermons but his general approach seems to have been blunt and 'in-your-face'. Asbury maintained that he 'roared and shouted and habitually shocked his hearers by preaching rigorously from the pornographic and sadistic sections of the Bible'.[70] He frequently graphically contrasted heaven and hell, sometimes warning specific individuals who sat in front of him, that they were in danger of eternal punishment. Dow also had a capacity for the unexpected which was well illustrated when the bench that he stood preaching on at Watson's Meeting House in Virginia gave way. Recovering dextrously, he noted, 'I observed it was a loud call for sinners to be in readiness, lest they should sink lower than the grave.'[71]

Dow's appearance was startling and sometimes terrified his hearers. He was tall and thin and his frequent lack of food and sleep left him emaciated and pale. He wore clothing which was invariably torn, shabby and ill-fitting. He was often hatless and sometimes shoeless. One of his contemporaries and a critic, Nicholas Snethen, wrote of him: 'His manners have been clownish in the extreme and his habit and appearance more filthy than a savage Indian; his public discourses a mere rhapsody, the substance often an insult upon the gospel.'[72] All of this combined with invective rhetoric made a powerful impact on his hearers, many of whom sought to make their peace with God when the 'anxious' were exhorted to prayer.

---

69 G. Herod, *Biographical Sketches* ([1855] Tentmaker Publications, 2002), pp. 188–9.
70 H. Asbury, *A Methodist Saint. The Life of Bishop Asbury* (Alfred A. Knopf, 1927), p. 227.
71 Dow, *Journal in the Dealings*, p. 713.
72 Asbury, *A Methodist Saint*, p. 231.

Revival Songs

Songs were a very important part of Dow's revivalism and the music that he brought with him from America contributed a great deal to his success. Dow published the words in booklet form but taught the tunes of what he called, 'A Collection of Spiritual Songs used at the Camp Meetings in the Great Revival of the United States of America'. According to Kent, the earliest known preface is reproduced in Herod's *Sketches* and is signed 22 February 1806.[73] It was printed by H. Forshaw in Liverpool in 1806 and must have been commissioned by Dow soon after he landed on English soil. The book was the first collection of revivalist songs to be printed in England and also the first containing songs from the Second Great Awakening in the Southern Colonies. Hugh Bourne was much taken with it and purchased a copy in April 1807. Such was his enthusiasm for the book that he reprinted all but two and a half of the songs in his own first hymnbook which he published in 1821. Kent points out that 19 of the original songs also appeared in Bourne's *Collection for Camp Meetings, Revivals etc for the use of Primitive Methodists* and without any acknowledgement to Dow. The songs, which emphasized religious feeling and experience, were widely used by Dow who set in motion the tradition of the singing evangelist. Kent gives as one example 'The Dying Pilgrim'.

> My soul's full of glory which inspires my tongue,
> Could I meet with angels I'd sing them a song.
> I'd sing of my Jesus and tell of his charms.
> And beg them to bear me to his loving arms ...
>
> Oh Heaven, sweet Heaven, I long to be there,
> To meet all my brethren and Jesus my dear.
> Come angels, come angels, I'm ready to fly,
> Come quickly convey me to God in the sky ...
>
> I'm going, I'm going, but what do I see;
> T'is Jesus in glory appears unto me.
> To Heaven, to Heaven I'm gone, I'm gone,
> Oh glory, oh glory, 'tis done. 'tis done.

Religious Exercises

Along with Barton Stone, James McGready and Peter Cartwright, Dow was accepting of the 'religious exercises' which emerged at the time of the Great Awakening. At some points in his journal, he describes the jerks, the dancing and falling exercises. It was his observation that those most often taken with the jerks were those whom God was recalling to Himself. Commenting on the

---

[73] Kent, *Holding the Fort*, p. 63.

jerks, Dow wrote, 'I have seen Presbyterians, Methodists, Quakers, Baptists, Church of England and Independents, exercised with the jerks; Gentlemen and Ladies, black and white, the aged and youth, rich and poor, without exception; from which I infer, as it cannot be accounted for on natural principles, and carries such marks of involuntary motion, that it is no trifling matter.'[74] Of particular significance was Dow's observation that the jerks that took place at meetings that he conducted tended to be among those who were lukewarm and half-hearted in their faith. 'The pious' and 'those who were given up to God' were 'rarely touched with it'. Dow also noted that when the back-slidden or the unbelievers were taken with the jerks they were usually 'alarmed and stirred up to redouble their diligence to God'.[75] In contrast Dow observed that the 'dancing exercise' was more common among the committed 'in whom it produced happiness, and a heavenly smile and solemnity towards God'.[76]

Publicity and House-to-House Visiting

Two other means, which Dow frequently used to bring people to his meetings, were publicity and house-to-house visiting. For instance, in his journal he recorded that on the way to Spencetown, 'I began immediately to visit the neighbourhood from house to house.'[77] He recalled that the people thought it strange 'but came to see where it would end'. Some years later at Savannah, Dow noted, 'I spoke to about seventy whites and blacks; but to get them collected, I took upwards of a hundred handbills and distributed them through the town.'[78] When at Pill-town in Ireland in August 1800 he passed out some 'rules for holy living in the streets'. On the following Sabbath morning he distributed 'upwards of a hundred handbills'.[79] In Dublin in January 1801 he 'got about three thousand handbills printed', the greater part of which he distributed 'among the quality and decent kind of people'.[80] After the time of revival at Congleton in Staffordshire, Dow went on to the Potteries where he spoke of the great usefulness of camp meetings and sold pamphlets giving details about them. Hugh Bourne purchased two pamphlets from him, one describing how camp meetings were held and the other being *A Defence of Camp Meetings* by the Revd S.K. Jennings AM.[81]

Publicity undoubtedly played an important role in Dow's impact and particularly so during his visits to England. Indeed shortly after landing at

---

74 Dow, *Journal in the Dealings*, p. 647.
75 Dow, *Journal in the Dealings*, p. 647.
76 Dow, *Journal in the Dealings*, p. 701.
77 Dow, *Journal in the Dealings*, p. 234.
78 Dow, *Journal in the Dealings*, p. 523.
79 Anon., *Eccentric Preacher*, p. 51.
80 Anon., *Eccentric Preacher*, p. 53.
81 J. Petty, *The History of the Primitive Methodist Connexion From its Origin to the Conference of 1860* (R. Davies, 1864), p. 18.

Liverpool in 1806, almost his first action was to have handbills printed. In this he was following the steps of Whitefield and others who had found that giving out leaflets and tracts, particularly those which contained positive accounts of previous meetings, did much to create faith and raise expectancy levels on the part of the hearers. The use of printed literature was to be a growing feature of nineteenth-century American revivalism. Indeed with the emergence of the great urban meetings organized by Moody in London and elsewhere printed publicity became a significant feature.

Postscript

Dow's significance as a revivalist is not easy to assess. In his earlier days he seems to have had some measure of the social graces and there was also a semblance of rationality in his behaviour and decision-making. Hugh Bourne recorded his impressions of Dow when first heard him preach at Harriseahead and then at Congleton in April 1807.

> His appearance was striking. His eyes bright and deep set: his hair dark and long, hanging over his shoulders; his visage elongated and well-defined; the tones of his voice were deep and solemn, and his style of address pungent and powerful. He not only preached with unusual effect; in social intercourse also he dealt faithfully and practically with the company around him, and communicated his views on various subjects with such clearness and cogency, that he was successful in promoting a revival of personal holiness, and also of converting work. His oral statements about the American camp-meetings were highly interesting, and he circulated tracts and pamphlets respecting them that extended and perpetuated the influence of his statements.[82]

As time progressed however Dow became increasingly unpredictable and fervent in the conduct of both his own life and his revival campaigns. By the time of his second visit to England his life had become a cocktail of high octane religious fervour and political invective mixed with intense suffering and hardship. It was suggested by Asbury and others that Lorenzo may have suffered epilepsy from his childhood days. This suggestion is certainly a way of accounting for the times when he fell to the ground while preaching with intense shaking, spasms and tremblings in his arms and legs. Dow was a preacher extraordinaire. He penetrated into all the frontier settlements of the American colonies and was a prominent figure in all the great camp-meeting revivals of the West and South. He knew how to hold the attention of very large

---

82 Anon., *The Life of Hugh Bourne Founder of the Primitive Methodist Connexion* (James B. Knapp, 1982) p. 56. See also W. Antliff, *The Life of the Venerable Hugh Bourne* (George Lamb, 1872).

audiences and few preachers could so quickly inspire their hearers to the jerks, dancing and the anxious rail. It was inevitable that when he became a national figure increasingly large crowds gathered out of curiosity to hear him. This, to some extent, caused him to be overly concerned with his own importance and quite possibly motivated his literary output of later years. But as C.C. Sellers observed, 'his delvings into book learning were largely superficial'. Indeed much of his writing was polemical in nature and ranged from attacks on Calvinism, Methodism and Roman Catholicism to remonstrations against social and political evils.[83] Dow's predictions of calamities, interpretation of dreams, guidance by sudden impressions and his wholehearted embracing of Freemasonry are hard to reconcile with orthodox Christianity. Against that can be set the fact that thousands came to faith through his ministry, not least in the British Isles, where Dow made a significant contribution to the development of Primitive Methodism. He will go down in the history as the great promoter of camp meeting revivals. William Antliff (1813–84)[84] in his Preface to the 1863 edition of Dow's *Nuggets of Golden Truth* paid him this tribute:

> How far we are indebted to Lorenzo Dow for the peculiarities of worship, and of church government, which have from the first prevailed among us as a section of Christ's church, it were not easy to decide. But, no doubt, the minds of our fathers were much impressed with appearance, the earnestness, the doctrines, and the disciplinary views of Lorenzo. Hence he having assisted, under God, to lay the foundation stones of the Primitive Methodist Church, we deem him worthy of lasting remembrance by the members of this church.[85]

---

83 Sellers, *Lorenzo Dow*, p. 216.
84 William Antliff (1813–84) was a largely self-educated Primitive Methodist minister who became the first Principal of the Sunderland Theological Institute and was President of the Primitive Methodist Conference in 1863 and 1865.
85 W. Antliff, Preface to Dow, *Nuggets of Golden Truth*, p. 8.

CHAPTER 3

Zilpha Elaw and Reformist Revivalism

Zilpha Elaw was born in the state of Pennsylvania. Her mother died when she was only 12 years of age and her father entrusted her upbringing to Pierson and Rebecca Mitchel. One day while she was singing and milking a cow she had a dramatic encounter with Christ. She expressed it as follows: 'one evening whilst singing one of the songs of Zion, I distinctly saw the Lord Jesus approach me with open arms, and a most divine and heavenly smile upon his countenance ... and he said, "Thy prayer is accepted and, I own thy name"'.[1] Zilpha was lastingly impacted by this encounter and wrote, 'From that day to the present I have never entertained a doubt about the manifestation of his love to my soul.'[2] In 1808 she joined the Methodists being received initially by the Revd J. Polhemos. He inquired as to whether there was any objections as to her being received into membership. There being none Zilpha joined a class which met some two miles away from her house. Although this meant frequent journeys in the dark, Zilpha found 'these nocturnal walks were to me seasons of sweet communion with my God'.[3] After she had completed six months of probation Zilpha was baptised by the Revd Joseph Lybrand and received into full-membership of the church.

In 1810 Zilpha married Joseph Elaw, 'a very respectable young man' but 'he was not a Christian, – that is, a sincere and devoted disciple of Christ, though nominally bearing his name'.[4] She wrote, 'My dear husband had been a member of the society to which I belonged, and had been afterwards disowned by them; but I could not regard him as a backslider from religion, for I am of the opinion that he had never tasted of the pardoning love of God through the atonement of Jesus Christ.'[5] Although he often pledged himself to rejoin the church and give himself to God's service he never fulfilled his promises. Joseph Elaw was a fuller by trade and his business concerns caused them to move to Burlington in the state of New Jersey which pleased Zilpha

---

1 Z. Elaw, *Memoirs of the Religious Experience, Ministerial Travels and Labours of Mrs Zilpha Elaw; Together with Some Account of the Great Religious Revivals in America* (first published by the authoress and sold by Mr T. Dudley and Mr B. Taylor, 1846; facsimile edition, Indiana University, 1986), p. 56.
2 Elaw, *Memoirs of the Religious Experience*, p. 56.
3 Elaw, *Memoirs of the Religious Experience*, p. 58.
4 Elaw, *Memoirs of the Religious Experience*, p. 61.
5 Elaw, *Memoirs of the Religious Experience*, p. 63.

since there was a Methodist Chapel close by where she was 'more plentifully able to enjoy the means of grace' and 'grew thereby'.[6]

Sanctified and Called to Minister

In 1817 Zilpha attended a camp meeting which proved to be a turning point in her Christian experience. She described the character of these meetings and their spiritual value at some length in her autobiography. She wrote:

> I, for one, have great reason to thank God for the refreshing seasons of his mighty grace, which have accompanied these great meetings of his saints in the wilderness. It was at one of these meetings that God was pleased to separate my soul unto Himself, to sanctify me as a vessel designed for honour, made meet for the master's use. Whether I was in the body, or whether out of the body, on that auspicious day, I cannot say; but this I know, that at the conclusion of a most powerful sermon delivered by one of the ministers from the platform, and while the congregation were in prayer, I became so overpowered with the presence of God, that I sank down upon the ground, and laid there for a considerable time; and while I was thus prostrate on the earth, my spirit seemed to ascend up into a clear circle in the sun's disc; and, surrounded and engulphed in the glorious effulgence of his rays, I distinctly heard a voice speak unto me, which said, "Now thou art sanctified; and I will show thee what thou must do".[7]

When she eventually came out of this experience of ecstasy she was conscious that all around her there were literally hundreds of others who were weeping and praying. This day marked the beginning of Zilpha's call to a wider ministry. Shortly afterwards many people came requesting that she pray for and minister to them. At the same time it became clear that she was to employ her time visiting families in their homes and pray for the sick and speak to them about salvation and eternal matters.[8]

In 1816 Zilpha had a severe fall and such was her condition that she was told that she would not recover from her injuries. In the event her health was fully restored and once more she resumed her 'household ministry work' for a further five years finding great happiness in it.[9] At this time her sister, Hannah, who was a Christian and lived in Philadelphia, fell seriously ill and Zilpha went with her daughter to spend time with her. Zilpha found a number of friends gathered round and praying for her night and day. As her sister lay on her deathbed she broke into song and as Zilpha recalled 'appeared to sing several verses; but the

---

6 Elaw, *Memoirs of the Religious Experience*, p. 64.
7 Elaw, *Memoirs of the Religious Experience*, p. 66.
8 Elaw, *Memoirs of the Religious Experience*, p. 67.
9 Elaw, *Memoirs of the Religious Experience*, p. 71.

Zilpha Elaw

language in which she sang was too wonderful for me, and I could not understand it'.[10] When she had finished her song of praise she informed Zilpha that she had seen Jesus and had been in the society of angels, and that an angel had come to her and told her that Zilpha must preach the gospel, and that she should go to a Quaker lady by the name of Fisher who would give her further guidance.

Hannah was insistent that Zilpha take up the call to preach immediately but Zilpha's circumstances were such that she deemed it impossible. In particular she worried about the care of her young daughter who was then about seven years of age. Among other concerns she had to endure 'sore trials' at the hand of her unconverted husband. She later wrote that because of her disobedience God used the rod to bring her into subjection to his will and she found herself 'upon a bed of affliction, with a sickness which, to all appearance, was unto death'.[11] Zilpha was 'on the verge of eternity' for a long period and underwent a painful operation which involved having her side burnt with caustic. It was

---

10 Elaw, *Memoirs of the Religious Experience*, p. 73. Zilpha noted in her autobiography that she subsequently learned of other Christians who when in the very arms of death broke forth into singing 'with a melodious and heavenly voice, several verses in a language unknown to mortals' (*Memoirs of the Religious Experience*, p. 74),

11 Elaw, *Memoirs of the Religious Experience*, p. 76.

many weeks before she recovered but through it all she felt the presence of the Holy Spirit within her in a powerful way. Finally she had a celestial visitation which resulted her submitting to what she already knew was God's call on her life. She described the visitation in the following lines:

> About twelve o'clock one night, when all was hushed to silence, a human figure in appearance, came and stood by my bed-side, and addressed these words to me, 'Be of good cheer, for Thou shalt yet see another camp-meeting; and at that meeting thou shalt know the will of God concerning thee'.[12]

Zilpha went on to describe how she put her hand out to touch the figure that had spoken to her only to find that it was not a human being but a supernatural appearance. She felt no fear but instead was overwhelmed with the sense of privilege at having had a glimpse of one of God's heavenly attendants. Some people seem to have questioned the validity of Zilpha's angelic encounter because in her subsequent reflection on the matter she wrote the following lines in support of angelic visitations.

> There are many sceptical persons who conceitedly, rashly, and idly scoff at the idea of apparitions and angelic appearances; but they ignorantly do it in the face of the most extensive experience, instinct, belief, and credible testimony of persons of every nation, and of all ages, as well as the inspired statements of the Scriptures.[13]

This, it should be noted, was not the only occasion on which Zilpha had an angelic encounter.[14] Some years later, after she had preached a sermon to an unwelcoming congregation in the town of Bath in the State of Maine, she reported, 'the Lord opened my eyes and I distinctly saw five angels hovering above and engaged in the praises of God: the raptures of my soul were too awful and ecstatic on that occasion for human description'.[15] Despite the fact that one of the Methodist ministers came a considerable distance to be with her because he was adamant that she was close to heaven, Zilpha felt assured of a full recovery on account of the heavenly visitation she had received. Her health gradually began to amend and she reflected, 'My spirit and temper were now

---

12 Elaw, *Memoirs of the Religious Experience*, p. 77.
13 Elaw, *Memoirs of the Religious Experience*, p. 77.
14 It is noteworthy that a number of revivalists claim to have had angelic visitations. Included among them are Maria Woodworth-Etter and Todd Bentley of Fresh Fire Ministries.
15 Elaw, *Memoirs of the Religious Experience*, p. 122. Zilpha also wrote of this encounter, 'I concluded that this wonderful manifestation was a token for good, and a proof that the Lord was well-pleased with the course I had taken.'

subdued, and resigned to the will of God.'[16] After about eight months she found herself sufficiently well enough to attend chapel, and it was there some time later that she saw an announcement of a coming camp meeting. Despite her state of weakness she resolved to attend, and to her great surprise her husband who was usually extremely hostile to such occasions raised no objection. Following an unexpected gift from her former guardian, Mr Mitchell, Zilpha was able to secure a ride in a carriage, travelling companions and a place in a tent with friends. Zilpha recalled that 'thousands were assembled ... and the mighty power of God was greatly displayed'.[17] At the conclusion of the main morning meeting people in every section of the estimated crowd of seven thousand were 'heaving bursts of penitential emotion with streaming eyes'. As they returned to their places in the camp Zilpha felt a strong prompting to go outside her tent. Immediately she did so, she started to exhort the people who remained in a state of distress by the preacher's stand. There was still a large crowd of ministers in the area, most of whom stood gazing in astonishment with tears running down their faces as they witnessed the power of Zilpha's address. After she had finished she heard the exact same voice that she had heard while on her sickbed, ' Now thou knowest the will of God concerning thee; thou must preach the gospel; and thou must travel far and wide.'[18] She reflected:

This is my commission for the work of the ministry, which I received, not from mortal man, but from the voice of an invisible personage sent from God. Moreover this did not occur in the night when the dozing slumbers of imaginative dreams are prevalent, but at mid-day, between the hours of twelve and two o'clock; and my ministry was commenced in the midst of thousands who were both eye and ear witness of the fact.[19]

Zilpha laid her call to preach before the ministers and they greatly encouraged her to proceed and to preach wherever the opportunity arose. Indeed she related, 'they saw no impropriety in it, and therefore advised me to go on and do all the good I could'.[20] Although almost all her black friends and associates abandoned her, probably, she felt, out of jealousy, the number of white brethren and sisters who flocked to her ministry increased almost daily. Zilpha's husband was grieved at her new role and advised her to decline the work, but she was now steadfastly resolved to follow the calling she had received, and it was not long before her black friends who had deserted her began to return with their support and encouragement.

On 27 January 1823 Zilpha's husband died, having a short time before his death offered words of apology for his behaviour towards his wife, and

---

16 Elaw, *Memoirs of the Religious Experience*, p. 78.
17 Elaw, *Memoirs of the Religious Experience*, p. 80.
18 Elaw, *Memoirs of the Religious Experience*, p. 82.
19 Elaw, *Memoirs of the Religious Experience*, p. 82.
20 Elaw, *Memoirs of the Religious Experience*, p. 83.

expressing the hope that they would meet again in a better world. He 'even acknowledged that Zilpha's conduct towards him had been irreproachable and expressed the hope that the Lord would sustain her'.[21] After her husband's burial, Zilpha was able to open a small school for black children, many of the pupils being drawn from the Society of Friends. All this time her mind remained strongly impressed with the commission which she had received from the Lord that 'Thou must preach the gospel, and thou must travel far and wide.'[22] A year or two passed and she related that still in the back of her mind was the journey she knew she must one day take to England. Some of the chapels in which she preached even made collections to provide her with sufficient resources for her endeavour, but it was to be another ten years before she finally made plans to set out for the 'old country'. For the time being she entrusted her daughter to the care of a relative and set out for Philadelphia and New York. Her heart being strongly bonded to the black slaves, Zilpha next made a preaching tour of the southern states and visited Baltimore and Washington in 1829. Her visit provided her with many opportunities to speak to both the poor and the wealthy. During a brief period of ministry at Annapolis, Zilpha was invited to preach in the small town of Mount Tabor. The gallery of the chapel was occupied by slaves and the main part of the building by proprietors. Despite the congregation being urged to restrain their feelings the people were unable to hold back their emotions. The people in the gallery wept aloud and raised their cries to heaven. The people in the body of the church also wept.[23]

After spending time at Hartford, Connecticut, Zilpha joined with many thousands of other Christians to attend a great camp meeting at Cape Cod. There many young men who came with the intention of mocking the proceedings were deeply affected and cried out for mercy under Zilpha's ministry. When the proceedings were over she remained on the Cape and preached in the Haverich Circuit. At every place large numbers of people came to hear her sermons, such that few buildings were able to contain them. She commented, 'As I drove from place to place, many an open wagon became my pulpit, from which I preached in the open air to listening multitudes.'[24] During the early part of 1830 Zilpha spent time in Massachusetts and preached in Boston, Salem and Lynn.[25] From 1834 Zilpha remained on the island of Nantucket where she preached in a Baptist chapel which was without a minister and 'the Lord wrought marvellously on the people' and she had the pleasure of seeing many of them baptised in the sea. She was also active in the Methodist circuit where the people 'were powerfully attended with the presence and operations of the Holy Spirit; and indeed a wonderful revival of the work of the

---

21 Elaw, *Memoirs of the Religious Experience*, p. 84.
22 Elaw, *Memoirs of the Religious Experience*, p. 86.
23 Elaw, *Memoirs of the Religious Experience*, p. 101.
24 Elaw, *Memoirs of the Religious Experience*, p. 101.
25 See Elaw, *Memoirs of the Religious Experience*, pp. 118–19.

Lord ensued'.[26] One morning in 1837 when still in her home area, and while she was out with friends, she had a remarkable vision which she recounted in the following lines.

> I appeared to be in a strange place and conversing with a stranger, when three enormous balls of fire came perpendicularly over my head, and each of them exploded and burst at the same moment: I instantly appeared to fall to the ground; but was caught up by an unseen hand, and placed upon an animal, which darted me through the regions of the air, with the velocity of lightning, and deposited me inside the window of an upper chamber. I there heard the voice of the Almighty, saying, "I have a message for her to go upon the high seas, and she will go". This occurrence took place just three years prior to my departure from America.[27]

Two years later the vision was confirmed by Mr Bedell who with his wife had come from England and was now working in Rhode Island. Zilpha had not been with them more than a quarter of an hour when both of them shared their impression that she was destined by the Lord to minister the gospel in a foreign land.[28] From this time onward she noted, 'wherever I went, the inquiry was continually made, if I was not shortly to embark for England'.[29] 'Many were the proofs', she wrote, 'besides those related in this work, that the Lord gave me for his purpose that I should come to England.'[30] Finally early in July 1840 she set sail for London.

In all her travels in America Zilpha seems to have encountered only minimal opposition to her preaching and holding revival services. In most instances her Methodist testimonial letters were a sufficient introduction to the circuit preachers. On other occasions the churches where she had held successful revivals gave her commendatory letters to take with her to the next places on her itinerary. In England the situation was somewhat different. At Liverpool for example, a Wesleyan minister's wife, a Mrs D., expressed the view 'that Paul ordained that a woman should not be suffered to speak in church: but to sit in silence'. Mrs D. was of the view 'that a preaching female ought to depart from the Methodist body, and unite with the Quakers'. When her husband came home and Zilpha presented her testimonials he said, 'Do you not know that we do not allow women to preach; and that there is nothing in the Scriptures that will allow of it at all?'[31] She met with the same opposition when she ministered at Shields. Although her ministry in that place was 'very gratifying' she recorded,

---

26 Elaw, *Memoirs of the Religious Experience*, p. 134.
27 Elaw, *Memoirs of the Religious Experience*, p. 137.
28 Elaw, *Memoirs of the Religious Experience*, p. 137.
29 Elaw, *Memoirs of the Religious Experience*, p. 138.
30 Elaw, *Memoirs of the Religious Experience*, p. 138.
31 Elaw, *Memoirs of the Religious Experience*, p. 147.

'I endured a considerable share of persecution from opponents of female preaching; some opposing my ministry out of mere caprice, and others from mistaken convictions.'[32] Zilpha herself justified her role on a number of occasions from various biblical texts asserting that, although in the ordinary course of church arrangement and order the Apostle Paul laid it down as a rule that females should not speak in church, the Scriptures made it abundantly plain that this was not intended to preclude 'the extraordinary directions of the Holy Ghost, in reference to female evangelists'.[33] She cited the examples of Phoebe, the deaconess in the church at Cenchrea, also the honourable mention of Tryphena and Tryphosa who laboured in the Lord with Paul. The prophet Joel had predicted that God would pour out his spirit on His handmaids and that they should prophesy and that this prophecy was fulfilled on the day of Pentecost. She also referred to Priscilla who took upon herself the work of a teacher, and the four daughters of Philip the Evangelist who were prophetesses and exhorters, probably assisting their father in the work of evangelism.[34]

Ministry in England

On Saturday 25 July 1840, Zilpha arrived at London Docks and the following day she set foot on British soil relating that she was much surprised to see shops open and many kinds of business being transacted with women crying out, 'fruits for sale'. She took up rooms in Wellclose Square and in the evening attended the Countess of Huntingdon's Chapel. Shortly afterwards she was able to make contact with the Wesleyans at St George's Chapel and was ushered in before one of their committees. Gradually opportunities for ministry began to open up for her. On the following Lord's Day she attended Salem Chapel with a Mrs T. and in the afternoon preached to a large crowd in Stepney-fields. A day or so later Mrs T. offered to provide a home for Zilpha so long as she resided in England and sent to her apartment for her trunk.

Zilpha preached in a number of small chapels in the Metropolis. She was then invited to Ramsgate and in consequence travelled through many towns and villages in Kent preaching the word. This was followed by an invitation from the Primitive Methodists in Yorkshire to go and labour among them. She reached Pontefract on 30 December where she was very kindly received by Mrs Clift and later met with Mr Colson, the superintendent minister, and Mr Crompton, his assistant. She reported that 'the weather was very inclement' and that she was presented with 'an abundance of labour which she entered into with much delight and vigour, though with considerable weariness and distress

---

32 Elaw, *Memoirs of the Religious Experience*, p. 155.
33 Elaw, *Memoirs of the Religious Experience*, p. 125. See also her discussion with a Wesleyan minister and his wife in Liverpool in August 1840: Elaw, *Memoirs of the Religious Experience*, p. 147.
34 Elaw, *Memoirs of the Religious Experience*, p. 125.

to the body'.[35] On 3 January 1841 she preached to a completely crowded chapel in Brotherton and returned to Pontefract the same evening. Notwithstanding these difficulties she found 'many seals on her ministry in Yorkshire' and particularly so in Leeds.

She preached in Leylands chapel in Leeds and then laboured with the Primitive Methodists at Quarry Hill where she attended several missionary meetings. She also preached for both the Wesleyans and the Primitives at Stanningley. Among other towns she visited in Yorkshire were Bradford, Shelf and Hull where she preached at Brewer Fields on 3 July and had the 'pleasure to witness the conversion of four souls from darkness to light'.[36] On the twenty-third of the month she went south to Wirksworth, accompanied by Sister W., and preached in the afternoon and evening of the following day.[37]

Early in August Zilpha found her way to Liverpool where she had been invited by a gentleman and his wife whom she had met while in Yorkshire. On arrival she found the lady and her daughter were away and that the gentleman only distantly remembered her. Zilpha therefore took lodgings and attended at Brunswick Chapel, but here also she met with a hostile reception from the circuit minister who could not accept the validity of women preachers. She therefore 'departed from this iron-hearted abode, somewhat distressed and wounded in the spirit and at a loss what step I should take next'.[38] The following morning however presented an altogether brighter horizon and a way opened up for her to go to Manchester within a few days. There she took lodgings at Chetham-Hill and preached at the Methodist chapel in Stanley Street on 28 August, and two days later in the Association Chapel in Stork Street 'to a numerous audience'.[39] She wrote that 'A great door and effectual was opened for me of the Lord, in Manchester; and many there became the crown of my rejoicing in Christ Jesus. I again became fully occupied in the service of my heavenly master, going from chapel to chapel, and from town to town.'[40] On 23 October Zilpha preached in the afternoon and evening 'to numerous audiences at Hayfield, with much freedom and the people were very attentive and much edified'.[41] A few days later Mr Ellery, the superintendent minister of Tonnon Street, invited her to speak at a meeting in his home, and then on 7 November she preached morning and afternoon at Tonnon Street Chapel, and gave a charity sermon in the evening at Berry Street Chapel in Salford.[42]

---

35 Elaw, *Memoirs of the Religious Experience*, p. 143.
36 Elaw, *Memoirs of the Religious Experience*, p. 146.
37 Elaw, *Memoirs of the Religious Experience*, p. 146.
38 Elaw, *Memoirs of the Religious Experience*, p. 148.
39 Elaw, *Memoirs of the Religious Experience*, p. 147.
40 Elaw, *Memoirs of the Religious Experience*, p. 149.
41 Elaw, *Memoirs of the Religious Experience*, p. 150.
42 Elaw, *Memoirs of the Religious Experience*, p. 150. An examination of the records of Tonnon Street and Chetham Street Methodist records revealed no mention of Zilpha's activities.

During her stay in Manchester Zilpha also went to Glossop and preached three anniversary sermons. When she spoke again on the following evening 'the place was excessively crowded'.[43] She went to Stockport to give some charity sermons on 5 December and the crowd was so large, that it was with great difficulty she reached the pulpit and 'many hundreds of persons were forced to retire who could not gain admittance'. She preached again on the eighth before returning to Manchester. She then went to Hollingsworth on 10 December preaching in the chapel at the afternoon and evening services. Zilpha wrote, 'I tarried in Manchester about nine months visiting and preaching in very many towns and villages in its vicinity and within ten or twenty miles around it ... I preached about two hundred times during my continuance here; and ultimately by His direction, took leave of my dear friends to see them no more in the flesh.'[44]

Huddersfield was to be the next sphere of Zilpha's work, and she arrived in the town by train on 13 June 1843 and stayed till the end of July. She began her labours by attending the Wesleyan class meeting of Mr Keys. On the seventeenth she went to Shelf and assisted in the Anniversary sermons of the Primitive Methodists and led several of their class meetings. She also preached in the Wesleyan Chapel 'where we enjoyed a very rich manifestation of the presence of God, and a delightful opportunity to our souls'.[45] On 29 July Zilpha made a short visit to Hull, preaching morning and evening to 'immense crowds'[46] before boarding a steamer for London. Some of the passengers requested her to preach to them, and the captain having granted permission, she held a meeting on the poop deck with many 'interested persons' in attendance. She remained in the nation's capital until the end of November preaching at Crosby Row Chapel, Whites Row Chapel and Timothy Row Chapel and for many other ministers and congregations.

During this time she received an invitation to return to the north of England, on this occasion to the town of Berwick. She boarded a ship on 27 November and after 'a very boisterous passage' she was kindly received by Mr G., the circuit superintendent. Zilpha reported 'many persons were converted to God under my ministry in this town'. From Berwick she went to Shields, writing that 'in heat and cold, through wet and dry weather, by night and day, I laboured in that part of God's vineyard, preaching Christ wherever the opportunity was afforded me'.[47] Although the success of her ministry was 'very gratifying', she encountered some who were opposed to female ministry.[48]

Zilpha remained in the North East for more than a year. She found Newcastle to be 'a very barren and rocky soil to work upon'. After preaching there on 28 January 1843 she wrote that 'the wickedness of the people is very great; and the

---

43 Elaw, *Memoirs of the Religious Experience*, p. 151.
44 Elaw, *Memoirs of the Religious Experience*, p. 152.
45 Elaw, *Memoirs of the Religious Experience*, p. 152.
46 Elaw, *Memoirs of the Religious Experience*, p. 153.
47 Elaw, *Memoirs of the Religious Experience*, p. 155.
48 Elaw, *Memoirs of the Religious Experience*, p. 155.

cry of it, like Sodom, must ere long reach unto heaven'.[49] However her visits to some of the surrounding towns and villages proved more responsive. During her Lord's day sermon at Middle Rainton 'the place was filled with the Holy Ghost' and this was followed on the next day by 'a delightful tea meeting'.[50] At Pittenton she preached to 'a very large audience' and the meeting was attended with 'much power and spiritual assurance'.[51] On 15 September having received 'a cordial welcome' she preached to 'a large assembly' and on the following day she preached the Lord's day sermon to 'a dense mass of people'. As she retired from the meeting she found herself filled 'with the love of God too full to conceal my emotion' and overhead she felt she heard 'a concert of angel voices singing the hymns of God'.[52] On nineteenth she held a meeting in the New Connexion chapel attended 'by a large and listening audience'.[53] On twenty-third she was at the Seceders Chapel and preached to 'an immense throng of people'. She recalled that 'the vapours which arose from so compacted a concourse, as it condensed, ran down the walls in streams of water'.[54] Following a sermon at Newbottle Wesleyan chapel Zilpha was attacked by a severe illness which confined her to bed for five months and it wasn't until the early summer of 1844 that she was able to recommence her labours in Shields, Newcastle and Sunderland.

On 31 July 1844 Zilpha embarked on a vessel bound for London where she was met by Mr and Mrs B.T. Her first residence was in Solomon's Terrace, Back Road, St George's-in-the-East but she was obliged to leave it on account of the intemperate habits of the residents. 'Drunkenness', she reflected, 'is an awful vice, and though debasing to both sexes, seems yet more unbecoming in a woman.' 'It is', she continued, 'a prolific parent of crime, being the origin of a thousand evils.'[55] It is at this point that Zilpha's autobiography comes to an end. On the penultimate page she writes that 'about the commencement of the present year, 1845, I removed to the residence of Mr T. Dudley, 19 Charter-House-Lane, where I enjoy a comfortable home.' Significantly the title page of her memoirs states that they were published in 1846 'by the authoress and sold by Mr B. Taylor of 19 Montague-St, Spitalfields and by Mr T. Dudley of 19 Charter-House Lane, Spitalfields'. The former gentleman seems likely to have been the Mr B.T. who met her on her arrival at London Docks, and Mr Dudley is clearly the owner of the home where she had taken up residence. In her last lines she relates that she had found a home at Jewin-Street chapel and had joined Mr Self's class, whom she refers to as 'an able and experienced leader'

---

49 Elaw, *Memoirs of the Religious Experience*, p. 156.
50 Elaw, *Memoirs of the Religious Experience*, p. 156.
51 Elaw, *Memoirs of the Religious Experience*, p. 156.
52 Elaw, *Memoirs of the Religious Experience*, p. 156.
53 Elaw, *Memoirs of the Religious Experience*, p. 157.
54 Elaw, *Memoirs of the Religious Experience*, p. 157.
55 Elaw, *Memoirs of the Religious Experience*, p. 159.

whose judicious counsel she highly prized. She felt 'a great attachment to each member of the class'.[56]

Zilpha Elaw and Revival

Zilpha Elaw understood revival in terms of large numbers of people coming to Christ and others who had become nominal in their faith making a renewed Christian commitment. While in the city of New Haven in the State of Connecticut people of every denomination were touched in large numbers. Zilpha commented that 'such a revival took place as filled the city with astonishment'.[57]

The Holy Spirit

For Zilpha Elaw revival was always a 'work of the Holy Spirit' in which both high and low, rich and poor, white and coloured, 'all drank of the living streams that flowed from the City of our God'.[58] Zilpha's meetings were often marked by religious exercises of various kinds. Commenting on her three-month stay in Hartford, Connecticut, she wrote, 'The excess of their emotions were such, that the order of worship was suspended; for some were calling upon the name of the Lord, some were groaning to receive the atonement of Jesus, while others were rejoicing in his salvation and giving glory to God.' She went on to observe that 'our services were not unfrequently [sic] interrupted by scenes of this description; for the operation of the Holy Ghost can no more be circumscribed within the limits of man's arrangement, than the wind and rain and sunshine can be restricted to man's times and opportunities'.[59] Zilpha pointed out that often the most abrupt and extraordinary changes in the weather produce far more benefits than the gentle and more settled periods. So too the Almighty often chooses to display the wonders of his grace in unaccustomed ways.[60]

Zilpha was convinced that unity, and unity among local Christians in particular, was a vital key to revival. 'O that the Christian community in Great Britain were all of one heart and one soul; only, but earnestly, contending for the faith once delivered to the saints; that there were no division among them ...'[61]

Preaching

As with most revivalists, preaching was central to Zilpha's revivalism. Her practice was to ask the Lord to fix the passage in her mind from which he wanted

---

56 Elaw, *Memoirs of the Religious Experience*, p. 159.
57 Elaw, *Memoirs of the Religious Experience*, p. 105.
58 Elaw, *Memoirs of the Religious Experience*, p. 96.
59 Elaw, *Memoirs of the Religious Experience*, p. 107.
60 Elaw, *Memoirs of the Religious Experience*, p. 107.
61 Elaw, *Memoirs of the Religious Experience*, p. 117.

her to preach. She relates that on a number of occasions she was still sometimes searching and asking God to show her the right text or chapter even as she was journeying to the chapel or place of preaching. Sometimes a passage or verse would be impressed upon her mind and yet she could think of nothing to add to it until she began to speak at the meeting. On one occasion when she was in the vicinity of Washington '2 Kings 20:1 flashed upon my mind', "Set thine house in order, for thou shalt die and not live."' She tried meditating on the passage but nothing came into her mind to add to it. 'My soul was barren', she wrote, and 'I was oppressed by a complete dearth of suitable ideas, and unable to obtain any spiritual opening or discernment of this text.' Because of this fact she thought she must abandon the text altogether and she began to search the Scriptures for a different verse. But even though she continued her search until twelve o'clock on Saturday night every other text 'was sealed up from me'.[62] From this Zilpha learned that 'when the Lord impresses a text on the mind of his servants, He will not be tempted by our solicitations to have another substituted'. When she arrived at the appointed place she found it already like a camp meeting with the platform erected and hundreds of persons assembled, and all things in readiness. While the congregation were singing she found herself still searching for a text but 'no other could I find than that which had been given me'. So when the hymn was finished she stood up and read the verse from 2 Kings which she had been given at first. Immediately she had done so 'a region of truths were unfolded to my view, such as I had never previously conceived of; and it occupied me an hour and a half to exhaust the fund of sentimental treasure, which the Divine spirit poured into my mind. It was, indeed, a time of refreshing from the presence of the Lord.'[63]

Follow up

Zilpha was a great believer in pressing those who attended her preaching to make a commitment. Her usual practice was to announce a prayer meeting immediately following the end of her sermon or address. After her sermon at New Lampton in the north of England on 15 September for example, she held a prayer meeting with the aim of exhorting those who were anxious regarding their spiritual state.[64]

House to House

During the revival that took place in New Haven, Connecticut Zilpha felt sufficiently emboldened to go from house-to-house preaching, even venturing into a 'house of ill fame' exhorting the inmates to repent of their sins and turn to Christ. Many of these unfortunate females, she recalled, 'became genuine

---

62 Elaw, *Memoirs of the Religious Experience*, p. 95.
63 Elaw, *Memoirs of the Religious Experience*, p. 95.
64 Elaw, *Memoirs of the Religious Experience*, p. 157.

disciples of Jesus'.[65] She also visited many of the alleys and courts on the outskirts of the town.

Sometimes Zilpha's house-to-house visiting provided opportunities to pray for the sick. While still in Hartford she was invited to visit and pray for a certain Mrs Adams. She found all the family gathered around her bed expecting to see her breathe her last. Zilpha prayed with great compassion and much power which left all the family bathed in tears. Contrary to their expectations Mrs Adams recovered, causing the local clergy who had opposed Zilpha's preaching to have further thoughts on the matter.

Holiness

As Zilpha understood it, revival began with the profession of 'entire sanctification and holiness of spirit'.[66] This experience, she urged, 'must be maintained'. Individual believers must be careful not to grieve the Holy Spirit of God: 'but ever remember that we are witnesses of that glorious passage of Scripture, "This is the will of God, even your sanctification " [1 Thessalonians 4:3]'.[67] Zilpha wrote of this doctrine as 'our high privilege and bounden duty'.[68] She found by experience that it could only be maintained by a ready obedience to the inner promptings in her spirit and by following the dictates of her conscience. 'How sweet', she wrote, 'is the path of obedience! God will bless while man obeys; "for what his mouth has said, his own almighty hand will do".'[69]

This holiness, Zilpha was adamant, must be in evidence in the life of every minister who 'really desires that his ministry may be effectual to convert and sanctify men'.[70] In a later passage she reiterated the point more strongly: 'When ministers aim at revivals in their flocks, they must first obtain them in their own souls; for he who has left his first love, is in no condition to communicate the glowing flame to others. He ... must stir up the gift of God in himself [and] ... render his body a temple of the Holy Ghost and equip himself with the whole armour of God [1 Corinthians 3:16, Ephesians 6:11].'[71]

Justice and Slavery

Zilpha was from her earliest days a champion of racial equality and a strong opponent of the slavery that existed in the southern states. As far as she was concerned, revival embraced 'the will of the Lord being done on earth, by his

---

65 Elaw, *Memoirs of the Religious Experience*, p. 105.
66 Elaw, *Memoirs of the Religious Experience*, p. 67.
67 Elaw, *Memoirs of the Religious Experience*, p. 68.
68 Elaw, *Memoirs of the Religious Experience*, p. 68.
69 Elaw, *Memoirs of the Religious Experience*, p. 70.
70 Elaw, *Memoirs of the Religious Experience*, p. 114.
71 Elaw, *Memoirs of the Religious Experience*, p. 115.

servants as it is in heaven'.[72] It was the case that from about 1820 Evangelicals in the south had sought to christianise the slaves but if possible without making them unhappy with their station in life.[73] Zilpha was in total opposition to their stance and before finally embarking for London, she, at some risk to her personal safety, visited the southern slave-holding states of America. There was always the fear of being captured particularly as the news of a black female preaching to the slaves would inevitably spread quickly. In the event her preaching was highly successful and in one town Zilpha even obtained permission to use a courthouse for public worship. During this time she visited Annapolis where she was led to speak at length on the subject of mortality and death. She was then succeeded by a black local preacher who was a slave and 'very impatient of slavery and anxiously sighed for liberty'. This brother was unexpectedly taken ill and died that same week, finding as Zilpha herself reflected, 'that rest where the prisoners hear not the voice of the oppressor; the small and the great are there, and the servant is free from his master Job iii.17–19'.[74] The incident caused Zilpha to comment on the oppression of slavery.

> Oh, the abominations of slavery! though Philemon be the proprietor, and Onesimus the slave, yet every case of slavery, however lenient its afflictions and mitigated its atrocities, indicates an oppressor, the oppressed, and the oppression. Slavery in every case, save those of parental government, criminal punishment, or the self-protecting detentions of justifiable war, if such can happen, involves a wrong, the deepest in wickedness of any included within the range of the second table.[75]

Zilpha spoke out strongly against the laws of the slave states which were such that any black person within their territories could be arrested and sold on behalf of the State unless they could produce papers in proof of their freedom. Zilpha expressed her gratitude to God that He had preserved her as she preached the Gospel 'in these regions of wickedness'. Not once was she even required to produce the documents of her freedom.[76]

Impacting the Culture

Zilpha Elaw was firmly of the view that where there was a revival of Christianity it would be clearly seen not just in major issues of social justice such as slavery, but also in quality of daily living and domestic behaviour. Referring to some of the time she spent in Massachusetts, she wrote:

---

72 Elaw, *Memoirs of the Religious Experience*, p. 90.
73 See Wolffe, *The Expansion of Evangelicalism* (Inter-Varsity Press, 2005), p. 164.
74 Elaw, *Memoirs of the Religious Experience*, p. 99.
75 Elaw, *Memoirs of the Religious Experience*, p. 98.
76 Elaw, *Memoirs of the Religious Experience*, p. 99.

The Lord's blessing on my visit to Salem was made apparent by the improvement which followed in the morals and habits of the coloured population; many of whom became truly devout, righteous, holy, godly, spiritual, and heavenly-minded: by devout, I mean, devotional and religious; righteousness consists in being and doing right; holiness is purity internally and practically.[77]

Conclusion

Zilpha made the observation that throughout all her labours in England she found far less favourable soil for the seed of the kingdom than she did in America. She put this down to the fact that 'the population in the United States have not been so extensively vitiated by the infidelity and sedition of the press' and the fact that America being a so much larger territory was not so easily contaminated as the more condensed mass of English society.[78] Nevertheless Zilpha wrote: 'I am justified in saying that my God hath made my ministry a blessing to hundreds of persons; and many who were living in sin and darkness before they saw my coloured face, have risen up to praise the Lord, for having seen my coloured face.'[79]

Although she had strong opinions about the validity of women preachers and, as has been noted, made a vigorous defence of her ministry, she is perhaps not as radical as some feminist writers have supposed. This is evidenced by the way in which she was very submissive to her husband, even despite his harsh and unreasonable behaviour towards her. The same attitude is seen for example in her comments on Mrs G. whom she met during her time in Huddersfield. Of her, she wrote: 'This lady is one of the genuine daughters of Sarah; chaste in conversation, subdued in temper and reverent to her husband. Oh, that many flighty, petulant, high-minded and insubordinate wives, who profess the religion of Jesus, would pay more attention to the duties of Christian wives, and like this lady, adorn the doctrine of God their Saviour.'[80]

Zilpha Elaw, like the great St Paul before her, was 'in labours often' though on British soil. She wrote of her time in England.

> My reader will perceive that I have not been an idle spectator in my Heavenly Master's cause. During my sojourn in England, I have preached considerably more than a thousand sermons. I have expended all my means in travels of no little extent and duration; devoted my time, employed the energies of my spirit, spent my strength and exhausted my constitution in the cause of Jesus; and received pecuniary supplies and

---

77 Elaw, *Memoirs of the Religious Experience*, p. 118.
78 Elaw, *Memoirs of the Religious Experience*, p. 144.
79 Elaw, *Memoirs of the Religious Experience*, p. 141.
80 Elaw, *Memoirs of the Religious Experience*, p. 153.

temporal remunerations in comparison with my time and labours a mere pittance, altogether inadequate to shield me from a thousand privations, hardships, target fires, vexatious anxieties and deep afflictions, to which my previous life was an utter stranger.[81]

Zilpha's Last Years

Up until the time of this present research Zilpha's last years were a blank page. Her autobiography which was published from London in 1850 ends with her resident in the capital's East End. John Wolffe noted that 'nothing is known of her subsequent life and she may well have died in obscurity before arriving back in the United States'.[82] A chance search however led me to the discovery that she in fact remained in England and married Mr Ralph Bressey Shum on 9 December 1850 in St Mary's Parish Church, Stratford Bow, the service being conducted by the rector, the Revd G. Driffield.[83] In the marriage register Ralph Shum is described as 'Gentleman' and his condition is given as 'widower'. Zilpha is listed as 'widow' but with no occupation given.[84] This is a little strange since she appeared on the 1841 Census return for Addingham in Yorkshire where she was holding revival services, and was described as 'Itinerant Preacher'.[85] Her date and place of birth were given as '1796 Foreign parts'. Ralph Bressey Shum was also listed in the 1841 Census for London along with his wife, Ann.[86] Ralph is stated to have been born about 1796, his residence given as 15 Houghton Street, St Clement Danes, Middlesex and his occupation listed as 'Pork Butcher'. Zilpha was listed in the 1871 Census as living at 33 Turner Street in Mile End.[87] *The Methodist Recorder* carried a brief report which stated that 'Mrs Zilpha Shum, formerly of Nantucket, North America' died on 20 August 1873'.[88] It also recorded that 'for many years she was a class leader and most consistent member of the Wesleyan Society in the St George's Circuit'.[89] Both *The Recorder* and the Register of Deaths note that she was in her eighty-first year.[90]

---

81 Elaw, *Memoirs of the Religious Experience*, p. 159.
82 Wolffe, *The Expansion of Evangelicalism*, p. 104.
83 I am indebted to the researches of Mr Rob Lewis of the Manchester Library and Information Service for leading me to the discovery of Zilpha's marriage.
84 See Marriage Register for the Parish of St Mary Stratford Bow, 1850 entry, No. 446.
85 *Census Return*, 'Township of Addingham', Yorkshire, HO 107/1315/1. Zilpha was resident in the home of John Brayshaw, a 'Cotton Weaver' and his wife, Elizabeth.
86 Ann's age is recorded as having been born about 1791.
87 See 1871 *Census*, Mile End. Also resident in the house was Francis Banham 'General Servant'.
88 *The Methodist Recorder*, 12 September 1873, p. 527.
89 *The Methodist Recorder*, 12 September 1873, p. 527.
90 See *Register of Deaths*, July, August and September 1873, Vol. 1c, p. 243.

CHAPTER 4

Charles Finney and the Beginning of Professional Revivalism

Charles Finney, one of America's great evangelists, was born on 29 August 1792 at Warren, Litchfield County in the state of Connecticut. Neither of his parents, Sylvester and Rebecca were Christians. When he was about two years of age, his parents who were farmers joined the westward migration and settled at Hanover, Oneida County, which Charles later recalled was then 'to a great extent, a wilderness'.[1] Charles spent two years at Hamilton Oneida Institute in Clinton intending to study law at Yale. He was at that early stage already proving to be a very able student and his head teacher advised him that he could qualify much more quickly without going to university. He therefore entered the law office of Benjamin Wright in 1818 in the town of Adams in New York State and was eventually admitted to the bar.

During his time at Adams, Finney attended the town's Presbyterian church and sat under the preaching of the hyper-Calvinist George Gale (1789–1861). He also began to take part in prayer meetings, at one of which he came under conviction that Jesus really meant it when he said, 'Ask and you will receive' and that 'the Bible is the true word of God'.[2] Finney recalled, 'I was brought face to face with the question whether I would accept Christ as presented in the Gospel, or pursue a worldly course of life.'[3] On Sunday 7 October 1821 Finney recollected that 'I made up my mind that I would settle the question of my soul's salvation at once, that if it were possible, I would make my peace with God.'[4] It was not until the Wednesday following that he finally found acceptance with God. By that time it had become clear to him that 'the offer of Gospel salvation' was 'an offer of something to be accepted'.[5] Instead of going to his office that morning he went after breakfast into a grove of woods north of the village 'where he cried to Him, "Lord, I take thee at thy word. Now thou knowest that I do search for thee with all my heart".'[6]

He returned to his office at lunchtime but found himself incapable of work and so took down his base viol as he often did, and played and sang some music. Fortunately for Finney his law practice was in the process of moving to

---

1 C.H. Finney, *The Memoirs of Charles Finney* (Zondervan, 1989), p. 4.
2 Finney, *Memoirs*, pp. 12–13.
3 Finney, *Memoirs*, p. 14.
4 Finney, *Memoirs*, p. 16.
5 Finney, *Memoirs*, p. 18.
6 Finney, *Memoirs*, p. 20.

another office and so he busied himself with packing books and removing furniture. When all the books and furniture were adjusted Finney bade goodbye to Benjamin Wright, his employer and made a good large fire in the open fireplace. As he went into the room 'it seemed as if I met the Lord Jesus Christ face to face'. He described his experience in the following lines:

> But as I returned and was about to take a seat by the fire, I received a mighty baptism of the Holy Ghost. Without expecting it, without ever having the thought in my mind that there was any such thing for me, without any recollection that I had ever heard the thing mentioned by any person in the world, at a moment entirely unexpected by me, the Holy Spirit descended upon me in a manner that seemed to go through me, body and soul. I could feel the impression, like a wave of electricity, going through and through me. Indeed it seemed to come in waves of liquid love, – for I could not express it in any other way. And yet it did not seem like water, but rather as the breath of God. I can recollect distinctly that it seemed to me, as these waves passed over me, that they literally moved my hair like a passing breeze.
>
> No words can express the wonderful love that was shed abroad in my heart. These waves came over me, and over me one after another, until I recollect I cried out, 'I shall die if these waves continue to pass over me'. I said to the Lord, 'Lord I cannot bear any more'. Yet I had no fear of death.[7]

After this overwhelming experience of God, Finney wrote, 'I was quite willing to preach the gospel.'[8] He began at once to share his new found faith whenever the opportunity arose. Many of the inhabitants of Adams who had believed him to be a hopeless case were profoundly challenged by his changed life. Soon afterwards his parents and his youngest brother, George, were converted. Finney wrote of those early days, 'I used to spend a great deal of time in prayer; sometimes, I thought, literally praying "without ceasing". I also found it very profitable, and felt very much inclined, to hold frequent days of private fasting.'[9]

Shortly after this Finney began theological studies tutored by his pastor, George Gale, with whom he soon entered into a theological dispute over the latter's belief in the limited atonement. From Gale he also gained some knowledge of Hebrew and Greek. He was examined by the St Lawrence Presbytery at Adams who unanimously voted to license him to preach the

---

7 Finney, *Memoirs*, pp. 23–4.
8 Finney, *Memoirs*, p. 28.
9 Finney, *Memoirs*, p. 39.

Gospel on 30 December 1823.[10] After he had given his first sermon, Gale said to him, 'Mr Finney I shall be very much ashamed to have it known, wherever you go, that you have studied theology with me.'[11] He subsequently spoke very harshly of Finney's views. Notwithstanding his mentor's opinions of him, Finney was ordained by the Presbytery of St Lawrence at Evans Mills on 1 July 1824.[12] In October the same year he married Lydia Andrews of Whitestown, Oneida County.

Campaigns in the North-Eastern States 1824–32

Since he had had no formal training for the ministry, Finney did not expect to be invited to labour in large towns and cities or to be invited to speak to cultivated congregations. 'I intended to go', he wrote at the start of the fifth chapter of his *Memoirs*, 'into the new settlements and preach in the school houses, and barns and groves, as best I could.' Accordingly, he set out on what proved to be almost a decade of conducting revivals in Upper New York State, an area on the margins of society subject to economic strains and political upheavals. It was known also as the 'burned-over district' on account of its previous history of religious excitement. Finney did however receive funding from 'The Female Missionary Society of the Western District the State of New York'. On 17 March 1824 they formally agreed to pay him a salary of $600 a year to labour as a missionary 'in the Northern parts of the County of Jefferson and other destitute places in the vicinity as his discretion shall dictate'.[13] He began in his own home area of Jefferson County, New York State, preaching in the villages of Evans Mills, Antwerp and Le Raysville. The impact was remarkable by any standard as recollections of his experience at Antwerp make abundantly plain. He wrote, 'The Lord let me loose upon them in a wonderful manner' and 'the congregation were either on their knees or prostrate'. Looking back on his time in Rome in 1825 he recalled, 'Convictions were so deep and universal that we would sometimes go into a house and find some in a kneeling posture and some prostrate on the floor. Some bathing the temples of their friends with camphor, and rubbing them to keep them from fainting and, as they feared, from dying.'[14] Gradually with the passing of the years, Finney began to receive invitations to the larger towns and cities such as Boston and Rochester. This first chapter of his life came to an end when he was invited to take up a full-time pastorate in New York City in May 1832 that lasted until 1837. During these years Finney's early revival campaigns were marked by a number of distinctive features, some

---

10 Finney, *Memoirs*, p. 54.
11 Finney, *Memoirs*, p. 54.
12 Finney, *Memoirs*, p. 77.
13 Letter of appointment, *Finney Papers*, Oberlin College Library, cited W.G. McLoughlin, *Modern Revivalism: Charles Grandison Finney to Billy Graham* (Ronald Press, 1959), p. 26.
14 Finney, *Memoirs*, pp. 103, 198 and 203.

Charles Finney

of which he expanded and developed during his later major urban campaigns and during his travels in England.

The Importance of Prayer

It soon became clear to Finney that prayer was a vital ingredient. At Rome in Oneida County where Finney went in 1826, preaching every day for three weeks, there was much emphasis on prayer and at some of the morning prayer meetings the church was full. 'Indeed', Finney recalled, 'the town was full of prayer. Go where you would, you heard the voice of prayer.'[15] At Auburn, Finney had a vision of what he was about to pass through, in consequence of which 'I shook from head to foot, like a man in an ague fit, under a full sense of the presence of God.'[16] He therefore took to closet [private] prayer and was rewarded with such a sense of God's presence that 'he felt as if he were Moses on Mount Sinai'.[17] Finney's campaigning at Troy during the autumn of

---

15 Finney, *Memoirs*, p. 168.
16 Finney, *Memoirs*, p. 195.
17 C.E. Hambrick-Stowe, *Charles Finney and the Spirit of American Evangelism* (Eerdmans, 1996), p. 57.

1826 and through to the spring of 1827 was 'marked by a very earnest spirit of prayer' and produced 'a multitude of conversions'.[18]

In-Your-Face Preaching

Finney was an imposing figure in the pulpit standing six feet two inches tall, slim and good-looking. According to one report 'his piercing eyes' stared out from their deep sockets with frightening intensity, and when he spoke 'guilt-ridden auditors quailed and fainted under his gaze'.[19] Finney quickly developed an abrasive in-your-face style of preaching. This was markedly in evidence when he visited Antwerp in 1824, a village known locally as Sodom. He chose his text from the story of Lot, 'Up get ye out of this place: for the Lord will destroy this city.'[20] He had not spoken for more than a quarter of an hour when 'the congregation began to fall from their seats; they fell in every direction and cried for mercy' and 'within less than two minutes the whole congregation was either on their knees or prostrate'.[21] At Evans Mills where Finney preached in the same year, the people 'thronged en masse to hear me preach'[22] which resulted in 'the conversion of the whole church' and 'nearly all the community of Germans'.[23] At the farming town of Gouveneur, in St Lawrence County, where Finney laboured from April–September 1825 it had earlier been revealed to Finney 'in a most unexpected manner' that 'God was going to pour out his spirit' on the town 'and that I must go there and preach'. He did so in obedience and with 'powerful effect' such that 'the great majority'[24] of the well-to-do inhabitants were converted to Christ. At Troy, Finney's preaching was described as 'overly abrasive' and his 'gestures violent'[25] with the result that the Revd Dr Lyman Beecher and the Revd Asa Nettleton raised public objections to some of his measures.[26]

When Finney went to Boston he was welcomed by Lyman Beecher who had previously so strongly opposed his revival services and what had been termed his new measures. He defended his changed outlook on the ground that Finney had corrected the excesses of his revival methods. That said, Finney's sermon entitled 'Sinners Bound to Change Their Own Hearts' did not endear him to the people of Park Street Congregational Church. 'I had never before seen professed Christians back away', he later wrote, 'as they did at that time in Boston, from preaching sermons.'[27]

---

18 Hambrick-Stowe, *Charles Finney*, p. 65.
19 NcLoughlin, *Modern Revivalism*, p. 17.
20 Finney, *Memoirs*, p. 101.
21 Finney, *Memoirs*, p. 102.
22 Finney, *Memoirs*, p. 64.
23 Finney, *Memoirs*, p. 77.
24 Finney, *Memoirs*, p. 130.
25 Hambrick-Stowe, *Charles Finney*, p. 65.
26 Finney, *Memoirs*, p. 226.
27 Finney, *Memoirs*, p. 347.

The Practice of Identifying Converts

At Troy where the revival was reported by opponents to have swept through the town 'like an epidemic, attacking in its worst form the most susceptible' an 'inquiry meeting' was established for the week with *The Troy Review* reporting attendances of between 20 and 160 each day.[28] At Rome in January 1826, Finney began the practice at the evening meetings of asking those who had been converted during that day to come forward and report themselves. This produced remarkable results: there was an average of 25 each day, with a total of nearly five hundred reported conversions in the space of the month. There is no doubt that there must have been considerable psychological pressure on the new converts to identify themselves in this way but it was a method that proved to be singularly effective. The result was that Finney developed and expanded it in his subsequent endeavours.

In January 1828 Finney went to Philadelphia at the insistence of James Patterson, the minister of the First Presbyterian Church, where his revival services took a 'powerful hold' with several hundred people from different denominations attending his 'anxious meetings'.[29] This device proved so effective that eventually Finney preached in all the city's Presbyterian churches with the exception of Arch Street. After several months it was decided to hold the meetings in only one place, and Race Street German Reformed Church was chosen since it was the largest building with a capacity for 3,000 worshippers. Finney preached there from mid-August until January 1829.[30] So effective were these meetings that in the summer of 1831 he made a further development when he received an invitation to undertake supply preaching at the Third Presbyterian Church in Rochester.

The religious life of this city, which was one of the fastest growing in the country, was in a 'low state'.[31] There Finney introduced the 'anxious seat', something which he claimed in his revised *Memoirs*, he had not used before 'except in rare instances'.[32] Finney asserted that he had occasionally asked people to stand up, but he believed that the 'higher classes especially' needed help 'to overcome their fear of being known as anxious inquirers'. In this new procedure, seats at the front of the building were left empty and those who were willing to renounce their sins and give themselves to God, were invited to do so at the end of the meeting by coming to sit on them.[33]

The 'anxious seat' was to prove a very effective feature of Finney's revival technique, as he observed that lawyers, physicians and merchants and indeed 'all the most intelligent class of society were more readily influenced to give themselves up to God by this means'. Out of total population of about ten

---

28 Finney, *Memoirs*, p. 210.
29 Finney, *Memoirs*, p. 248.
30 Finney, *Memoirs*, p. 255.
31 Finney, *Memoirs*, pp. 299 and 301.
32 Finney, *Memoirs*, p. 306.
33 Finney, *Memoirs*, p. 307.

thousand in 1831 there were estimated to be eight hundred converts with some one thousand two hundred uniting with the churches of Rochester Presbytery.[34] Finney himself later recalled that 'the revival was so powerful, it gathered in such great numbers of the most influential class in society'.[35] Among those converted were 14 lawyers, 24 merchants and physicians, a General, 3 Colonels, a sheriff and a cashier of the bank.[36] The city's leading prosecuting attorney, who was himself converted, subsequently reported that 'I have been examining the records of the criminal courts, and I find this striking fact, that whereas our city has increased since that revival threefold, there is not one third as many prosecutions as there had been up to that time.'[37] A Mr C.P. Bush also reported, 'The courts had little to do, and the jail was nearly empty for years afterwards.'[38] Additionally, the town's theatre, which was thought by many to be a place of corruption, was reported by *The Troy Review* to have remained closed from 1832 until the later 1850s.[39] Rochester marked the maturing of Finney's revivalistic techniques, and by the time the revival ended, Finney had an established reputation as an evangelist in demand in both the East and the West.

The Remarkable Presence of God

The impact of Finney's revivalism was remarkable by any account. At Utica Finney preached for several months during 1826 from the pulpit of the First Presbyterian Church while staying at the house of the pastor, Samuel Aikin.[40] Finney noted that 'the word took immediate effect, and the place became filled with the manifested influence of the Holy Spirit'.[41] Men who entered the town on business, 'felt as if God pervaded the whole atmosphere', and some were converted without even attending the meetings.[42] The revival reached a cotton manufactory at Oriskany Creek, a little above neighbouring Whitesborough. It was owned by a Mr Wolcott, an unconverted man of high standing and good morals. Finney was invited to look around the buildings and while he did so, so many came under conviction and burst into tears that Mr Wolcott said to the superintendent, 'Stop the mill, and let the people attend religion; for it is more important that our souls be saved than that this factory run.'[43] Accordingly

---

34 Finney, *Memoirs*, p. 318 and note 88. Rochester was the first place where all the Presbyterian churches gave their support to Finney.
35 Finney, *Memoirs*, p. 323.
36 Finney, *Memoirs*, p. 327, note 118.
37 Finney, *Memoirs*, p. 318.
38 Finney, *Memoirs*, p. 319 note 91.
39 Finney, *Memoirs*, p. 318.
40 Murray, *Revival and Revivalism*, p. 172.
41 Murray, *Revival and Revivalism*, p. 172.
42 G.S. Eddy, *A Spiritual Awakening: The Life and Lectures of Charles Finney* (Morgan and Scott, 1915; Eerdmans, 1996), p. 9.
43 Harding, *Revivals of Religion Lectures*, pp. 11–12.

the gates were closed and machines shut down and a meeting held where many of the men made immediate decisions for Christ. The minister of the Presbyterian church at Whitesborough subsequently issued a pamphlet in which it was stated that the number of converts in the district, during the revival numbered 3,000.[44]

In the spring of 1829 when Finney was holding special services in Philadelphia many of the lumbermen who floated timber into the city started to attend his meetings. They returned to the forest regions along the Delaware River and prayed for an outpouring of the Holy Spirit. 'Their efforts', Finney wrote, 'were immediately blessed and revival began to take hold and spread among the lumbermen.' Finney later recalled that 'it spread to such an extent that in many cases persons would be convicted and converted who had not attended any meetings, and were almost as ignorant as the heathen'.[45]

Pastorate in New York City

Finney's campaign at Boston marked the end of the itinerant phase of his life. Together with his wife and growing clutch of children he was now ready for a more settled environment. It came in the form of a call to the pastorate in New York City. In March 1832 Finney received a letter of invitation from a group of men led by Lewis Tappan and William Green. They proposed to take the Chatham Garden Theatre and convert it into a chapel and premises which could accommodate various charitable societies. The expense of changing the saloons into lecture rooms amounted to nearly $7,000. Finney moved with his family to the city and began preaching on 6 May 1832. The response was immediate, Finney noting that 'the Spirit of the Lord was poured out upon us, and we had an extensive revival that spring and summer'. It was such that Lewis Tappan reported that within three months there was such an improved moral change in that part of the city that every grog shop in the area had to close.[46] In the summer following however there was a severe outbreak of cholera in the city and many fled into the surrounding countryside. Finney who had been formally installed as pastor on 28 September 1832 was himself shortly afterwards seized with the cholera. He was confined to bed for several weeks and supply preachers had to be employed in his place. By the end of October however he was much recovered and preached for 20 evenings in succession with such great effect that some four to five hundred people declared themselves as 'inquirers'. The Chatham Street congregation was so large that very soon a group was sent off to plant the Fourth Free Presbyterian Church on 5 January 1834. Finney found

---

44 Harding, *Revivals of Religion Lectures*, p. 12. Harding comments in a footnote that the superintendent was in fact Finney's brother-in-law.
45 Finney, *Memoirs*, p. 260.
46 *Christian Register* [Boston] 28 February 1832 cited Finney, *Memoirs*, p. 357 note 7.

his congregation 'who were largely from the middle and lower class',[47] to be united, praying, working people who were ready 'to go out into the highways and hedges and bring people to hear preaching'.[48]

Following the publication of his *Lectures on Revival,* a book packed with detailed information on how to promote and sustain revivals, Finney inevitably became increasingly alienated in his conflict with the 'Old School Presbyterians' and eventually severed his connections with the presbytery altogether in 1836. In the mean time a new church had been building for his use since 1835. Finney was therefore released from Chatham Street Chapel on 2nd March, 1836 and installed in the new purpose-built and theatre-like Broadway Tabernacle on 10 April.[49] As things turned out however, Finney had not been in his new post for very long when the call came to take up an altogether different role as a College Professor.

The majority of students at Lane Presbyterian Seminary in Cincinnati, who were strongly abolitionist, were forbidden to discuss the matter and 75 of the 103 therefore parted company with the institution. At this point Arthur Tappan made a proposition that if Finney would come west and instruct them he would foot the bills. The result was the founding of Oberlin College for which a charter had earlier been granted by the Ohio legislature on 28 February 1834. Finney became a professor of theology after the trustees agreed to allow the college 'to receive colored people on the same conditions that we did white people' and 'never to interfere with the internal regulations of the school'.[50] Initially, it was agreed that Finney would spend his winters in the college and continue his evangelistic work in New York from April to November. As things turned out his links with the church had to be ended on 6 April 1837 when his health failed.

Oberlin College 1835–75 and a Place for Women

In July 1835 Finney was installed as Professor of Theology along with the Revd John Morgan who became Professor of Bible and Church History and the Revd Asa Mahan who became President. The necessary buildings were soon in place, including Tappan Hall, a four-storey brick building with a central cupola. The college was named after Jean Frederick Oberlin, a Strasbourg pastor, who had pioneered colonies in the Vosges region of France and whose biography had recently been published.[51] Although abolition was not incorporated into the vision of the college 'colored students' [as Finney calls them in his autobiography] were allowed in on equal terms. They boarded in the same halls

---

47 Finney, *Memoirs,* p. 362.
48 Finney, *Memoirs,* p. 359.
49 Finney, *Memoirs,* p. 378.
50 Finney, *Memoirs,* p. 380.
51 Finney, *Memoirs,* p. 236 note 21.

and ate at the same tables in the dining room.[52] Oberlin became noted for its support of abolitionism and was well known as a stopping place for slaves who were escaping northwards to Canada.[53] Finney recalled 'several slaves had been secreted here' and their friends aided their escape 'through fields of high-standing corn and through woods'.[54]

While he was at Oberlin the issue of holiness teaching came to the fore. Finney confessed himself dissatisfied 'with my own want of stability in faith and love' and 'felt himself weak in temptation'.[55] He sought the Lord during the winter of 1836 and the spring of 1837 and the Lord brought him 'into a large place' and gave him 'divine sweetness in his soul'.[56] Finney was much taken with Wesley's *Plain Account of Christian Perfection* which he judged to be 'an admirable book'.[57]

An important impact of Finney's tenure at Oberlin was the increasing respect with which women and the female students were treated. The college stood for 'female reform', indeed it was possibly the first co-educational college in the world.[58] Some of the earlier revivalist practices such as allowing women to exhort, pray, preach and sing in public were fostered in the classes and curriculum at Oberlin. Finney was of the view that the Scriptures did not prevent women from speaking or praying at meetings where both men and women were present.[59] In his open-style classes at Oberlin Finney encouraged women to take an active part in discussions. The founders of the College believed in education for young women and the institution had a strong female department. Lydia Finney also played an important role in some of the women's organizations at Oberlin, which included the Oberlin Female Anti-Slavery Society, the Female Society of Oberlin for the Promotion of Health, and the Oberlin Female Moral Reform Society.[60] A number of Oberlin graduates became prominent feminists in later life. Among them was Lucy Stone who had promoted *The Liberator* and other anti-slavery periodicals on campus. Stone later took the public eye when she worked out a marriage contract which provided equal rights for herself and her husband, Henry B. Blackwell.[61] Others who made a significant contribution to women's rights were Antoinette Brown who was the first woman graduate to be ordained, and Sallie Holly who became a prominent anti-slavery lecturer. From the beginning of his ministry Finney

---

52 Finney, *Memoirs*, pp. 411–12.
53 Finney, *Memoirs*, p. 412.
54 Finney, *Memoirs*, p. 413.
55 Finney, *Memoirs*, p. 391.
56 Finney, *Memoirs*, p. 393.
57 Finney, *Memoirs*, p. 391 note 37.
58 See L.S. Dayton and D.W. Dayton, '"Your Daughters Shall Prophesy": Feminism in the Holiness Movement', *Methodist History*, 1876, Vol. XIV, No. 2, p. 71.
59 Dayton, '"Your Daughters Shall Prophesy"', p. 71.
60 Hambricke-Stowe, *Charles Finney*, p. 179.
61 See Dayton, '"Your Daughters Shall Prophesy"', p. 71.

had given place to women. As early as 1827 the Oneida Presbytery had criticised his decision to allow females to pray in the presence of men and to pray for individuals by name.[62]

Hambrick-Stowe also noted that evangelical women played a key role in promoting the revival in Philadelphia by organizing bands of visitors and praying with women for the conversion of their husbands.[63] Significantly Finney had found when in his New York pastorate that 'our ladies were not afraid to go and gather all classes from the neighbourhood round about into our meetings'.[64] During his later revival meetings in England Finney's wife took on an increasing role preaching at large gatherings for women.

Visits to England

During the Oberlin period, Finney made two visits to England. The first took place from 1849–51 just after his second marriage to Elizabeth Atkinson in November 1848[65] and the second between January 1859 and August 1860. Prior to his first trip Finney had become keenly aware that many in Britain, and particularly in Wales, were appreciative of his *Lectures on Revivals of Religion*. One publisher in England alone sold 80,000 volumes of the *Lectures* and they were translated into Welsh where they were influential in promoting a number of local revivals.[66] Encouraged by friends on both sides of the Atlantic the Finneys left New York on 20 October 1849. Charles Finney had been given a specific invitation from Mr Potto Brown and his pastor Mr Harcourt to come to the small village of Houghton near Huntingdon. Brown was a Nonconformist mill-owner and philanthropist who was concerned for the souls of his wealthy and influential friends, many of whom he invited to come and meet with Finney in his home.[67] Finney reported in his autobiography that that 'a revival commenced and spread' and 'the work spread among those who came from the neighbouring villages'. In December Finney went to Birmingham and began a series of meetings in Mr Roe's[68] Baptist church, reporting that 'revival swept through the congregation, and a very large proportion of the impenitent were turned to Christ'.[69] During this period of three months Finney also spent time

---

62 George Gale to Finney, 14 March 1827 cited McLoughlin, *Modern Revivalism*, p. 30.
63 George Gale to Finney, 14 March 1827 cited McLoughlin, *Modern Revivalism*, p. 80 f.
64 Finney, *Memoirs*, p. 359.
65 His first wife died on 17 December 1847.
66 Eddy, *A Spiritual Awakening*, p. 13.
67 C.G. Finney, *An Autobiography* (Hodder and Stoughton, 1832), p. 322.
68 Finney reported that Roe's church was one of the few close-Communion Baptist churches in England. See Finney, *An Autobiography*, p. 324.
69 Finney, *An Autobiography*, p. 324.

with the minister of Carr's Lane Chapel, the Revd John Angell James, a man of great influence in the social and political affairs of the city.

Finney then moved to London in April 1850 and began preaching for Dr Campbell who ministered at Whitefield's Tabernacle. Campbell was a strange individual who was also editor of *The British Banner* and *The Christian Witness*. He often wrote critically in these periodicals of those he invited to occupy his pulpit. Finney fared better than most since Campbell compared him to Whitefield remarking that it was appropriate that 'Mr Finney should commence his labours in this Metropolis in an edifice reared by George Whitefield, the most eminent Evangelist that England ever produced.'[70] Campbell also reported that Finney's visit resulted in 'a great number of the most interesting cases of conversion' and recorded that he 'preached a great deal on confession and restitution; the results of which were truly wonderful'.[71] While at the Tabernacle Finney made full use of inquiry procedures asking 'those, and those only, who are not Christians, but who are anxious for salvation to attend a meeting for instruction'. Hambrick-Stowe wrote of Finney's preaching as follows: 'Struck by what he saw as "the moral desolation of the vast city", Finney focussed his preaching less on the second blessing of holiness – which he knew would alienate him from some of his supporters – than on the primary need for salvation from sin.'[72] Finney and his wife finally departed for home in April 1851 with 'a multitude of people who had been interested in our labours, gathered upon the Wharf. A great majority of them were young converts'.[73]

On the occasion of his second visit, Finney and his wife arrived on 1 January 1859 at Liverpool where they were met by their friend Potto Brown who escorted them to Houghton and St Ives, 'where we saw precious revivals'.[74] They then moved to London to Borough Road Chapel where Mr Harcourt, the former minister of Houghton, was now labouring. Finney reported that the work there 'deepened and spread till it reached every household belonging to that congregation'.[75] *The Revivalist* reported that 'for nearly two months the Revd C.G. Finney, of Oberlin, Ohio, has been preaching at Borough Road Chapel, during which time he has regularly delivered six sermons a week. The attendance has been well sustained throughout, and on Sunday evenings the chapel has been crowded, and on the last more so if possible than any other previous occasion.'[76] The same article concluded that 'it is evident that the labours of Mr and Mrs Finney have been attended by the divine blessing to a great extent. Many professors of religion have been quickened into new life,

---

70 Hambrick-Stowe, *Charles Finney*, p. 244.
71 Finney, *Memoirs*, p. 515.
72 Hambrick-Stowe, *Charles Finney*, p. 247.
73 Finney, *An Autobiography*, p. 343.
74 Finney, *An Autobiography*, p. 374.
75 Finney, *An Autobiography*, p. 375.
76 *The Revivalist*, 1859, p. 80.

backsliders have been restored, and hardened sinners have been melted into penitence, and led to Christ.'[77]

Following this the Finneys spent three months in Edinburgh where attendances 'kept steadily at 400 to 450 each week-night evening' with 2,000 being present at the Sunday meeting.[78] *The Revivalist* reported that on one evening when Mr Finney asked those who were prepared to profess their faith in the Saviour publicly to stand up. At least two hundred did so holding up their right hands in testimony.[79] Then following a brief period in Aberdeen, Finney accepted an invitation to Bolton also staying there for a three-month period. There in the Temperance Hall which the Bolton Methodist-Congregational Evangelical Revival Committee had secured, he preached twice on Sundays and on four week-night evenings. Finney urged the people to canvas the whole town and 'to go two and two and visit every house; and, if permitted, to pray in every house'.[80] Each evening Finney called for inquirers to come forward and 'great numbers' did so from 'the dense masses that filled every nook and corner of the building'.[81] He noted that 'all classes' were drawn into these services.[82]

Significantly, Finney who was often in earlier days accused of creating excitement by his preaching and exhorting, found himself having to calm things at some of the Bolton meetings. The Methodist brethren there seemed to take the view that the greater the excitement the more rapidly the work would be extended. In consequence they would pound the benches and pray exceedingly loudly. Eventually, Finney, who was of the opinion that they were putting off those who might otherwise be inquirers, urged the disturbers to quieten down, observing that many more were converted as a result.[83]

During the course of the Bolton campaign Finney's wife took a significant part in the proceedings. Some of her daytime meetings in the Temperance Hall were largely attended. On some occasions the hall was almost full and the ladies from the various denominations encouraged her in the work. *The Revivalist* reported that during the campaign at Borough Road Chapel in London, 'Mrs Finney conducted a series of meetings for women, in the afternoon, which have been productive of much good.'[84] Women such as Mrs Finney who took a public role in preaching at large open meetings were undoubtedly paving the way for greater acceptance of women in the public sphere. In this particular function it is reasonable to see in their activities a precursor to the movement for the emancipation of women which increasingly surfaced with the passing of the century.

---

77 *The Revivalist*, 1859, p. 80.
78 *The Revival Advocate*, Vol. 2, No. 6, June 1859, p. 718.
79 *The Revival Advocate*, Vol. 2, No. 6, June 1859, p. 718.
80 Finney, *An Autobiography*, p. 386.
81 Finney, *An Autobiography*, p. 386.
82 Finney, *An Autobiography*, p. 386.
83 Finney, *An Autobiography*, p. 387.
84 *The Revivalist*, 1859, p. 80.

Despite both being exhausted by their endeavours in Bolton, the Finneys went on in April to Manchester. There, although Finney saw evidence of God's Spirit assisting the work, he felt a real breakthrough was held back on account of the Methodist and Congregational brethren not working together as harmoniously as they might. By August the Finneys were worn out, and decided that the moment was right for them to return to America. Arrangements were therefore put in place and on 3 August they sailed on board the *Persia* for New York.

Finney's Preaching and Writing

In addition to his college commitments, Finney was also responsible for pastoring the Oberlin congregation. Despite the opposition over doctrinal matters, Finney recalled, 'we not only prospered in our souls here as a church, but we had a continuous revival'.[85] 'Our students', he continued, 'were converted by scores from year to year.'[86]

During his time at Oberlin, Finney revised some of his views on revival with the publication of his *Letters on Revival*. They were first issued in a series in *The Oberlin Evangelist* and later printed as a separate volume. They were intended as a supplement to the *Lectures on Revival* and were to some extent a corrective to his earlier views. Hambrick-Stowe posited that they could have been written as a response to John W. Nevin's *The Anxious Bench*, a critique of new measure revivalism that was published in 1843, although there is no evidence that Finney ever read it. In the same period Finney also began writing his *Systematic Theology* the first volume of which was published in July 1846 with the second appearing in August 1847.

Finney's Final Days

On his return home from England in 1851, Finney was unanimously elected President of Oberlin College following the death of Asa Mahan. He held the position until 1866 and continued as pastor at Oberlin First Congregational Church until 1872. He was married for the third time in October 1865 to Rebecca Rayl, a widow and Assistant Principal of the Oberlin College female department. Although he had been a Mason in his younger days, he published a strong attack against the order in 1869 entitled *The Character, Claims and Practical Workings of Freemasonry*. He felt very strongly that it was entirely wrong for a husband to pledge to conceal from his wife things he freely shared with other men at the Lodge. He died peacefully on 16 August 1875.

---

85 *The Revivalist*, 1859, p. 405.
86 *The Revivalist*, 1859, p. 405.

Finney's Understanding of Revival

Finney's basic understanding of revival was of significant numbers of people making an immediate decision to have faith in Christ's forgiveness and to turn their lives over to his rule. Such a revival included the presence of the Holy Spirit in individual believers causing them to live lives of holiness which extended to every aspect of their living. This included habits that might be injurious to their health such as smoking, chewing or snuffing tobacco, late nights and too much eating between meals.[87]

A Human Endeavour

Finney's prominence and influence in the history of revivals stems from his emphasis on 'means' or 'new measures' to achieve revival. In truth however, Finney did not develop 'new means', he simply took what others had already been using and systematised them in his writing and practice. Finney identified the means that he employed in his campaigns as prayer, public preaching, visitation and inquirers' meetings. Finney was strongly of the view that humanity has the ability to make choices and to work in cooperation with the Holy Spirit. He therefore used these 'means' to hold people's attention and to stir and captivate their minds. As far as Finney was concerned all revivals have a dual aspect in that they are works of God which demand a human response. What made Finney so prominent in this debate was what many saw as an over-emphasis on the human contribution. At the beginning of his first lecture on 'Revivals of Religion' he stated:

> Religion is the work of man. It is something for man to do. It consists in obeying God. It is man's duty. It is true God induces him to do it. He influences him by His Spirit, because of his great wickedness and reluctance to obey. If it were not necessary for God to influence men, if men were disposed to obey God, there would be no occasion to pray: 'O Lord, revive Thy work'.[88]

At another place in the lectures Finney stated boldly that 'a revival should be expected whenever it is needed'.[89] He was adamant that Christians were to be blamed if there was no revival, for God 'has placed His Spirit at your disposal'.[90] Again, he emphasized that revival is 'not a miracle, nor dependent on a miracle in any sense. It is a purely philosophical result of the right use of

---

87 C.G. Finney, *Lectures on Systematic Theology* (Oberlin, 1878; Eerdmans, 1953), pp. 312–16.
88 C.G. Finney, *Revivals of Religion Lectures by Charles Grandison Finney*, Lecture 1 (Marshall, Morgan and Scott, 1910; Oliphants, 1928), p. 1.
89 McLoughlin, *Modern Revivalism*, p. 36.
90 Finney, *Revivals of Religion*, p. 134.

the constituted means – as much as any other effect produced by the application of means.'⁹¹ In his *Memoirs*, when recalling the revival at Rome, Finney stated them as follows:

> I have said before that the means that I had all along used thus far in promoting revivals, were much prayer, secret and social, public preaching, personal conversation, and visitation from house to house for that purpose: and when inquirers became multiplied I appointed meetings for them, and invited those that were inquiring to meet where I gave them instructions suited to their necessities.⁹²

None of these were in actual fact new. Indeed they were all utilised in the Second Great Awakening. What Finney did was to combine and systematise them. In short, Finney 'codified what others had made common practice'.⁹³

Revivals Can Be Promoted

Finney was clear that when these means were put forward 'without wildness or fanaticism' and are responded to, revivals occur. Thus he wrote:

> Revivals were formerly regarded as miracles. And it has been by some even in our own day .... For a long time it was supposed by the church that a revival was a miracle, an imposition of Divine Power, with which they had nothing to do, and which they had no more agency in producing than they had in producing thunder, or a storm of hail, or an earthquake. It is only within a few years that ministers generally have supposed that revivals be promoted by the use of means designated and adapted specially to that object. It has been supposed that revivals came just as showers do, sometimes in one town, and sometimes in another, and that ministers could do nothing more to produce them than they could to make showers of rain come on their town, when they were falling on a neighbouring town.⁹⁴

A little further in on in his second section, Finney went on to point out that such understandings of revival have had a detrimental effect on the level of religious life and practice.

> Revivals have been greatly hindered by mistaken notions concerning the sovereignty of God. Many people have supposed God's sovereignty to be something very different from what it is. They have supposed it to be

---

91 Finney, *Revivals of Religion*, p. 5.
92 Finney, *Memoirs*, p. 158.
93 W.R. Cross, *The Burned-Over District* (Harper and Row, 1965), p. 172.
94 Finney, *Memoirs*, pp. 12–13.

such an arbitrary disposal of events, and particularly of the gifts of the Holy Spirit, as precluded a rational employment of means for promoting a revival. But there is no evidence from the Bible that God exercises any such sovereignty. There are no facts to prove it, but everything goes to show that God has connected the means with the end, through all the departments of His government, in nature and grace.[95]

At another place in the lectures he stated boldly that 'a revival should be expected whenever it is needed'. Finney who saw revival rather in local terms, a town, village or local community, was one of the first to argue that revivals could be planned and got up by the use of appropriate means including obviously sustained prayer and preaching but also by the use of so called 'new measures' which included publicity and the use of the penitent form. Finney was always quick to remind others that prayer was an absolute necessity before a revival could take place. In a letter sent to *The Revivalist* from St Ives, Finney wrote that 'Prayer, closet prayer, social, public, earnest, agonising, prevailing prayer, praying everywhere, lifting up holy hands without wrath or doubting, has been the great fundamental fact in the use of means.'[96]

Concern for Social Justice

In keeping with this emphasis on human endeavour, Finney's understanding of revival was integrally tied to issues of social justice. He was firmly of the view that to overlook social justice was to cause God to withhold his blessings. At New York Finney was one of the founding members of The New York Anti-Slavery Society in 1833. Both he and his congregation were strongly opposed to slave-holding and Finney frequently spoke against it. Finney welcomed blacks and refused to serve communion to slaveholders at the chapel believing this to be 'a decidedly good influence on individuals and the church as a whole'.[97] His sermons on the subject of slavery were vivid as he spoke for example of 'the two millions of degraded heathen in our land' who 'stretch forth an agonising cry to God'.[98]

In the spring of 1834 Finney's health broke and he was obliged to take a sea voyage. On his return he was alarmed to find that *The New York Evangelist*, a pro-Finney revival paper, had floundered on account of its advancing the slavery question too rapidly. In an attempt to save it, Finney proposed 'to preach a course of lectures to my people on revivals of religion'.[99] They proved the very thing, with Joshua Leavitt, the paper's editor, reporting the substance of each address. Such was the demand for the lectures that they were afterwards

---

95 Finney, *Memoirs*, p. 14.
96 *The Revivalist*, 1859, p. 32.
97 Hambrick-Stowe, *Charles Finney*, p. 142.
98 Hambrick-Stowe, *Charles Finney*, p. 142.
99 Finney, *Memoirs*, p. 372.

published in May 1835 as a book entitled Finney's *Lectures on Revival*. They were reprinted in England and translated into French and later German and read extensively in Europe. In America 12,000 copies of the *Lectures*, which controversially described revival as 'an essentially human activity', were immediately sold. In the *Lectures* Finney demonstrated an acute awareness of the dangers of antinomianism which were often attached to the doctrine of perfectionism. 'On account of Christian perfectionism', he wrote, 'misguided believers have run into so many wild notions.'[100] Among them were James Boyle and Humphrey Noyes.[101]

Although Finney fully recognized the dangers inherent in 'perfectionist' teaching, he persisted with the terminology which was clearly evidenced in biblical texts such as 'be ye perfect' and 'may the God of peace sanctify you wholly'. Finney did not believe sanctification meant a change in 'the substance of the soul or body'. For Finney 'entire sanctification' was not a permanent 'higher' Christian state from which it was impossible to fall. It could be lost when the believer ceased to live the consecrated life.

Finney's Preaching

Finney's preaching was designed to stir the emotions of his hearers. When he gestured, people in his congregations sometimes ducked as if he were throwing things at them. When he described the fall of sinners he often pointed to the ceiling and as he let his finger slowly drop people at the back of the building would sometimes stand to watch the final entry into hell. He sought to bring those who were not Christians to a point where they would be convicted over their sinfulness and in consequence turn to Christ for forgiveness. He believed that conversion was a work of man and that it happened in a specific moment.[102] Finney held the human frame to be naturally sluggish and that rational thinking was heavily influenced by the physical senses. It was therefore quite proper, in his view, to use means that would stir the senses and in so doing recall the attentions of those who were on the point of disengaging with the message. Finney instructed ministers of the gospel 'to address the feelings enough to secure attention, and then deal with the conscience, and probe to the quick. Appeals to the feelings alone will never convert sinners.'[103] But he added, 'If

---

100 Hambrick-Stowe, *Charles Finney*, p. 184.
101 Finney, *Memoirs*, p. 392, note 42.
102 Finney, *Lectures on Systematic Theology*, p. 290: 'What is implied in regeneration. 1. The nature of the change shows that it must be instantaneous. It is a change of choice or intention. This must be instantaneous. The preparatory work of conviction and enlightening the mind may have been gradual and progressive. But when regeneration occurs, it must be instantaneous.' See also p. 217: 'There are many passages which represent the conversion of sinners as the work of men.'
103 Finney, *Lectures on Systematic Theology*, p. 241.

attention flags at any time, appeal to the feelings again, and rouse it up; but do your work with conscience.'[104]

Finney firmly believed that preaching should be conversational. 'Preaching to be understood', he wrote in his Lectures, 'should be colloquial in style. A minister must preach as he would talk, if he wishes fully to be understood.'[105] Looking back to his early days as a preacher Finney recalled that 'they used to complain ... that I talked to the people in a colloquial manner, that I said "you" instead of preaching about sinners'. However his reply was, 'Show me the fruits of your ministry, and if they so far exceed mine as to give evidence that you have found a more excellent way, I will adopt your views.'[106] Although the central aspect of Finney's revival preaching was always bringing the sinner to repentance, he sometimes widened its practical application and preached on confession and restitution. For example, during his first visit to London which began in May 1850, he reported that 'almost every form of crime was thus searched out and confessed. Hundreds, and I believe thousands, of pounds sterling were paid over to make restitution.'[107] Finney repeated this practice at Bolton in 1860 where one gentleman admitted that he had made restitution of £1,500.[108] Finney recalled that he had had similar instance following one of his addresses at Rochester, New York.[109]

The 'Protracted Meeting' and the 'Anxious Seat'

In addition to what were considered to be generally accepted 'means', Finney often added 'other measures' when he considered it expedient. Such were the 'anxious seat' and the 'Protracted Meeting'.[110] It was these two means which aroused the most discontent on the part of the Old School Calvinists. The 'Protracted Meeting', as Finney practised it, was essentially a three- or four-day gathering. Sometimes the schedule included three sermons a day and as many prayer meetings. In the 'Protracted Meeting' sometimes several ministers would work together sharing the preaching, leading and ministry. Finney first utilised Protracted Meetings about the time of the Rochester revival.[111] He regarded

---

104 Finney, *Lectures on Systematic Theology*, p. 241.
105 Finney, *Revivals of Religion Lectures*, p. 233.
106 Comment by W.H. Harding (ed.), *Revivals of Religion* (Oliphants, 1928). p. 163, note 1.
107 Finney, *An Autobiography*, p. 343.
108 Finney, *An Autobiography*, p. 388.
109 Finney, *An Autobiography*, p. 389.
110 Both these two measures had been used in the Second Great Awakening. What Finney termed the 'anxious bench' was more often spoken of as the 'anxious pen' at camp meetings. The protracted meeting was basically an urban equivalent of the more rural camp meeting.
111 The first four-day protracted meeting for revival was said to have been held by William C. Walton in Alexandria, Virginia in October 1828. See also Finney, *Memoirs*, p. 340, note 62.

them as an important means of creating a strong impression of divine things on the minds of the people.

Finney used the 'Anxious Seat' during the Rochester revival. In this procedure those who were 'anxious' to renounce their sins then and there were invited to come forward at, or towards the close of the meeting, and sit on seats at the front which had been left empty for the purpose. Trained helpers would meet with them there and pray for them. The Anxious Seat was objected to because it often created excitement and emotional shouts and tears from the penitents. It was also claimed that conversions arising out of such an environment wouldn't last. Others argued that the Anxious Seat also represented a doctrine of conversion which over-stressed the human will. Preaching at Park Street Chapel in Boston, Finney had said that 'if a man resolves to be a lawyer; then he directs all his plans and efforts to that object'. Similarly, 'the simple volition of the sinner's mind through the influence of motives ... is all that is necessary to make a sinner a Christian'.[112] Perhaps more startling was Finney's sermon preached in 1831 entitled, 'Make Yourself a New Heart'. As far as his Calvinist opponents were concerned, Finney had effectively removed divine initiative from conversion.

As variants on the Anxious Seat, Finney also, on occasion, held 'Anxious Meetings' in 'Anxious Rooms', perhaps in a church vestry or room adjoining the church building or meeting house. The object of such occasions was in essence the same, to bring the sinner to a point of decision to renounce sin and embrace Christ in personal commitment. It was success at this one crucial point that everyone expected of the revivalist. As long as people were committing their lives to Christ in a public and definite manner the revivalist would be invited to continue his labours.

Publicity and Music

Finney, along with many other preachers, made wide use of publicity. In the 1820s he had relied on the *Western Recorder* for reliable news reports of his labours. Later when he moved east, he turned to *The New York Evangelist* for support. These two papers together with *The Oberlin Evangelist* he used as the means of correcting misrepresentations of his teaching and theology and of promoting revival in more distant places. His published books, particularly *Lectures on Revival*, enjoyed huge sales in England and created an appetite for deeper Christian experience. The *Lectures* were first published on 15 May 1835.

Finney was also acutely aware of the importance and value of music. In particular he looked for music with easy melodies which would stir the emotions. When he came to New York in 1832 he teamed up with Thomas

---

112 C. Finney, *The Biblical Repertory and Theological Review* (1832) cited Murray, *Revival and Revivalism*, p. 295.

Hastings of Utica as his music and choir director. In addition to being an excellent conductor, Hastings was writing new hymns which were beginning to catch on with the wider public who were drawn into his campaigns.

The Use of Independent Meeting Places

One valuable strategy that Finney learned during his time in England, and his second visit in particular, was the use of independent premises in which to hold his meetings. Finney wrote, 'I found it to be true in England wherever I tried it, that the best way to promote revivals of religion was to hold independent meetings; that is, meetings in large halls, where they can be obtained, to which all denominations may come.'[113] Finney believed that in the United States people would generally attend public meetings but in England he was of the view that 'the true way to labour for souls there is to have no particular connection with any denomination; but to preach the true Gospel, and make a stand in halls, or even in streets when the weather is favourable, where no denominational feelings and peculiarities can straiten the influences of the Spirit of God'.[114] Hambrick-Stowe took the view that in this matter Finney had anticipated the later city-wide campaigns of Dwight L. Moody and those who followed his work.

A New Understanding of Revival

Charles Finney ushered in a new understanding of revival which greatly influenced both his contemporaries and subsequent revival preachers. In earlier days in the previous century, Jonathan Edwards, who had been at the centre of the Great Awakening in New England, had explicitly declared that human agency had no more ability to produce revival than it had 'in producing thunder or storm of hail or earthquake'.[115] Finney in effect reversed this understanding. He compared working for revival with that of a farmer toiling in expectancy of a harvest.

The great majority of the subsequent generations of nineteenth- and twentieth-century preachers of revival were in the Finneyan tradition. James Caughey, the Pearsall Smiths, Phoebe and Walter Palmer, Moody, Torrey and Sunday all believed that revival could, to a lesser or greater extent, be planned. All of them utilised some or most of the measures that Finney had developed and refined. Thus Iain Murray wrote: 'Certainly, before the end of the nineteenth century this form of evangelism and its attendant "revivals" was so established across the United States that few could remember anything different.'[116]

---

113 Hambrick-Stowe, *Charles Finney*, p. 262.
114 Hambrick-Stowe, *Charles Finney*, p. 262.
115 McLoughlin, *Modern Revivalism*, p. 85.
116 Murray, *Revival and Revivalism*, p. 278.

Significantly, this Arminian emphasis resonated with a nation which was discovering what could be accomplished in almost every field by human endeavour.

It was the case that Finney's new emphases and 'new measures' represented a departure from Old School Congregationalism and Presbyterianism and therefore to some extent provoked division. Asa Nettleton and others of the Old School held that the revivalist's sole responsibility was to instruct sinners in the truth of the gospel and urge them to pray and repent in the hope that God had predestined them for salvation.[117] Finney's contrasting emphasis on the human will and the ability of any individual to respond to the invitation to give their life to Christ, ran counter to their Calvinistic views which saw revival in terms of a sovereign move of God in which the divine Spirit took hold of the individual. For those like Finney's former pastor, George Gale, who subscribed to the Westminster Confession, regeneration was essentially a passive experience. Their problem however was that Finney's great effectiveness appeared to increasing numbers of people to demonstrate the rightness of his understanding. A major break of some kind was therefore inevitable. It came in 1874 when the Presbyterian Church formally split into two groups known as the Old and New Schools. The Old School retained 2,025 churches and 141,000 communicants.[118]

Finney seems to have endured overly harsh criticism at the hands of some Calvinist theologians and historians. That said, it needs to be remembered that he tempered his views with the publication of his *Letters on Revival* which first began to appear in 1845. Here he warned against enthusiasts who are guided by their impulses rather than by enlightened intelligence.[119] He stressed the need 'to keep excitement down as far as is consistent with a full, thorough and powerful exhibition of truth'.[120] He emphasized 'the want of personal holiness, power in prayer and in preaching the word'.[121] Significantly, he also warned of the danger of 'so much dependence upon means and measures, so much of man and so little of God'.[122] In truth, Finney was of the view that there is a dual aspect to any revival, a divine initiative and a human response. This is why he was unapologetic in his instruction to Christian workers. 'Whenever you have reason to believe that a person within your reach is awakened', he wrote, 'do not sleep till you have poured in the light upon his mind, and tried to bring him to immediate repentance.'[123]

In summary, Finney was a very versatile and gifted individual. He was an organizer, college professor and president and a leader of men, who

---

117 McLoughlin, *Modern Revivalism*, p. 32.
118 McLoughlin, *Modern Revivalism*, p. 274, note 1.
119 C.G. Finney, *Letters*, 12 March 1845.
120 Finney, *Letters*, 23 April 1845.
121 Finney, *Letters*, 16 July 1845.
122 Finney, *Letters*, 17 December 1845.
123 Finney, *Revivals of Religion Lectures*, p. 162.

communicated with all levels of society. Above all he was a revivalist and, on account of his so called 'new measures', which strictly speaking were not new, he is rightly regarded as the author or founding figure of 'revivalism'. He was perhaps the first individual to make revivalism into a profession. As early as 1830 some of his contemporaries observed that he had proved himself a master of respectable, efficient, carefully organized revivalism. He was a gifted preacher whose sermons and addresses were compelling listening. His theological and popular writings did an enormous amount to raise people's expectancy and desire to awaken churches and communities. Like many revivalists both before and after him, Finney was a social reformer with a deep concern for the abolition of slavery, the promotion of temperance and equality for women, a fact which was seen particularly in the life of Oberlin College. Probably no one since the days of George Whitefield had had such success as a preacher in their endeavour to convert souls to God than Finney had. In fact Charles Hambrick-Stowe entitled one of the chapters in his study of Finney as 'Whitefield Redivivus'.

CHAPTER 5

James Caughey and Holiness and Temperance Revivalism

James Caughey was a remarkable revivalist preacher effective in both England and North America. Richard Carwardine has called him 'the king of revivalist preachers'. When he returned to America after six years of revival campaigning in Britain and Ireland he was to claim that some 20,000 souls had been justified and 9,000 'entirely sanctified'. There was no Victorian biography of Caughey and he left no memoirs, with the result that he hasn't received the attention that has been devoted to other to other nineteenth-century revivalists. Caughey did however leave a number of writings which provide valuable insights into his times in England as well as descriptions of his revival methods.[1]

Early Days

James Caughey was born about the year 1810 and was a native of Ireland who emigrated to America in his youth. In 1830 he went to work in a flourmill at Troy in New York State. He was converted in 1832[2] and some two years later was admitted as a preacher on probation by the Annual Conference of the Methodist Episcopal Church which that year was held at Troy. Shortly before his ordination as a deacon in 1834, Caughey was profoundly influenced by reading a passage from the writings of Dr Adam Clarke. So strong was the experience that he had found himself calling out, 'God have mercy upon me a sinner! Save me Lord, or I perish! Heal my soul for it hath sinned against thee!' From this moment forward Caughey was a changed man.

In 1839 shortly after being appointed to the Whitehall circuit he had another remarkable experience. Having just taken up his new work he desired to take a wife 'but the more he sought to do so, the more he felt distress and the loss of God's presence'. He described his feelings in the following lines: 'The world was a blank, a bleak and howling wilderness to my soul, without the smiles of my saviour.' He sought God for the answer for three days and then on 9 July

---

1 *Letters on Various Subjects*, 5 volumes (Simpkin, Marshall, 1844–7), *Revival Miscellanies* (Houlton and Stoneman, undated), *Arrows from my Quiver* (W.C. Palmer Junior, 1868), *Glimpses of Life in Soul-saving* (W.C. Palmer Junior, 1868), *Earnest Christianity Illustrated* (J.P. Magee, 1855), *Methodism in Earnest being the History of a Great Revival in Great Britain* (Charles H. Pierce, 1850), *Showers of Blessing from Clouds of Mercy* (W.C. Palmer, 1868).
2 J. Caughey, *Earnest Christianity Illustrated* (J.P. Magee, 1855), p. 9.

1839 he received a remarkable revelation. It was 'spoken to my heart, but in a manner, and with rapidity, I cannot possibly describe'.

> These matters which trouble thee must be let entirely alone. The will of God is, that thou shalt visit Europe. He shall be with thee there, and give thee many seals to thy ministry. He has provided thee with funds. Make thy arrangements accordingly; and, next Conference, ask liberty from the authorities; and it shall be granted thee. Visit Canada first; when this is done, sail to England. God shall be with thee there, and thou shalt have no want in all thy journeyings; and thou shalt be brought back safely again to America.[3]

This impression left Caughey in no doubt. He wrote, 'I fell on my knees before the Lord, my whole mind consenting to the orders .... O, the sweetness of that communion I then enjoyed with God.'[4] Caughey sought and obtained permission from his Conference in 1840 to visit Europe. Before setting out he visited Quebec and Montreal where 500 were converted under his labours in a few weeks. Caughey's initial visit to England lasted from 1841 to 1847. He then returned to America for a decade before making three shorter visits to the 'Old Country'. By the late 1860s his health was failing and he retired to Highland Park in New Jersey.

Caughey's first campaign was his most effective. He published an account of it in 1850 entitled *Methodism in Earnest being the History of a Great Revival in Great Britain.* In this book he stated that 'twenty thousand souls professed faith in Christ, and ten thousand professed sanctification in about six years' in connection with his labours. On his return to America from this visit Caughey spent his summers in literary labours at his residence in Burlington, Vermont, while during the winter months he preached successively in New York, Albany, Providence, Lowell, Fall River, Warren and Cincinnati and Toronto, Quebec and London in Canada.[5]

Caughey returned to Britain in 1856 and made other visits before his retirement in 1866. On these latter occasions although his revival preaching was effective he never achieved the same level of results that attended his first visit.

Early Labours in America and the British Isles 1840–7

Before setting out for England Caughey was obedient to the revelation that he had received at Whitehall in 1839 and visited Quebec and Montreal. In a letter dated 30 October 1840 Caughey related how on the night of 8 October he had reached La Prairie, a village on the banks of the St Lawrence, opposite Montreal

---

3 Caughey, *Earnest Christianity*, p. 15.
4 Caughey, *Earnest Christianity*, p. 16.
5 Caughey, *Earnest Christianity*, p. 18.

James Caughey

where 'there was a very gracious influence during the service'. The next morning he crossed the river to Montreal where 'I received a hearty welcome from many of my old friends'. He spent 18 days there preaching 18 sermons in consequence of which 'about twenty souls were converted to God'. Caughey then moved on to Quebec City where he spent 12 weeks and 'preached nearly one hundred sermons'.[6] He then returned to Montreal passing through Three Rivers where he preached 86 sermons, a temperance sermon, and 'delivered five lectures on total abstinence from all intoxicating drinks'. More than two hundred sinners were converted to God, and one thousand persons united with the Montreal Young Men's Total Abstinence Society.[7] In all 500 persons were converted during Caughey's labours in Canada.[8]

Caughey arrived in Liverpool on 29 July 1841 and straight away visited the Wesleyan Conference which happened to be meeting at that time in Manchester. He then went first to Ireland and laboured in Dublin, Limerick, Cork and Bandon. Then re-crossing the channel, he held meetings in Liverpool, Leeds,

---

6 Caughey, *Letters on Various Subjects*, Letter IV, 16 March 1841, p. 30.
7 Caughey, *Letters on Various Subjects*, Letter IX from St John's, Canada, 2 April 1841.
8 Caughey, *Earnest Christianity*, p. 16.

Hull, Sheffield, Huddersfield, York, Birmingham, Nottingham, Lincoln, Boston, Sunderland, Gateshead, Scarborough, Chesterfield, Doncaster, Macclesfield, Wakefield and some other minor towns.

From this it is obvious that the settings for Caughey's activities were the towns and cities of the industrial north of the country. He operated for the most part within the Wesleyan Methodist circuits which embraced these places. It was only in 1846 that he began to devote his energies outside the parent body of Methodism's control. In truth, the early 1840s were a time when Wesleyan Methodism was rising up the social hierarchy and many leading ministers, especially Jabez Bunting their dominant voice, frowned on revivalist excitement and sought to halt the work of men such as Caughey. There is no doubt that Caughey, for his part, also treated the English Methodist Conference rulings with a degree of lightness. Additionally, having his own funds he didn't feel overly intimidated by threats of discipline or suspension from the Connexion. The Annual Wesleyan Conference held a vigorous debate over Caughey's ministry in their circuits but no formal resolutions were carried.

At the beginning of 1846 Caughey entered his sixth year of itinerant work in Britain and the Wesleyan Conference finally lost its patience. At the prompting of Jabez Bunting, William Atherton brought forward a resolution that 'the American bishops be affectionately requested to call Caughey back to the United States on the ground that he has now been for several years in this country, and has visited many of our principal circuits, subject to no ecclesiastical supervision, responsibility or control, such as those to which all other Methodist ministers ... are required to submit; – [and] that such irregularity ...'[9] The Wesleyan Conference of 1847 expressed their deep concern that the impact of Caughey's style of revivalism had been 'to produce serious discords of opinion, feeling, and conduct among Brethren, and to create that internal disunion which is truly and scripturally condemned as divisive and schismatical'.[10] The Conference went on to speak of it as 'this great evil'. The real nub of their concern appeared in what followed that 'revivals have the effect of alienating in some degree the affections of our people from the well-accredited, long-tried, and officially-responsible Ministers and Pastors of our churches, – of lessening them in public estimation, – and of diminishing their legitimate and beneficial influence'.[11] The Conference went on to reprint and agree to enforce the Minute of 1807:

Q. XXI Have our people been sufficiently cautious respecting the permission of strangers to preach in our congregations?

---

9 Carwardine, *Transatlantic Revivalism*, p. 128.
10 *Wesleyan Methodist Conference Minutes*, 1847, Q XXXIX, p. 552.
11 *Wesleyan Methodist Conference Minutes*, 1847, Q XXXIX, p. 552.

A. We fear not; and we, therefore, again direct that no stranger, from America or elsewhere, be suffered to preach in any of our places, unless he come fully accredited, if an Itinerant Preacher, by having his name entered on the Minutes of the Conference of which he is a member; and if a Local Preacher, by a recommendatory note from his Superintendent.[12]

Caughey's exclusion from the Wesleyan circuits created a good deal of opposition and early on he took engagements from those who refused to abide by the Conference ruling. Even after he received a request from the American bishops to return home Caughey remained in England doing revivalistic and temperance work in churches connected with the Primitive Methodist Connexion in the North Midlands and in some Methodist New Connexion and Wesleyan Methodist Association churches.

Campaigning in Britain

Of his time in the summer of 1841 at Liverpool where he was very happily provided for in the homes of Messrs Fannin and Banning, Caughey wrote: 'I spent five months in Liverpool, preached one hundred and twenty times, delivered five temperance lectures and a few missionary speeches ... more than thirteen hundred persons found peace with God.'[13] This number, according to the Revd J.H. James, in a private letter addressed to the Revd Daniel Wise, was greatly understated 'for prudential reasons'.[14]

At Leeds Caughey laboured for a month at Brunswick Chapel where 20 souls were converted on the first night. He wrote that 'we have not witnessed a single pause in the revival. Sinners are converted, and believers are sanctified daily'.[15] He estimated that 'the total number professing to have obtained justification was about six hundred'. Of these, 244 'were cases of sanctification'.[16] Caughey also preached at Oxford Place Chapel, the largest Methodist place of worship in the world with seats for two thousand five hundred persons. 'Such a mass of people' he wrote, 'was a most sublime and imposing scene. The Lord graciously assisted my voice, so that I could be heard in all parts of the congregation.'[17] Caughey looked back on his time at Leeds with great affection: 'I know not which to admire most, this or the society at Brunswick.' He found that the Oxford Place Society were 'a truly loving, gracious people' whose 'hospitality and many acts of kindness left an indelible impression upon my heart'.[18] The results of what Caughey called 'the great revival at Leeds' were spectacular.

---

12 *Wesleyan Methodist Conference Minutes*, 1847, Q XXXIX, p. 552.
13 Caughey, *Methodism in Earnest*, p. 278.
14 Caughey, *Methodism in Earnest*, p. 278.
15 Caughey, *Methodism in Earnest*, p. 292.
16 Caughey, *Methodism in Earnest*, p. 293.
17 Caughey, *Methodism in Earnest*, p. 317.
18 Caughey, *Methodism in Earnest*, p. 317.

Three hundred persons were enabled to declare that 'the blood of Jesus had cleansed them from all sin: and an equal number professed justification'.[19]

While at Leeds, Caughey also spent time at St Peter's Chapel where 'two hundred persons obtained the blessing of salvation' and 'one hundred and ninety individuals professed justification' of whom 50 were already members in the St Peter's circuit. Caughey observed that St Peter's Chapel had a high percentage of poor who were 'clothed in the coarsest of garb' and that 'they were more noisy during the services than in any other circuit in town'.[20] At Hull the revival advanced with 'rapidity and power' Caughey reporting that 'the congregations were large, beyond anything I had yet seen in a revival'.[21] In *Earnest Christianity* Caughey recalled that on the Sabbath morning 'the town was stirred wonderfully – a congregation of three thousand in the morning and a perfect jam at night! Blessed by God!'.[22]

On 10 March 1844 Caughey recorded:

> We administered the Lord's Supper at Buxton Road chapel. The crowd of believers was so great that we despaired of ever having them round the altar. It was therefore concluded to distribute the elements to the people in the pews, so ... we succeeded in giving the sacrament to about fourteen hundred people, with great quietness and order, but with an extraordinary influence from above, with many expressions of praise and thanksgiving to Him who died and rose again.[23]

During his time in the Hull West Circuit Caughey related that the people were powerfully impacted his message. One evening during his campaign, he declared, 'If we are sanctified by faith, why not now, this very moment?', 'an influence, evidently from Heaven came upon the people suddenly'.[24]

> The scene was, beyond description, grand and sublimely awful .... Poor sinners were amazed and fled; but some fell down, some distance from the chapel, in terror and agony. Many however, remained, venturing the publican's plea, 'God be merciful to me a sinner!' .... The Superintendent minister, the Rev Thomas Martin, who was with me at the time in the pulpit, was so overpowered, that he could do nothing but weep and adore.[25]

Careful records were kept of the revival in Hull from which it was ascertained that 2,300 persons obtained justification, of whom 1,700 were from

---

19 Caughey, *Methodism in Earnest*, p. 318.
20 Caughey, *Methodism in Earnest*, p. 319.
21 Caughey, *Methodism in Earnest*, p. 340.
22 Caughey, *Earnest Christianity*, p. 97.
23 Caughey, *Methodism in Earnest*, p. 367.
24 Caughey, *Methodism in Earnest*, p. 341.
25 Caughey, *Methodism in Earnest*, p. 342.

the world. More than a thousand united with the Wesleyan church in Hull'.[26] As Caughey finally departed from the area he was moved by the unbounded affection of the new converts and the multitude that surrounded his carriage as he left Great Thornton Street Chapel.

At Sheffield Caughey ministered at Ebenezer and Carver Street chapels with a pleasing response. He also held services in July 1844 at Brunswick Chapel. At Ebenezer where Caughey spent the greater part of May, 323 persons were justified out of the world and 163 from Methodist circuits.[27] At Carver Street his reported results were more impressive with a total of 825 justified and 335 sanctified.[28] At Carver Street in June 1844 Caughey wrote:

> The scene of my labours at present is Carver Street Chapel. The work of God is advancing with increased rapidity and power. The first Sabbath we spent in this place of worship, one hundred and sixty-seven persons professed salvation. Since then hundreds have been saved. The work is indeed glorious, beyond anything I have seen before in the space of time.[29]

Caughey reported that the figures for the first quarter for 1845 for the Sheffield Wesleyan Methodist district 'showed an increase on the past year of one thousand four hundred and twenty-five members, and one thousand and twenty eight on trial'.[30]

In May 1846 Caughey was at Wesley Chapel in Nottingham where the young William Booth heard him speak. Although he had already been converted, the future founder and leader of the Salvation Army was profoundly stirred by what he heard and it created in him a deep desire to be an evangelist and see souls saved. Booth later penned the following lines about Caughey:

> He was an extraordinary preacher, filling up his sermons with thrilling anecdotes and vivid illustrations, and for straightforward declarations of scriptural truth and striking appeals to the conscience, I had up to that time never heard his equal; I do not know that I have since. For three months we were expecting him, during which time remarkable stories of the wonderful results that had attended his ministry elsewhere were continually reaching us, and for months before he came meetings were held to pray for a blessing on his labours. His visit was consequently the constant topic of conversation, and everybody was on the tip-toe of expectation when he arrived.

---

26 Caughey, *Methodism in Earnest*, p. 372.
27 Caughey, *Methodism in Earnest*, p. 389.
28 Caughey, *Methodism in Earnest*, p. 392.
29 Caughey, *Methodism in Earnest*, p. 389.
30 Caughey, *Methodism in Earnest*, p. 416.

The result answered the anticipation. There were such crowds and rushes to hear the Gospel as we had never dreamed of seeing. There were wonderful meetings, wonderful influences, and wonderful conversions. Multitudes were saved, many of whom became the most useful members of the society. All this had a powerful influence on my young heart. The straightforward conversational way of putting the truth, and the common-sense method of pushing the people up to decision, and the corresponding results that followed, in the conversion and sanctification of hundreds of people, made an ineffaceable impression on my mind, filling me not only with confidence in the power of God to save all those that come unto him, but with an assurance of the absolute certainty with which soul-saving results may be calculated upon when proper means are used for their accomplishment.

I saw as clearly as if a revelation had been made to me from Heaven that success in spiritual work, as in natural operations, was to be accounted for, not on any mere abstract theory of Divine Sovereignty, or favouritism, or accident, but on the employment of such methods as were dictated by common sense, the Holy Spirit and the Word of God.[31]

The Wesleyan Methodist authorities became increasingly concerned at Caughey's influence and at their Conference of 1846 Jabez Bunting moved and carried a resolution that the American bishops be requested to recall him. Such however was the 'Caughey influence' that he remained in England until 1847 returning a decade later in 1857 as the hero of the Wesleyan Reformers[32] and on further occasions in the 1860s. Figures for his campaigns in Sheffield from August 1857 to May 1858 were: 'Converts out of the world, 3,378; converts in the church, 742; sanctified, 1,889'.[33] Caughey who had stated that 'The Staffordshire Potteries are on my heart' laboured with great success at Hanley and Newcastle-under-Lyme in the latter part of 1858.[34] He then moved on with 'great success' to the Lever Street Circuit in Manchester from 26 December to Sunday 27 March 1859 preaching every Sunday twice and on the evenings of Tuesday, Wednesday, Thursday and Friday with an enthusiasm 'of that quiet, undemonstrative kind, that is much more felt than seen'. As a result of his endeavours an estimated 1,582 persons 'professed to receive good, and have their names recorded'. Of these 999 persons were brought 'out of the world', 843 of them promising to join various churches.[35] Then at the end of June and the first week of July, Caughey was briefly at Hull and at Louth where he urged on members 'the great importance' of 'knowing the time and place of their

---

31 G. Railton, *Twenty-One Years in the Salvation Army* (Salvation Army, 1891), p. 8.
32 See Kent, *Holding the Fort*, p. 38.
33 *The Revivalist*, 1860, pp. 41–2 cited Murray, *Revivals and Revivalism*, pp. 395–6.
34 *The Revivalist*, 1860, pp. 41–2 cited Murray, *Revivals and Revivalism*, p. 27.
35 *The Revivalist*, 1860, pp. 41–2 cited Murray, *Revivals and Revivalism*, p. 75.

conversion'.[36] In October 1859 Caughey was at Hanley where, according to *The Revivalist*, 'under his ministry, believers have been quickened, sanctified, and raised to holy enterprise, and the fire of devotion burns brighter, and with greater intensity in many hearts'.[37] At the close of his time in the town 680 enrolled for a special service as 'having received spiritual good in some form' from Caughey's ministry.[38] After spending one Sunday in Sheffield and one in Liverpool he left for America on 23 July 1860.

He returned to Lincolnshire in the summer of 1861 preaching in the new United Methodist Free Chapel at Market Rasen and also at Lincoln where 'about 500 persons professed to have obtained pardon'.[39] This was followed by short visits to Ripley, Ilkestone and Nottingham 'where a spiritual revival of very unusual power manifested itself'.[40] In consequence of his preaching in these places '1,450 professed to be justified by faith'.[41] In November 1861 Caughey was in Burton-on-Trent 'where scores of sinners were converted to the Saviour'[42] and at Derby where there was 'outward excitement' and 'powerful meetings'.[43] April 1862 witnessed his arrival in Bristol where he spent nearly three months preaching with remarkable effect in the Broadmead Room and Milk Street Chapel, with 'upwards of one thousand persons being justified and between two and three thousand receiving the blessings of a clean heart'.[44] At one of the Bristol meetings the room was so crowded that Caughey was forced 'to crawl in through the window to get into the building, and afterwards make his exit by the same window'.[45] He travelled via Wolverhampton and Nottingham[46] to Walsall where he preached in the Guildhall with 'backsliders coming and shouting, "Glory be to God!" and some weeping and singing' and some 'as soon as they got into the vestry, fell on their knees, and prayed as they never prayed before'.[47] This level of success did much to alleviate his Methodist critics.

Caughey and the Meaning of Revival

Caughey defined 'revival' as 'the Spring Season of the Church of God' accomplished by the instrumentality of 'extraordinary effusions of the Holy

---

36 *The Revivalist*, 1860, pp. 41–2 cited Murray, *Revivals and Revivalism*, p. 141.
37 *The Revivalist*, 1859, p. 16.
38 *The Revivalist*, 1859, p. 16.
39 *The Revivalist*, Vol. VII, No. 9, September 1861, p. 141.
40 *The Revivalist*, Vol. VII, No. 9, September 1861, p. 182.
41 *The Revivalist*, Vol. VII, No. 9, September 1861, p. 182.
42 *The Revivalist*, 1862, p. 44.
43 Murray, *Revivals and Revivalism*, Vol. VIII, No. 2, 1862, p. 29.
44 Murray, *Revivals and Revivalism*, Vol. IV, No. 4, 1862, p. 77.
45 *The Revivalist*, 1862, p. 77.
46 Murray, *Revivals and Revivalism*, Vol. VIII, No. 5, May 1862, p. 93.
47 Murray, *Revivals and Revivalism*, Vol. VIII, No. 8, August 1862.

Spirit'.[48] Such effusions might on occasion include 'animal excitement' which should not cause undue concern.[49] He was of the view that revival contained a human element in that preparation is necessary but essentially it is God's work. 'It is sweet to reflect', he wrote, 'that whether Paul may plant, or an Apollos water, ... it is God who giveth the increase .... The work is ours to do, but the deed is God's, else all our work is in vain.'[50] 'Many', he wrote, 'desire a revival, but they are unwilling to work for it. I know an animal that is very fond of fish, but would rather do without them than wet her feet.'[51] In another place Caughey explicitly stated that human endeavour is needed in revival work. 'We must', he wrote, 'not only strike the iron till it is hot, but strike it till it is made hot. Great occasions must not be waited for, but we must make use of ordinary opportunities.'[52] On occasion Caughey spoke of 'the laborious matter-of-fact work in a revival'.[53] When Caughey's 1859 campaign at Sheffield was described as a 'Pentecost' and 'a great revival', the *Wesleyan Times* believed that it was evidence that revivals could be generated by the right human endeavours. The paper stated: 'In commenting upon the labours of Mr Caughey, we have always said, that there is no reason but the unfaithfulness of others, why similar scenes should not be witnessed wherever God has established a Christian church.'[54]

Revivals, as Caughey perceived them, had a spontaneous aspect to them: 'They may be gradual in preparation, but instantaneous in accomplishment.'[55] In another place, Caughey suggested, 'A revival is a year of spiritual health, and is usually attended by the smiles of heaven, temporally as well as spiritually, coming down upon a region all around like sunshine.' Here Caughey clearly saw revival in broader terms, impacting a 'region' and resulting in 'temporal' as well as spiritual blessings. In this he resonated with the Wesleyan revivals of the previous century in which the social and cultural aspects of many English communities were impacted by Wesley's preaching. Caughey was also ever ready to stress the importance of the Holy Spirit in all spiritual endeavour.

> I am now fully persuaded that in proportion as the spirit of God shall condescend to second my efforts in the Gospel message, I shall be successful; nor need I expect any success beyond. No man has ever

---

48 Caughey, *Revival Miscellanies*, p. 200.
49 Caughey, *Revival Miscellanies*, p. 210.
50 Caughey, *Arrows*, p. 37.
51 Caughey, *Revival Miscellanies*, p. 17.
52 J. Caughey, *Helps to the Life of Holiness and Usefulness or Revival Miscellanies* (J.P. Magee, 1852), p. 233.
53 Caughey, *Revival Miscellanies*, p. 198.
54 Cited by *The Revivalist*, 1859, p. 75 cited by Murray, *Revival and Revivalism*, pp. 380–1.
55 *The Revivalist*, 1859, p. 75 cited by Murray, *Revival and Revivalism*, p. 35.

been signally useful in winning souls to Christ, without the help of the Holy Spirit.[56]

Elsewhere Caughey wrote of revival occurring when 20, 30, 50 or 100 get converted to God within a few hours, days or weeks.[57]

Sanctification

Revival for Caughey was always going to include holiness or sanctification. As he saw it, unless the subjects of revival look like God, the revival isn't likely to be of God. It was this doctrine which John Wesley so continuously emphasized declaring that he had come to spread 'scriptural holiness' throughout the land. Caughey as a true son of Wesley preached for sanctification in all his revival campaigns. He wrote on one occasion, 'I preach upon the subject once a week, on Friday nights; the impulse of which is felt for several days, especially on the sabbath.'[58]

Where Caughey encountered opposition even among some Wesleyans was his insistence that sanctification could be appropriated by faith and indeed could be received in an instant. He did however urge that 'people should never attempt to believe you have what you know and feel you have not'. Rather he counselled, 'But do attempt, and with all your might, to believe that you do receive it, and he who has the power to do it will cut the work short in righteousness, and save you to the uttermost.'[59] He reminded those who heard his revival sermons of the salvation principle which is 'faith alone'. Thus 'sanctification' follows the same pattern as 'justification'. It is 'not of works, lest any man should boast. It is the gift of God'. As such, it is to be received by faith. 'God is able to save to the uttermost', which Caughey took to mean, 'to purify you from all sin, and fill all your heart with love.'[60] This purification God is not only able to do, but willing to do it 'now'. Caughey wrote with emphasis, 'Not when you come to die, not at any distant time; not tomorrow but to-day. God will then enable you to believe it is done according to his word.'[61]

In a sermon entitled 'Helps to Belief in Sanctification' Caughey asks the question, 'By what means may a wavering mind establish itself in the belief of entire sanctification?' To this he replied, 'By a proper knowledge of the word of God, and a profound reverence for it', and 'by believing the truth.' Caughey then quoted extensively from the Scripture to sustain his point. Among the texts he selected were John 17:17, 'Sanctify them through Thy truth' and 2 Thessalonians 2:3, 'Because God hath from the beginning chosen you to

---

56 Caughey, *Earnest Christianity*, p. 11.
57 Caughey, *Revival Miscellanies*, p. 227.
58 Caughey, *Glimpses of Life in Soul Saving*, p. 375.
59 Caughey, *Earnest Christianity*, pp. 198–9.
60 Caughey, *Earnest Christianity*, p. 377.
61 Caughey, *Earnest Christianity*, p. 377.

salvation through the sanctification of the Spirit and belief in the truth.'[62] In another address entitled 'Is sanctification Gradual or Instantaneous?' Caughey answers, 'it is gradual in three respects, and it is instantaneous in one'.[63] It begins from the moment of our justification as we gradually die to sin and live to God. Then after we are entirely sanctified, 'we ascend, all through life, to higher degrees of it'. Finally, after death, we shall rise still higher, and 'progress eternally in the love of God'. In this phase there will be no falling back, it will be a steady progress forward. Caughey then focuses his attention on the second phase which he sums up succinctly in the following lines.

> In one respect entire sanctification is instantaneous; that act of the Holy Ghost, accorded to our faith, by which sin is entirely expelled from the soul – when the blood of Jesus Christ cleanseth from all sin – is 'an instantaneous deliverance from all sin, and includes an instantaneous power then given always to cleave to God. Thus, an excellent man remarked, it is gradual in preparation, but instantaneous in reception. And the more earnestly we long for this unspeakable blessing, the more swiftly the preparation increases.[64]

We come to this second phase, Caughey says, 'instantly, and not by degrees'. Just as we are justified by faith, so we are also 'sanctified by faith' (Acts 26: 18). The progress to this experience is gradual but 'there is a last moment and a first: a last moment when sin is not dead, and a first moment when it is'.[65] Caughey cites John Wesley's testimony on the doctrine. He carefully examined the matter in London where he 'found six hundred and fifty two of our society who were exceedingly clear in their experience, and whose testimony I could see no reason to doubt'. 'Everyone of these', John Wesley stressed, 'has declared that his deliverance was in a moment.'[66] From this point in his address, Caughey moved on to ask, 'But does God want us to be holy now? – to love Him with all out heart now – this moment?'. Caughey replies, 'Most certainly. To suppose to the contrary would be to set God a trifling with us, and us trifling with God!'.[67] He concludes by making it clear that the way to prosper from this instantaneous moment of 'entire sanctification' is 'entire consecration – offering up all your thoughts and actions as a spiritual sacrifice to God, acceptable to Him through the blood and intercession of His well-beloved son'.[68] When believers surrender all known sin as an offering on the altar of God's love, 'it is a spiritual sacrifice

---

62 J. Caughey, *Revival Sermons and Addresses* (R.D. Dickinson, 1891), pp. 300–3.
63 Caughey, *Revival Sermons and Addresses*, p. 317.
64 Caughey, *Revival Sermons and Addresses*, p. 318.
65 Caughey, *Revival Sermons and Addresses*, p. 320.
66 Caughey, *Revival Sermons and Addresses*, pp. 321–2.
67 Caughey, *Revival Sermons and Addresses*, p. 323.
68 Caughey, *Revival Sermons and Addresses*, p. 325.

to God, acceptable to Him'. It results in 'an entire deliverance' and is 'one of the great blessings on this side of heaven'.[69]

Caughey's version of entire surrender, it should be noted, included denying oneself aspects of worldliness such as the pleasures of the dance floor and alcoholic drink.[70] At a missionary meeting in Birmingham, Caughey had urged support for the Evangelical Alliance which 'had opposed the extravagant waste of money on dance and opera'.[71] Whilst in the town he had also been a strong advocate of temperance. Speaking at a meeting in the Town Hall in February 1846 Caughey, 'who was received with great applause' said that the evils of intemperance had become so general that 'a systematic and combined effort ought to be made a common cause'.[72] Caughey also believed, along with many other revivalists of the era, that achieving holiness involved putting to death wrong traits within people. Thus he wrote, 'Shun all evil companions. Take care of the beer houses.'[73] He often spoke at temperance meetings. At Liverpool in February he spoke at a temperance tea party in the Music Hall declaring that the one essential ingredient in the foundation of true greatness in the nineteenth century was 'total abstinence from all that could intoxicate'.[74] Years later at Wolverhampton in April[75] 1862 he delivered one of his 'telling Temperance Lectures' after which 'above a hundred signed the pledge'.[76]

Caughey's teaching on 'entire consecration' was to find fuller development in the altar theology of his contemporary, Phoebe Palmer. For Caughey, therefore, revivals were integrally linked with holiness and were always going to be a good thing despite the extremes of emotion and excitement that often accompanied them. In a piece entitled 'Reconnoitring Infidel Positions' he wrote: 'A great revival of religion ... awakens the attention, like a blaze of lightning and thunder among the clouds, setting some quaking and others querying.'[77]

---

69 Caughey, *Revival Sermons and Addresses*, p. 325.
70 See his sermon at Hanley in 1859, *The Revivalist*, 1859, p. 26.
71 *Birmingham Gazette*, 27 April 1846.
72 *Birmingham Gazette*, 9 February, 1846. See also *Birmingham Gazette*, 20 April 1846 which reported Caughey's address at the Birmingham Temperance Society's thirteenth Annual Festival. Caughey stated that 'strong drink had mocked the world to the present hour, but thank God, there were those whom it had not mocked'. He 'exhorted all parents present to keep the temptation of all strong drink from their children, and exhorted the Sunday school teachers to use their influence in the cause.'
73 *Birmingham Gazette*, 29 April 1846.
74 *The Liverpool Mercury*, 24 February 1843.
75 *The Revivalist*, 1862, p. 93.
76 *The Revivalist*, 1862, p. 93.
77 J. Caughey, 'Reconnoitring Infidel Positions', *Arrows in My Quiver* (W.J. Palmer Jr, 1868) p. 204.

Revival Methods

Richard Carwardine in his study of transatlantic revivalism wrote, 'With Caughey the day of the revival technician who was paid for his services had arrived.'[78] In his earlier writings Finney had laid down certain means which needed to be in place in preparation for a revival to occur, but with the passing of the years he modified his views and gave greater place to the divine element. Caughey however, as Carwardine has pointed out, used the term 'revival campaign' suggesting that he aimed to give revivalism 'a more premeditated professional character'.[79] Certainly some of the methods which he utilised in his work appeared blunt and on a number of occasions he was accused of terrorising his hearers.[80]

Preaching

The central aspect of Caughey's labours was preaching. In a letter dated 25 April 1842 written from Cork to a friend in America he wrote, 'We are resolved by the help of God, to push our principles to the utmost for an extensive revival. Hammer on the rock enough, and it must break in pieces.'[81] That said, Caughey had an impressive pulpit manner which was easy and natural. His voice was varied and 'when tremulous with emotion, it had a bell-like ring never to be forgotten'.[82] His style was often blunt and to the point. He urged fellow preachers to avoid 'theological technicalities' and to give people 'straightforward facts'. 'Like a stone in the sand', he declared, 'a fact may imbed itself in the mind, and stamp upon it an indelible impression of the truth of that which had thus been illustrated.'[83] Caughey urged that clergy must neither underestimate their hearers with 'sermons which are destitute of brains' nor over-estimate them and 'put meat which their teeth cannot chew, nor the stomach concoct'.[84] He also urged that 'the important doctrines of repentance and regeneration' must be 'distinctly, fervently and experimentally preached'.[85]

Caughey also had a capacity to be very straight in his preaching which at times was almost 'in-your-face'. On one occasion he warned the older members during one of his revival campaigns with the following:

> Old age is no good age to repent. When the fingers are hard and stiff, it's not easy to learn to play an instrument; When the heart is grown hard in

---

78 Carwardine, *Transatlantic Revivalism*, p. 128.
79 Carwardine, *Transatlantic Revivalism*, p. 128.
80 See for example, J. Caughey, 'Revivals and the Terrors of God', *Revival Miscellanies* (Houlton and Stoneman, undated), pp. 89–100.
81 J. Caughey, *Letters on Various Subjects* (Simpkin, Marshall, 1846) p. 211.
82 Carwardine, *Transatlantic Revivalism*, p. 118.
83 Caughey, *Revival Miscellanies*, p. 223.
84 Caughey, *Revival Miscellanies*, p. 233.
85 Caughey, *Revival Miscellanies*, p. 203.

wickedness .... Poison long in the stomach is hard to get out .... Sunset is no good time to begin a day's work, and what is done is done to great disadvantage.[86]

Whereas Moody was later to put emphasis on God's love and the loving Father, Caughey preached hell with much greater insistency. In his view, if hell is a reality and is believed to be so by the preacher, it cannot be safe to keep it from the sinner's view. He cited John Wesley who began to preach the doctrine and raised a storm of protest but was soon surrounded by thousands of penitents.[87] 'Hell', Caughey said was incorporated into his discourses, 'because it cannot well be avoided.'[88] Caughey felt strongly that

The real hell, as described in the Scriptures, is not uncovered in all the terrific horrors which belong to it; nor in such a manner as to render inapplicable that satirical couplet:-

'Smooth down the stubborn text to ears polite
And snugly keep damnation out of sight.'

Hell is not unfolded so as to make the heart and soul of many sinners in that congregation tremble before the Lord God of Hosts; exhorting, if possible, the awakened and agonising cry —

What must be done.
To save a wretch like me?
How shall a trembling sinner shun
That endless misery?[89]

In a sermon entitled 'Purification by Faith', Caughey warned his hearers, 'Beneath you yawns the lake that burneth with fire and brimstone; stand where you are you cannot; time will force you thence. Salvation is before you; it is nearer than it will ever be again; lay hold of it – cling to it with the firmness of a death grasp'.[90] The bluntness of Caughey's eschatology with vivid portrayals of the damned pulling on the weight of their chains in the smoke-filled abyss[91] led to accusations that his hearers had been terrorised into conversion. Caughey was nevertheless happy to stand by his convictions. In a piece entitled 'Revivals and the Terrors of God' he admitted that 'some may be frightened into a religious life'. On the other hand, he reasoned, many whose conversion was occasioned by

---

86 Caughey, *Earnest Christianity*, p. 117.
87 Caughey, *Revival Miscellanies*, p. 204.
88 Caughey, *Revival Miscellanies*, p. 203.
89 Caughey, *Revival Miscellanies*, p. 49.
90 J. Caughey, *Revival Sermons and Addresses* (Richard D. Dickinson, 1891), p. 93.
91 Caughey, *Revival Sermons*, p. 50.

'a fright' remained in the faith until the end of their days. The Apostle Paul, he pointed out, declared that 'knowing the terrors of the Lord we persuade men'.[92] Reflecting on the matter further, Caughey wrote that 'it is not an easy matter to terrify a sinner sitting in a comfortable chapel, in good health, and with no prospect of dying soon'.[93] In his *Revival Miscellanies* Caughey asked a rhetorical question: 'Tell me, is hell thus delineated in the place of worship where you usually worship God? If hell be a reality, and is believed to be so by a preacher, is it safe to keep it out of the sinner's view, or to represent it less terrible than it is?'[94] As far as he was concerned hell was an essential ingredient in the preacher's armoury. 'Leave that link out', he declared, 'and the chain is broken,'[95] Caughey also felt it was important to remind his hearers that natural disasters, calamities and violent storms also serve as reminders of judgement.[96] Indeed he even spoke on one occasion of cholera being a revivalist![97] Although this was undoubtedly an effective means of filling up the anxious benches at the end of his meetings, it was a blunt weapon which produced a crude form of manipulation.

There was however another side to Caughey's preaching: he had a real ability to illustrate his points with a good story or well-drawn anecdote. 'Through the whole of my life', he wrote, 'I have been of the opinion that the poor, and, indeed, that all ranks of people, are best taught by tales and parables.'[98] Preaching an address entitled, 'The "Besetting Sin" Detected', he referred to wise men of Troy who advised Priam to send Helen to the Grecians, and not to allow himself to be captivated by her fascinations, as it was likely she would be the cause of a fatal war. 'Hear me then inquirer', Caughey continued, 'dismiss from thy soul this bosom sin; away with it to the devil, to whom it belongs!'[99] On another occasion at the close of an address entitled 'The Sting of Sin' he used the illustration of a small crowd waiting on the quayside for the return of a vessel. 'A sail! A sail! Shouts one and there is an air of expectation. As the sight of the homeland opens to the sailors their hearts swell with joy and they shout out, 'Home! Home!'. 'Welcome! Welcome! tempest-tost mariners, the crowd respond.' 'Faintly indeed', Caughey concluded, does this 'shadow forth the scene witnessed when a soul is entering heaven – when it passes full-sail into the port of glory'.[100] Caughey devoted time to finding good illustrations because he believed that when important truths 'enter first like a picture into the imagination ... they are stamped on the memory'.[101]

---

92 Caughey, *Revival Sermons*, p. 90.
93 Caughey, *Revival Sermons*, p. 91.
94 Caughey, *Revival Miscellanies*, p. 204.
95 Caughey, *Revival Miscellanies*, p. 203.
96 See Caughey, *Revival Miscellanies*, chapter 6 'Revivals and the Terrors of God'.
97 Caughey, *Revival Miscellanies*, p. 259.
98 Caughey, *Revival Miscellanies*, p. 215.
99 Caughey, *Revival Sermons*, p. 234.
100 Caughey, *Revival Sermons*, p. 40.
101 Caughey, *Revival Miscellanies*, pp. 223–4.

Direct Words to Particular Individuals

Caughey had a strange uncanny ability to break off his discourses on occasion and speak directly to individuals in the congregation. Understandably this practice sometimes caused considerable alarm. Reflecting on his campaign in Sheffield, he recorded that 'the Lord has enabled me, of late, to describe particular characters, during the course of my sermons, with wonderful, and in some cases, with what appeared miraculous accuracy'.[102] This resulted in accusations that members of the congregations had been 'spilling the beans' on some of those they had either brought or knew would be attending the revival services. Caughey instanced the case of a man sitting in the gallery at one of his meetings. In the midst of his sermon he had a strong impression of a man with the words, 'A Roman Catholic in the gallery!' He paused and quickly urged on such a man the way of salvation. The man scrambled for his hat and left but not before he had heard the truth. Another pointed incident occurred as Caughey preached a sermon entitled, 'God's Speedy Judgement upon the Wicked'. Without warning Caughey made the following interjection in the second section of his discourse.

> Now, there are several characters here before me to-night; my discourse will particularly concern them. I will describe them. The first is a man who has heard me often before, both here and elsewhere. The next is one who has heard me before, but not here: .... Another is a woman who has heard me once before only, and that in this chapel: she was here on Sunday night. The last is an old grey-headed man, who has never seen my face before, either here or anywhere else. For these four I have a message. They will find it in Jeremiah 28 v 16. Well, here it is; now are you ready to receive my message? Then you shall have it – 'This year thou shalt die!' That is my message.[103]

In a similar way he warned his hearers at Hanley in 1859 that there some of their number 'had turned their backs on love feasts and fellowship meetings' and that he had a strong impression that 'God was going to weed them out'. He then went on to give some remarkable instances of judgements which had befallen others who had not given heed to his previous religious impressions. He urged them to turn that very night.[104] In an atmosphere that was described as 'almost an electric shock' Caughey warned that those Hanley individuals 'had bartered their souls to the world' and on them would come 'domestic bereavement, commercial disaster, or failing health'.[105]

---

102 Caughey, *Methodism in Earnest*, p. 395.
103 Caughey, *Revival Sermons*, p. 170.
104 *The Revivalist*, 1859, p. 26.
105 *The Revivalist*, 1859, p. 24.

These kinds of pointed directives are not unlike some of the personalised messages given by some of the Kansas City prophets on their visits to England with the American evangelist, John Wimber, at the time of the London Docklands Conference. Both had the effect of riveting the attention of the rest of the audience, making them much more ready to respond to the appeal to make a commitment to Christ or receive prayer for sanctification, or in Wimber's case Holy Spirit ministry. That said, the words of the Kansas prophets were gentle in comparison to Caughey's somewhat unpredictable outbursts.

Caughey attracted a certain amount of criticism on account of his having impressions and revelations. Caughey defended them stating that 'it pleased my good and gracious Lord, in answer to many prayers, and tears, and earnest cries, to make known to me his mind on a particular subject that distressed me'.[106] 'Surely', he continued,' there is nothing, to a devout Christian, objectionable in this.'[107] Such 'new revelations', Caughey understood, to be 'impressions, persuasions, or doctrines not warranted in the Scriptures, or contrary thereto.'[108] He related that he did not regard impressions with implicit confidence, but rather as Dr Johnson said of dreams: 'Do not wholly believe them, for they may be false; do not wholly reject them, for they may be true.'[109] When asked if he regarded impressions as superior in their claims to the written word, Caughey answered 'unequivocally, No'.[110]

Immediate Decisions and After Meetings

S.G. Dimond in his examination of the conversions recorded in Wesley's journal observed that almost all were sudden.[111] Caughey was in this tradition; he believed in striking while the iron was hot. He favoured 'After Meetings' of various kinds but always as an immediate response to his revival message. He was of the opinion that datable conversions were likely to be more lasting but his insistence on the matter led to many making re-commitments at the altar rail. Typical of Caughey's style was his sermon entitled 'God's judgement on

---

106 'Letter from J. Caughey on Impressions, Revelations & C', *Methodism in Earnest*, p. viii.
107 'Letter from J. Caughey on Impressions, Revelations & C', *Methodism in Earnest*, p. viii.
108 'Letter from J. Caughey on Impressions, Revelations & C', *Methodism in Earnest*, p. viii.
109 'Letter from J. Caughey on Impressions, Revelations & C', *Methodism in Earnest*, p. ix.
110 'Letter from J. Caughey on Impressions, Revelations & C', *Methodism in Earnest*, p. ix.
111 S.G. Dimond, *The Psychology of the Methodist Revival* (Oxford University Press, 1926). Having examined all the instances of the conversion of both individuals and groups (about 700 in total) recorded in Wesley's *Journal*, Dimond wrote, 'In Methodism, conversions are mainly instantaneous.' See p. 5.

James Caughey and Holiness and Temperance Revivalism

the Wicked'. Coming to the climax of his message he warned his hearers that they might be only 'within a breath' of the judgment. Then in his very next sentence he cried out, 'There is the penitent form; who will go to it? Who will flee? ... Who will escape for his life? Lord lay hold of them'.[112]

Where no benches were available, Caughey made use of the altar rail or the sanctuary area surrounding the Communion table. Penitents would crowd in and then, assisted by local preachers and ministers, there would be exhortations for 'a more copious outpouring of the Holy Spirit'.[113] On some occasions in order to illicit a response Caughey would walk up and down the aisles and shout, 'Come out, man! and save your soul now'.[114]

Chapter 3 of Caughey's *Revival Miscellanies* is entitled 'Revival Preaching' and contains a section on the importance of calling people out publicly at the conclusion of the meeting. Caughey poses the question, 'Why call persons forward to be publicly prayed for? Could not God convert them in any other part of the chapel, as well as the communion rails?' He then proceeds to give his reply with eight short points:

1. Because there are 'distinctions' in reality, produced by the spirit of God, before we make them by separation.
2. If God has told us to pray for one another, that we may be healed, is it not reasonable that we should know who they are that require to be healed?
3. By this means we are made acquainted with their particular state of mind .... We are thus enabled to give them instruction suitable to their circumstances, and to spread their whole case before the Lord.
4. Sympathy is thereby excited in the hearts of praying men ...
5. Frequently such a test as that as coming forward to be prayed for leads to a decision, the consequences of which may be eternal.
6. The public avowal of their determination to leave the ranks of sin ... and raises a barrier against their return, not unfrequently has a very powerful influence upon those awakened sinners who conclude to remain in their seats.
7. We find that those who take such a decided step obtain, by doing so, a much greater earnestness of soul than those awakened sinners who conclude to remain in their seats.
8. That God could convert them in 'any other part of the chapel', we do not deny; but nineteen out of twenty of those who get saved in this blessed work of God have thus come forward to be prayed for publicly.[115]

---

112 Caughey, *Revival Sermons and Addresses*, pp. 175–6.
113 Caughey, *Methodism in Earnest*, p. 370.
114 Carwardine, *Transatlantic Revivalism*, p. 120.
115 Caughey, *Revival Miscellanies*, pp. 216–17.

Even those few Wesleyan Methodist ministers who were reticent to give Caughey their wholehearted endorsement recognized in the words of Benjamin Gregory that 'he had a grace-gift rich and rare ... the gift of bringing the undecided to decision' which was indicated by his favourite text: "How long will ye halt between two opinions? if the Lord be God, follow Him," etc.'[116] What concerned some of his colleagues such as the Revd William Atherton, who was President of Conference in 1846, was Caughey's 'machinery of revival'. In particular they had serious misgivings regarding his use of 'decoy penitents'. It was the evangelist's practice to call together a number of people from nearby circuits and extract from them a promise that as soon as they heard his call to penitents to come forward they would immediately crowd up to the communion rail in order to encourage others to do the same. Notwithstanding the hundreds who responded to Caughey's altar calls, Atherton and others regarded the practice as 'unworthy trickery'.[117]

Prayer Gatherings

Caughey laid stress on prayer of every kind, both individual and corporate, as being vital to revived Christianity. In his *Revival Miscellanies*, Caughey included a chapter entitled 'Methods of Promoting a Revival' which included a section on the importance of prayer. He related that two individuals prayed secretly together for the revival of their church and how after the ninth week they saw 'the beginning of a great work of God' in which 'scores of converted souls were added to the little society'.[118] Caughey encouraged prayer gatherings to intercede for revival services. If the effectual fervent prayer of one righteous man avails so much with God, he said, how much more will the united prayer of the whole church accomplish?[119] During his campaigns, Caughey often organized prayer meetings for those seeking sanctification or desiring to consecrate their lives to God. At Huddersfield on 3 January 1845, for example, a meeting was held for new converts. They were invited to the altar rail in groups and prayed for individually. This was followed by a prayer gathering for mourners and a number were reported as being 'saved'.[120]

---

116 B. Gregory, *Side Lights on the Conflicts of Methodism* (Cassel, 1898), p. 344. Benjamin Gregory (1820–1900) who was President of the Wesleyan Conference in 1879 based his book on notes taken by the Revd Joseph Fowler on the conference debates between 1827 and 1852.
117 Gregory, *Side Lights*, p. 345.
118 Caughey, *Revival Miscellanies*, p. 210.
119 Caughey, *Helps to the Life of Holiness*, p. 228.
120 Caughey, *Earnest Christianity*, p. 152.

Answering His Critics Openly

During his campaigns in England in particular, Caughey met with much opposition. His sermons were analysed and criticised. His methods were said to involve 'terrorism' and excessive emotionalism. His campaigns were the subject of considerable debate at the Annual Methodist Conferences and in 1846 a recommendation was made by them that the American bishops recall him home. At Hull 'the enemies of Christ' gave out parody handbills inviting the town's inhabitants to Kingston New Theatre to hear 'Yankee Humbug'. Caughey however was made of strong emotional stuff and took to answering his critics openly. He would often do this immediately before commencing to preach. As the Revd Daniel Wise commented, his style on these occasions was 'very abrupt'.[121] For example, in dealing with a complainant who felt he had been disrespectful to the elderly, Caughey replied: 'Let "One truly grieved" hearken!- "Disrespect for the aged"? Not so! I dare not! God has commended, "Honor the face of the old man". Did I not quote Solomon ...'[122] Again he spoke to 'A Protesting Hearer', 'Come, come, sir; pray try to look at your principles ...'[123] During his labours at Rochdale in December 1860 he had some particularly strong words to those 'fault-finders' who had been grumbling about his preaching: 'God would be necessitated to do what he had frequently done during his ministry elsewhere, send death in among them, to snatch away hearers, for the purpose of rousing the people to yet greater zeal, and to bring his hearers to their senses.'[124] Such indeed was the case, one hearer 'fell dangerously ill' and another 'was a corpse' in less than half an hour of leaving the chapel.[125]

Publicity

Like those who came before and after him, Caughey was acutely aware of the importance of publicity. He stated that he had known places where they had no revival, but accounts given by those who had attended revival services in other places had stirred people's spirits and resulted in a fresh outpouring of God's blessing.[126] 'Descriptions and accounts of revival in the Christian press', Caughey contended, 'fan the revival flame in the hearts of ministers and people.' He was clear that

> Often the effects are thrilling and powerful beyond description. An entire church will be thrown into a state of sanctified excitement, after reading

---

121 Caughey, *Earnest Christianity*, p. 110.
122 Caughey, *Earnest Christianity*, p. 115.
123 Caughey, *Earnest Christianity*, p. 119.
124 *The Revivalist*, 1861, p. 25.
125 *The Revivalist*, 1861, p. 25.
126 Caughey, *Revival Miscellanies*, p. 225.

or hearing an account of a revival in some city or town with which they are acquainted. 'The revival in ____ ' is talked of in the counting-house, work-shop, parlor, and kitchen; and why should it not? Is it not a mighty and glorious event …?[127]

As Caughey saw it, what is thus read and talked about caused people and churches to begin to ask why they may not have a revival of a similar kind in their locality. Caughey bemoaned the fact that the religious periodicals in England didn't appear to have columns or pages set apart for reporting revivals.[128] He wrote that he would have considered it 'a serious disaster' to the church of God in America if accounts of revivals were suppressed. He was of the opinion that such accounts were often written by the preacher or minister in charge and were therefore reliable. Any unreliable information would be swiftly counteracted by other magazines or local newspaper reports.

Follow Up

For Caughey 'revival' is both the work of God's Holy Spirit and human endeavour. On the one hand he is adamant that 'no man has ever been signally useful in winning souls to Christ without the help of the Spirit'.[129] On the other, he asserted, revivals can be planned and promoted with special prayer, preaching, publicity, music and perhaps above all follow up to ensure people's commitment and growth as Christians. 'We must do God's work in his time' but it is vital not to be content with one glorious meeting. In Caughey's view the ordinary Sunday services were insufficient to sustain a revival. In the *Revival Miscellanies* he stated that 'My opinion is, you will look in vain for extensive revival unless you "follow the blow" with a succession of sermons and prayer meetings.' He quotes Hannibal of whom it was said 'he knew how to obtain victory, but not to improve victory'. Gideon by contrast knew how to improve victory and improve the advantage given him by God.

Once having helped his hearers to commit their lives to Christ, Caughey stressed the importance of continuous nurture. On leaving Hull for example, he recorded that before he left the town several opportunities were afforded him 'of exhorting the leaders to take special care of the new converts'.[130] At the end of his time in Manchester in March 1859 he arranged a special service to which all who had professed to find forgiveness of their sins were invited to meet him on the final Friday. Admission was by ticket. After a period of singing and a short address Caughey then invited those present to come forward in small groups and kneel around the communion rail. After a few brief words each

---

127 Caughey, *Revival Miscellanies*, p. 225.
128 Caughey, *Revival Miscellanies*, p. 226.
129 Caughey, *Earnest Christianity*, p. 11.
130 Caughey, *Methodism in Earnest*, p. 373.

person was then asked if they were at peace with God and if they had united with a Christian church. A verse was sung while they retired and another group came forward. A record was then taken of each person and their name and address: 602 promised to join the United Methodist Free churches, 109 with the Wesleyans, 17 with the New Connexion, 19 with the Congregationalists and the rest in smaller numbers with other churches.[131]

Caughey's Significance as a Revivalist

James Caughey was a self-educated man who gained a great deal through his extensive reading. He had a vivid imagination and a real ability to communicate. The Revd Daniel Wise wrote of him:

> His mind possesses great force; his manner is earnest and persuasive; his gesticulation natural. His voice possesses remarkable compass; if not richly musical, it is very pleasant, and the more it is heard the more it charms. His discourses bear the mark of originality. It is true they often flash with the intellectual jewels of great writers, but these are faithfully acknowledged; and his sermons, both in thought and structure, are manifestly the offspring of his mind.[132]

For all the criticisms Caughey received both at the hands of the Wesleyan Methodists and his hearers from unchurched backgrounds, he proved remarkably effective among the lower middle class groups in both England and America. It is clear that even though a substantial percentage of his converts had been nominal church members prior to his campaigns, the number meeting in class in the Methodist circuits of the north of England grew significantly in the middle years of the nineteenth century. In places he also attracted a substantial number of the labouring poor. Commenting on his time at Hanley, *The Revivalist* stated that his congregations included 'all classes in Pottery society; but great numbers of outsiders – "the common people" – the commonest of the people'.[133]

Richard Carwardine in his *Transatlantic Revivalism* adjudged Caughey to have had a number of negative impacts on mid-nineteenth-century English Wesleyan Methodism.[134] It can of course be argued that in the long run the great disruption brought about by the Reformers, many of whom were stirred by Caughey's revivalism, helped to democratise later post-Buntingite Wesleyan Methodism. Carwardine readily acknowledges that Caughey preached with remarkable effect in Sheffield, including at the elegant Carver Street Chapel, replete with galleries and organ. Here there were some eight hundred 'justified'

---

131 *The Revivalist*, 1959, p. 92.
132 Caughey, *Methodism in Earnest*, p. 11.
133 *The Revivalist*, 1859, p. 25.
134 See Carwardine, *Transatlantic Revivalism*, pp. 121–33.

and 'sanctified'.[135] At Brunswick Chapel there was 'a most extraordinary effusion of the Holy Spirit' in which there was a total of 1,260 'justified' and 'sanctified' between 7 July and 2 August 1844.[136] Carwardine points out that though most of his Sheffield converts were described as 'from the world' the majority of them attended Methodist services regularly. One thing that is clear however is that even in the mid-1840s there were many Wesleyan Methodist ministers who were still prepared to endorse Caughey's revivalism and speak warmly of the overall effects of his ministry. The Revd John Haswell,[137] for example, reported to the Conference of 1844 that he had invited him to Sheffield for a month where there had been 'no extravagances' and 'great fruit from his ministry night after night'.[138] Alexander Bell[139] also paid 'very high tribute' to Caughey's preaching and success. He had 'never seen anything equal to it'. That said, by the following year the overall tenor of conference was considerably more critical and Jabez Bunting proposed 'that a letter be sent to the American bishops requesting that they would recall Mr Caughey, whose visit has been so unusually protracted in this country, where he is under no authority'.[140]

Although Caughey's passage in Sheffield was smooth, Carwardine suggests his success exacerbated underlying and growing tensions within Wesleyan Methodism. The steadily advancing prosperity and respectability was turning away from the Pentecostal excitements of campaigns of men like Caughey. When the Wesleyan Conference finally pronounced against him, they stated their concern that irregular movements could damage good order and pastoral care. Carwardine maintains that Caughey was certainly at fault in his treatment of the English Conference which never recognized his labours. That said, the Quarterly Meeting of the Sheffield West Circuit unanimously 'acknowledged the goodness of God in rendering the course of special services now in progress, so effectual in promoting a revival of his work'. It went on to speak of 'the affectionate, enlightened, and powerful ministrations of the Rev James Caughey' and resolved 'that its warmest thanks are due to Mr Caughey for his kind acceptance of an invitation to visit this circuit, and his subsequent efficient labours in it'.[141] In retrospect however, it may be too easy simply to rest the blame on the low-church circuits of the connexion. It has also to be recognized that the Conference had become progressively authoritarian in the decades prior to Caughey's arrival. It is arguable that the catastrophic split of 1849–50, the worst in Methodist history, was in any case inevitable. Caughey for his part was

---

135 Caughey, *Methodism in Earnest*, p. 392.
136 Caughey, *Methodism in Earnest*, p. 407.
137 John Partis Haswell (1790–1870).
138 Gregory, *Side Lights*, p. 368.
139 Alexander Bell (1788–1851).
140 Gregory, *Side Lights*, p. 401.
141 *Quarterly Meeting Minutes of the Sheffield West Circuit*, 24 June 1844.

humble in his bearing, saying of the ministers at Hull, 'I felt I could rather take my place at their feet.'[142]

Caughey left England peacefully urging his sympathisers to be 'quiet, kind and loving'. He returned to his homeland and took charge in Providence, Rhode Island where there were soon several hundred converts. He continued to write and his publications went through several editions in both England and America. As has been noted above Caughey subsequently returned to England the hero of the Wesleyan Reformers in 1857. There can be no doubt, as Carwardine observed, that Caughey was indeed 'a revival technician'.[143] When it came to the arts of persuasion he had at his fingertips a whole gamut of well-honed skills, which ranged from startling stories and compelling gestures, to graphic portrayals of hell and the use of decoy converts to encourage others to make public commitments of faith. Indeed Caughey may have been the first revivalist to use the term 'campaign' to refer to meetings he held.

---

142 *Quarterly Meeting Minutes of the Sheffield West Circuit*, 24 June 1844, p. 373.
143 Carwardine, *Transatlantic Revivalism*, p. 128.

CHAPTER 6

Walter and Phoebe Palmer (1807–74) and Holiness Revivalism

The Context of Holiness

The middle years of nineteenth-century America were a time of optimism and perfectionism. Industrialisation was bringing progress and improvement in many aspects of people's lives. Something of this was beginning to rub off on Christian theology and practice. In former times Jonathan Edwards had considered that seven weeks was too short a time to reflect on whether a person had been chosen or elected by God. But now in the early nineteenth century the Methodists and later Charles Finney and the New School Presbyterians believed 'this very moment is the time for salvation'. After responding to fire and brimstone sermons, converts were encouraged to go on to 'perfection'. Among the leaders of these perfectionist or holiness revivals was Phoebe Palmer together with her husband, Dr Walter Palmer and her sister, Sarah Lankford. Her work carried this doctrine across the United States, Canada and the British Isles.

Marriage and Early Christian Experience

Sarah and Phoebe were born to Henry and Dorothea Worrall in New York City. Sarah Worrall was their third child and born on 23 April 1806. Phoebe, their fourth, was born on 18 December 1807. Sarah was converted in 1819 and later married Thomas Lankford. Phoebe came to faith sometime before her seventeenth birthday. Walter Palmer was converted at the age of 13 in 1817 in the Methodist Church. He was a medical doctor who specialized in homeopathic treatments. Dr Walter Palmer first appears in Phoebe Worrall's diary in 1827 when she speaks of their engagement. Not long after, they were married.

The Palmers shared their home with the Lankfords from 1831–40 and again later for an unspecified period. The two sisters were devoted to each other and close observers noted that there was never any sign of tension in their shared household which was often filled with visitors. 1835 was an important year for in the spring Sarah Lankford, who had married Thomas Lankford in 1831, received 'Entire Sanctification'. In the autumn of that year the 'Tuesday Meetings for the Promotion of Holiness' began. They were originally intended for women only, since the custom of the day was that women were only allowed to teach women. In many Christian circles women did not speak in mixed assemblies, indeed they did not even give testimonies when men were present. That the Tuesday meetings should have come to include men was both unexpected and controversial. Through the prayers and fasting of her sister, Sarah, Phoebe received the gift of entire sanctification in 1837. Not long after, on 26 July 1837, Dr Palmer was 'entirely sanctified' at a camp meeting.

The Tuesday Meeting for the Promotion of Holiness was dramatically opened to men in 1839. Their inclusion helped to break what had become a major social and spiritual taboo of the mid-nineteenth century. The Tuesday Meetings increasingly became the preserve of Phoebe Palmer when the Lankfords moved in 1840 to Caldwell which was situated on the main road some fifty miles north of New York City. In later times when Walter and Phoebe were away from home Sarah Lankford came down to lead the Tuesday Meetings.

It was in the 1840s that Phoebe began her evangelistic travels across the United States and Canada. Up until that point she had made her children a priority and only travelled as her family responsibilities became lighter. In 1855 the Palmers' daughter, also Phoebe, married Joseph Knapp the founder of Metropolitan Insurance. Phoebe Palmer Knapp became a part of the Tuesday Meetings and served as organist for many years. She wrote many hymns and also composed the tunes both for her own words and those of others. Most famously she provided the music for Fanny Alstone's highly popular song 'Blessed Assurance Jesus is Mine'. During the 1850s Dr Palmer took off one summer month from his successful medical practice to travel with his wife. However they were much in demand and soon found it necessary to travel together in both the summer and the autumn. After Mrs Worrall, Phoebe and Sarah's mother, died in 1857 the Palmers began to take on commitments that were further afield in Eastern Canada and during the period 1859–63 they made a tour of the British Isles.

Phoebe's Publications

During the 1840s and 1850s Phoebe Palmer turned her writing skills to the doctrine of 'entire sanctification'. The books she wrote made her a familiar name to those seeking 'entire sanctification'. Faith in Its Effects and The Way of Holiness introduced many to the experience of Christian perfection as well as helping to establish her as a conference and camp meeting speaker. In time her publications sold so well that Dr Palmer was able to stop practising medicine and join his wife in evangelistic work in the British Isles. The situation was such that, when the Palmers returned to New York in 1865, Dr Walter was able to purchase the *Guide to Holiness* periodical and establish his wife as editor. This journal had originally been promoted by Sarah Lankford who had persuaded the Revd Timothy Merritt to begin it.

Dr and Mrs Palmer continued to travel and hold holiness revival meetings until Mrs Palmer's health began to fail. Phoebe's health first began to deteriorate in 1871. She suffered from a form of kidney failure known as Bright's Disease. In August 1874 when they returned from their travels she knew she was terminally ill. Her suffering was further exacerbated by blindness before she

Phoebe Palmer

finally died on 2 November 1874 following a heart attack. Following her death Walter Palmer took up the editorship of *Guide to Holiness*. In 1876 he remarried. His bride was Phoebe's sister, Sarah Lankford, whose husband had died some years previously. The marriage was recorded as a comfort to both and a blessing to Christian community at large. Following a period of failing health Dr Palmer turned the editorship of *Guide to Holiness* over to George Hughes in 1880. Hughes later wrote Walter Palmer's biography.

The Palmers' Influence

The Palmers were great social entertainers and were close friends with three Methodist bishops, Edmund Janes, Leonidas Hamline and Jesse Peck. Phoebe Palmer frequently corresponded with the Hamlines. Another habitual guest whom they influenced was Dr Thomas Upham who was to have a significant impact on the Keswick Convention in England. Timothy L. Smith noted that 'wherever they went, their great prestige with the bishops and church officials enabled these two laymen [sic] to win the confidence of the Methodist ministry'.[1]

It was Dr Palmer's lucrative medical practice which enabled Phoebe to travel but he himself was also anxious for the conversion of sinners and the sanctification of believers. For this reason he was always very happy to accompany her when circumstances permitted and to take a supporting and active

---

1 T.L. Smith, *Revivalism and Social Reform* (Harper and Row, 1965), p. 123.

role in her meetings. Dr Palmer endorsed his wife's activities above what was the acceptable norm of the age. Phoebe's biographer, Charles White, wrote of her uniqueness as follows:

> In an age when it was deemed unseemly for a woman to speak in public, she addressed thousands. In a day when men doubted the capacity of a woman's mind for logic, she edited a popular magazine and wrote well-researched and closely reasoned books on Christian doctrine. In a day when women were often forbidden to speak in church, she urged on both female and male believers the duty of public testimony for their Lord.[2]

All this was in an age when the Bronte sisters found it necessary to use male pseudonyms for their writings.

Besides being an advocate of 'entire sanctification' through hosting, traveling, preaching and publishing, the Palmers involved themselves in Methodist benevolent and philanthropic enterprises and Jewish, Christian and Foreign Missions. Theirs was not simply an introverted spirituality; they were also supporters of church planting activities in the slums of New York, prison ministry and temperance societies.

The travels of Phoebe Palmer and her ministry in New York City with the Tuesday Meetings made a profound impact on the Methodist Church. As a result of her influence both the Salvation Army and the Keswick Higher Life Movement of England came to lay greater stress on holiness teaching.

Phoebe Palmer, Sarah Lankford and Sanctification

It needs to be noted that 'Entire Sanctification', 'Christian Perfection' and 'Holiness by Faith' all refer to the same phenomenon. They were terms used inter-changeably by the two sisters and their circle. Sarah Lankford was the first of the two sisters to receive 'Christian Perfection'. The following excerpt from her personal testimony recounts her experience.

> The baptism of the Holy Ghost came in its glorious fullness; it seemed as a baptism of love almost to the overwhelming of the physical frame, accompanied with an inexpressible consciousness of purity, a consciousness only understood by those who have received it.

> Since that blessed day, May 21, 1835, I think there has not been one hour in which my soul has not been sweetly resting in the precious. Though the witness of the Spirit has not been withdrawn for an hour, yet there have been instances when sudden temptation has assumed so much the appearance of

---

2 C.E. White, The Beauty of Holiness: Phoebe Palmer as Theologian, Revivalist, Feminist and Humanitarian (Ph.D. thesis, Francis Asbury Press, 1986).

sinful emotion as to cause keen pain; but I have been invariably enabled almost instantly to appropriate that blood which cleanseth from all sin.[3]

In August 1835 Sarah Lankford began the Tuesday Meetings for the Promotion of Holiness at the house which she and her husband shared with Phoebe and Walter Palmer in 54 Rivington Street, New York City. It was not until 26 July 1837 however that her sister, Phoebe, received 'Christian Perfection'. Although she attended the Tuesday Meetings, Sarah Lankford felt particularly burdened for her sister on 26 July 1837. She later wrote:

> I sought an interview with dear sister Phoebe before breakfast, telling her I intended spending the day in special fasting and prayer for her ... she playfully replied, 'I must have my breakfast; but I will pray' ... I went to my room, wept, and made this record: 'This day shall be spent in fasting and prayer for my precious sister, asking that she may see the vanity of earthly joys and know more of spiritual life .... A little before three p.m. that darling, almost twin sister, said to me, with streaming eyes, 'Never did I see the vanity of earthly joys as today'.[4]

It was later that same day that Phoebe received 'entire sanctification'. She recorded the momentous experience in her diary for 27 July 1837, the day following:

> I never made much progress in the career of faith until I most solemnly resolved, in the strength of the Lord, Jehovah, that I would do every duty, though I might die in the effort. Between the hours of eight and nine o'clock yesterday I was led by the Spirit to the determination that I would never rest, day or night until I knew that the spring of every motive was pure and that the consecration I made of myself was wholly accepted.[5]

A little later in the same entry she went on to record the climax of her consecration:

> 'Glory be to the Father! Glory be to the Son! Glory be to the Holy Spirit for ever!' O, into what a region of light, glory and purity, was my soul at this moment ushered! I felt that I was but a drop in the ocean of infinite love, and Christ was all in all.[6]

---

3 S.O. Garrison (ed.), *Forty Witnesses. Covering the Whole Range of Christian Experience* (1888), p. 190.
4 G. Hughes, *The Beloved Physician: Walter C Palmer MD and His Sun-Lit Journey to the Celestial City* (Palmer and Hughes, 1884), p. 15.
5 Garrison, *Forty Witnesses*, p. 300.
6 Garrison, *Forty Witnesses*, p. 305.

After Phoebe received the gift of perfect love both she and her sister led the Tuesday meetings together. This custom continued until Mrs Lankford and her husband left New York City. The meetings were only open to women until December 1839. It then happened that Phoebe L. Upham brought her husband, a philosopher and college professor, to the meeting. Phoebe Palmer and Sarah Lankford were able to answer his many questions and through this help and encouragement he received assurance of 'entire sanctification'. He later wrote, 'I shall ever recollect the time. It was Friday morning, the 27th of December' and 'I was distinctly conscious of a new but powerful and delightful attraction toward the divine mind. This, I believe, is a common form of interior experience among those who have enjoyed the blessings of sanctification.'[7] It was Upham's remarkable experience through the ministry of the two women that led to men being invited into the Tuesday Meetings which continued in the care of Sarah and Phoebe for over sixty years. Among the men who found their way there were a number of bishops and pastors. In time many of their number, including Dr and Mrs Upham, replicated the Tuesday Meetings in their own areas.

The Tuesday meetings began at 2.30 p.m. and with the passing of the years the initial exercises were always conducted by a minister or pastor. After this opening period, anyone could request to speak, sing or propose united prayer. Testimonies of Christian perfection were given. The rooms were often crowded and it was not unusual for from six to ten clergy to be present on each occasion. Minister and pastors often sat quietly throughout the meetings. Some were afraid of being scorned or dubbed as 'Palmerites' as those who associated with the Palmers were known.

Phoebe Palmer's Theology

Phoebe Palmer's theology of Christian Perfection was not complex. The Bible was central and her interpretation of the text common sense. She aimed at a theology which could embrace both clergy and laity. Phoebe wrote of her approach in the third person as follows:

> She afterward found that God did not require her to believe anything but what was thoroughly substantiated by the requirements of his written word ... it was ... her duty ... by a careful searching of the Scriptures, in order to prove the validity of each step as successively taken.[8]

Holiness was not an option. 'We spoke of the necessity of entire sanctification, that it was not left optional with God's redeemed people whether they be holy; the

---

7 Garrison, *Forty Witnesses*, pp. 275 and 281.
8 P. Palmer, *The Way of Holiness* (Lane & Scott, 1951; 52nd ed. N.Y. Palmer and Hughes, 1867), pp. 82–3.

command is absolute, "Be ye holy".[9] Mrs Palmer stressed that sanctification was to be claimed by the individual immediately. Her text for justifying this was 2 Corinthians 6:26, 'Now! Is the accepted time, now is the day of salvation.' This interpretation was not a common one but it is what she used. 'Entire Salvation', and she stressed 'entire salvation',[10] also termed 'perfection in holiness' or 'perfection in love', is she argued the first great commandment (Luke 10:27) to love God with all one's heart, soul, mind and strength.

Those seeking 'entire sanctification' must be determined. It must be their personal decision to receive it and it was their right to say, 'I must and I will have it now.'[11] Receiving 'entire sanctification' was the only way to become 'totally converted'. It was however a state from which one could not 'fall away from God'. If one had only been 'justified' salvation was still only tentative. If you wanted to be used by the Lord in the conversion of members of your household and others, 'get wholly sanctified', she said.[12]

Phoebe Palmer taught the experience of 'entire sanctification' or holiness by means of an 'altar theology' which drew on the Old Testament sacrificial system. When the animal was placed on the altar of sacrifice it became God's property. It also became holy because it was God's property and everything which was placed on the holy altar became holy. In Phoebe Palmer's teaching every aspect of a person's life, including all worldly desires, dreams, hopes, possessions, goals and ambitions had to be surrendered in a conscious and deliberate way to God. And just as the sacrificial lamb became holy when it was placed on the temple altar, so the Christian believer, the moment that individual offered their lives in conscious surrender to God, became holy. This experience of deliberate and personal submission and becoming holy was often one in which the emotions were powerfully touched. Believers were overwhelmed with feelings of love, often they cried out and sometimes they sank to the ground or experienced a burning sensation, the fire of God's Spirit. In her book *The Way of Holiness*, Phoebe Palmer, referring to herself in the third person, described the mechanics of this 'altar theology':

> And by the determination to consecrate all upon the altar of sacrifice to God, with the resolve to enter into the bonds of an everlasting covenant to be wholly the Lord's for time and eternity, and then acting in conformity with the decision, actually laying all upon the altar, by the most unequivocal Scripture testimony, she laid herself under the solemn obligation to believe that the sacrifice became the Lord's property; and by virtue of the altar upon which the offering was laid, became 'holy' and acceptable.[13]

---

9 P. Palmer, *Full Salvation* (undated; Schmul Publishers, 1979 edition), p. 172.
10 See Kent, *Holding the Fort*, p. 323.
11 Palmer, *The Way of Holiness*, p. 234.
12 Palmer, *Full Salvation*, p. 39.
13 Palmer, *The Way of Holiness*, p. 63, also pp. 62–70, 243.

It was the giving up of all the desires of this world for the Lord which was the sacrifice the believer laid upon the altar. Mrs Palmer made full use of biblical texts with sacrificial terminology. For example, Romans 12:1-2 where Christians are exhorted to be 'living sacrifices'; Matthew 23:19 which states that the altar sanctifies the gift; Exodus 29:37 which asserts that whatever touches the altar is holy and perhaps most important, Hebrews 13:10 which declares that Jesus Christ is a more sacred altar than the altar of the tabernacle. In an article written much later in her life in *Guide to Holiness* magazine, Phoebe Palmer drew the parallel between the Christian believer's sacrificial act of consecration and the Old Testament sacrificial system.

> The presentation of an offering suggests the necessity of an Altar. Under the Jewish dispensation the sacrifice was brought and bound to the altar. The moment it was laid there, it became virtually God's property, to be used only in the service of the sanctuary. And scarcely could an act more sacrilegious be conceived of, than an attempt to resume a sacrifice, and use it for secular or common purposes. The offering became "wholly acceptable" by virtue of the altar on which it was laid, and not through the worthiness of the offerer, or the greatness of the gift.[14]

After making the sacrifice, the believer could expect the gift of entire sanctification. From this point onwards all thoughts and actions were to be done in accordance with God's will and out of perfect love.

In practice Phoebe Palmer also found 'one act of faith not sufficient to insure a continuance in the "way of holiness" but that a continuous act of faith was requisite'.[15] Again writing in *Full Salvation* Phoebe emphasized, 'The cost of holiness was the blood of the Son of God, and greatly does he mistake who supposes that it can be preserved short of "Eternal Vigilance".'[16]

Revival Campaigns in North America and Britain

Phoebe Palmer's biographer, Richard Wheatley, wrote of the year 1840: 'In this year, Mrs Palmer began the long series of evangelistic expeditions, which only terminated in the last year of her mortal life, by brief visits to Rye and Williamsburg.'[17] From this year forward through to the close of 1858, Phoebe held revival services sometimes alone and sometimes with her husband in more than eighty major towns and cities in America and Canada. Then in 1859 she turned her attentions to England.

---

14 'Did the Lord Release You?', *Guide to Holiness*, September 1874, p. 79.
15 Palmer, *The Way of Holiness*, p. 69.
16 Palmer, *Full Salvation*, p. 49.
17 R. Wheatley, *The Life and Letters of Mrs Phoebe Palmer* (W.C. Palmer, 1876), p. 258.

In that year, together with her husband, Dr Walter Palmer, she set out for what proved to be a four-year series of meetings. She had by this time become well known both in England and on the continent on account of her writings. For this reason Phoebe's arrival in the 'Old Country' was keenly awaited. On her return from what had proved to be a successful campaign, she published an account of her time in England under the title Four Years in the Old World. The Methodist Quarterly Review said of this volume:

It is a pleasant record of much that was seen and done ... when theatres are emptied, rum shops closed, policemen left idle, blasphemers taught to pray, defrauders compelled to make restitution, and thousands of awakened souls made joyful in the Redeemer's love, the work must be confessed to be of God.[18]

During their time in England and Ireland the Palmers spent most of their time campaigning in Wesleyan Methodist churches and circuits holding meetings in more than fifty major towns and cities. In the services which they held people were exhorted to have faith in Christ and, if they were already believers, to seek for 'entire sanctification'. Their meetings seem to have achieved a high level of response. At Newcastle-on-Tyne, where the Palmers began their labours in September 1859,[19] Phoebe recorded that 'The number of the newly blessed, as taken by the secretaries of the meeting, now amounts to about thirteen hundred.'[20] The Wesleyan Methodist Magazine reported that 'altogether 1,400 names of persons were taken down' at the meetings and almost all were visited in their homes.[21] In a letter to Mr E. Squire, dated 16 September and published in The Revivalist, Phoebe wrote: 'Hundreds are coming out to the meetings .... Would that you could witness the multitudes which nightly congregate there. The place seems filled with the awful presence of God.'[22] Phoebe went on to report that 'they have come, laying their all upon heaven's altar, and the holy fire has descended, and scores have been able to testify that the consuming, purifying fires of the Spirit have descended, and by the manifestation of their lives, are declaring, "The zeal of thine house has eaten me up".'[23] She estimated that between three and four hundred souls 'have been gathered out of the world, and translated into the kingdom of God's dear Son, during the last five days'.[24] In a subsequent letter from Hull on 4 November Mrs Palmer gave further details of events at Newcastle-on-Tyne.

---

18 Cited by Wheatley, *Life and Letters*, p. 398.
19 See 'Revival in Newcastle-upon-Tyne', *Wesleyan Methodist Magazine*, August 1860, pp. 738–40.
20 Palmer, *Four Years*, p. 104.
21 *Wesleyan Methodist Magazine*, August 1860, p. 739.
22 *The Revivalist*, 1859, p. 169.
23 *The Revivalist*, 1859, p. 170.
24 *The Revivalist*, 1859, p. 169.

The number of newly blest, as given by the secretaries of the meeting, now amounts to about thirteen hundred. Yesterday fifty names were recorded; the day previous about the same number, and thus the work goes on. We find great advantage from taking the names newly-enlisted in the service of Christ. Not only does it furnish work for the beloved and indefatigable Pastors of the flocks worshipping at the various Wesleyan Chapels, in this place and the region round about, but it furnishes needful work for the scores of newly-baptised disciples .... One evangelical church whose membership has gathered largely with us, had an increase of one hundred and thirty at their last communion service, a Sabbath or two since; and we do not doubt but other denominations have shared in similar manner.[25]

Among other encouragements that Phoebe reported was the presence of a minister of the Church of England, whose parish was close to London had been present at Newcastle for several days. He related to her that he had received such 'a baptism of fire' that 'he could scarcely have endured more'.[26] Another gentleman came down from Scotland 'groaning after the witness of inward purity'. During the course of one of the meetings he was enabled to experience 'the full baptism of the Spirit'.[27] Their time in Newcastle was followed by a period in Sunderland and North Shields where the theatre had to be closed as the crowds tuned away from what Phoebe termed 'this nursery of vice'.[28] The Palmers' campaign had a significant impact on the Wesleyan circuits of the North East with the Wesleyan Methodist Magazine stating that 'an increase of 1,593 members, with 1,851 on trial, will be reported to this District, – the largest it has known for many years'.[29]

At Stroud, which the Palmers visited in early October 1860, 'a little town of about 6,000 inhabitants', one circuit minister reported: 'I have now the names of two hundred and fifty persons who have obtained pardon or purity since you came to Stroud, and a few more have been added to the list.'[30] In January 1861 Dr and Mrs Palmer spent time in Leamington where 'night after night the communion rails were crowded with persons seeking salvation' and 'about two hundred professed to have received good during the services'.[31] At Liverpool in November 1861 it was reported that, 'Dr and Mrs Palmer have been favoured with glorious revival seasons in Richmond Hall, where the work of sanctification and conversion has progressed as it usually does in connexion

---

25 *The Revivalist*, 1859, p. 186, letter from Phoebe Palmer 4 November.
26 *The Revivalist*, 1859, p. 186.
27 *The Revivalist*, 1859, p. 187.
28 Palmer, *Four Years*, p. 152.
29 *Wesleyan Methodist Magazine*, August, 1860, pp. 738–40.
30 Palmer, *Four Years*, p. 336.
31 *The Revivalist*, Vol. VII, No. 1, January 1861, p. 12.

with their novel and effective ministry.'[32] The Revivalist reported that 'between twenty and thirty are coming forward every night'.[33] From Liverpool the Palmers went on to Bridgend pausing briefly at Madeley Wood Chapel where the Revd J.W. Fletcher lived, laboured, and died. Under their ministry 'the Lord poured out His Holy Spirit in a wonderful manner upon his people'. On the Sunday afternoon 200 expressed their earnest desire to have 'the full baptism of the Spirit'. All those who were able to surrounded the altar and, according to a contemporary report, 'it would be difficult to describe the manifestations of the power of the presence of Him who baptiseth with the Holy Ghost'.[34] At the evening service which followed Dr Palmer invited all those who were seeking Jesus to rise in their seats. It was estimated that at least three hundred did so and remained standing.[35] By any standards the results achieved by the Palmers were encouraging. A mere addition of figures of those who testified either to having been justified or sanctified comes to over 14,000.

On their return to America in the autumn of 1863, the Palmers were greeted by invitations which poured in from all parts of the country. Phoebe and her husband immediately embarked on what proved to be a gruelling schedule of revival services in America. Some of the meetings which they held evoked religious exercises reminiscent of earlier times. On 13 December Phoebe recorded, 'We spent eight days at Baltimore City, holding two meetings daily as usual. Many were blest; about fifty with full salvation. With a large number of these, the tide of glory was overwhelming, and they sank down under the weight of glory; other leaped and shouted. Like the Samaritan cleansed of his leprosy, they glorified Christ with a loud voice'.[36] They lasted for over a decade during which time they visited more than eighty major towns and cities in Canada and the USA. It was perhaps no surprise that after returning home from camp meetings in Illinois and Ohio Mrs Palmer should have been unwell. She died soon afterwards in November 1874.

Phoebe Palmer's Understanding of Revival

Revival as Sanctification

As might be expected Phoebe Palmer saw 'revival' very much in Methodist terms. It was people in large numbers being 'justified' and 'sanctified'. In fact she laid particular stress on the latter, proclaiming sanctification, she maintained, as taught by Wesley. Commenting on the meetings she and her husband had run at Loughborough in Leicestershire, she wrote:

---

32 *The Revivalist*, 1862, p. 29.
33 *The Revivalist*, 1861, p. 182
34 *The Revivalist*, 1862, p. 44.
35 *The Revivalist*, p. 44.
36 Wheatley, *The Life and Letters of Phoebe Palmer*, p. 444.

We had a meeting of extraordinary power last Sabbath. About a hundred rose to express their determination not to rest without the Holy Ghost. Many have received. This alone is the true heaven-laid basis for a revival, on the same principle that the baptism of fire prepared the one hundred and twenty for aggressive movements against the host of sin.[37]

In this context Phoebe is quite clear that 'full sanctification' alone is 'the true heaven-laid basis of revival'. Revivals, as she perceived them, were something which required human endeavour and co-operation. In *Guide to Holiness* for October 1874 Phoebe related how they asked 'who would pledge themselves – though it might be at the trouble of asking twenty before they could get one promise – they would be at pains to bring one next day'.[38] In what followed Phoebe noted 'a daily increase of spiritual power ... bringing the unsaved to the Saviour of sinners'. In what she described as 'this revival' not 'all the professed disciples of Jesus were at this time recipients of the grace of entire sanctification; but I believe many were'.

In the same article Phoebe went on to indicate that 'entire sanctification' is in essence 'withdrawal from the world'.

Now what is entire sanctification? Does it not suggest a separation from the world to holy purposes? And when the Church members separate themselves from the spirit of the world, and set themselves apart for the great work of soul-saving, did not the Holy Spirit set the sanctifying seal? Surely God takes all we give Him'.[39]

Phoebe recognized that revivals may sometimes be accompanied by charismatic gifts and other phenomena. When she and her husband first arrived in Belfast on 19 July 1859 she described how they had encountered a revival in a Presbyterian church.

Now, you may go into a Presbyterian Church but a few minutes walk from where I write, and you will hear young men and maidens, old women and children, speaking with tongues touched with living fire, of the wonderful works of God .... Here you may witness the slaying power, and listen to the piercing cry for mercy, equal to, if not exceeding anything that has been heard among Methodists even in the days of the devoted Abbot.[40]

Although the Palmers' teaching on the Baptism of the Holy Spirit had strong echoes of later Pentecostalism there were some differences. There is no record

---

37 Palmer, *Four Years*, intro to Chapter XXVI, pp. 437–8.
38 *Guide to Holiness*, October 1874, p. 107.
39 Palmer, *Four Years*, p. 45.
40 Palmer, *Four Years*, p. 45.

of any of those who were 'filled' at their meetings ever having spoken with tongues. Once believers entered into this experience they were exhorted to maintain it by a constant and steady faith and by pursuing holiness. In contrast, classic Pentecostals maintained their experience by continuing to use their newfound gift of speaking, and by the development and practice of other charismata.

Revival Methods

The central focus of the Palmers' meetings and revival services was the altar. Their aim was to bring each occasion to a climax in which 'seekers' after justification ('trusting Jesus for the first time') or for 'sanctification' were to come out publicly before the congregation. They would either gather round or kneel at the altar. Sometimes they would be asked to make a public commitment of their purpose in coming. The Palmers would pray for them and other helpers would join in giving prayer and counsel. Much of this was very similar to the camp meetings held by the Methodists in the United States. At Newcastle-upon-Tyne on the afternoon of 14 September 1859, it was reported that 'the communion rail was full all round compassing the pulpit'.[41] It was also reported that generally on these occasions Mrs Palmer 'modestly walks within the rails of the communion, not to preach according to the modern acceptation of that term, but simply to talk to the people, which she does with all the gracefulness of an intelligent Christian lady'.[42]

There were a number of other aspects or features in the Palmers' campaigns. One of these was hand raising. At Penrith in the North of England, for example, in April 1860 the accommodation was too small for those who wished to express their desire for the full baptism in the Holy Spirit. Dr Palmer therefore asked all who wished to signify their determination that they would never rest without this blessing, to raise their right hand, 'and keep it upraised until the recording angel might note it down in the book of God's remembrance'.[43]

The Palmers were very keen to ensure that those who made a response at their meetings were followed up by their own clergy and pastors. For this reason she wrote, 'We find great advantage from taking the names of newly-enlisted in the service of Christ. Not only does it furnish work for the beloved and indefatigable Pastors of the flocks worshipping at the various Wesleyan Chapels, in this place and the region round about, but it furnishes needful work for the scores of newly baptized disciples.'[44]

Another aspect of the Palmer campaigns were testimonies. Often towards the close of the services Dr Palmer asked those who came forward as seekers what

---

41 *The Revivalist*, 1859, p. 171.
42 *The Revivalist*, 1859, p. 171.
43 Palmer, *Four Years*, pp. 229–30.
44 *The Revivalist*, 1859, p. 186.

the Lord had done for them. One will say amid tears of joy Jesus 'has taken my feet from the miry clay', and another, 'He has pardoned all my sins', 'Oh! I do believe. Jesus is my Saviour: glory be to Jesus!' It was Walter Palmer's custom to repeat them to the congregation, 'so that through the thanksgiving of many, praise may redound to God.'

Singing played a significant role in all the Palmers' holiness revivals. Many of the songs called on the congregation to surrender their lives in wholehearted sacrifice to God. On occasion, those who had come forward to consecrate themselves to God were then invited to make their pledge in a song which expressed surrender. This happened at Manchester in April 1863. All who had pledged themselves were then invited to sing:

> Take my poor heart, and let it be
> Forever closed to all but Thee;
> Seal Thou my breast, and let me wear
> The pledge of love forever there.[45]

A further step was taken in song when the same group were invited to confess the faith of their hearts by singing:

> Saviour from sin, I thee receive
> From all indwelling sin:
> Thy blood I steadfastly believe
> Doth make me thoroughly clean
>
> 'Tis done; then did'st this moment save,
> With full salvation bless;
> Redemption through thy blood I have,
> And spotless love and peace.[46]

Singing also featured at the conclusion of many of the Palmers' meetings. When they found that people were unwilling to leave at the close Phoebe reported that on such occasions they often sang 'Revival Melodies' such as had been sung during the awakenings in America and Ireland.[47]

Drink and Dealing with Evil

In her early years Phoebe was a strong advocate of the temperance movement and wrote a number of poems on the dangers of drink in the 1830s. The following is a verse from 'The Man that Drank the Adder Up':

---

45 Palmer, *Four Years*, p. 672.
46 Palmer, *Four Years*, p. 673.
47 Palmer, *Four Years*, p. 152.

> The Bible has pronounced the woe
> On him who loves strong drink,
> And though I'm young, too well I know
> That man is on the drink
> Who puts the poison to his lips;
> Who tarries long at wine
> And takes the cup and si-p-s and si-p-s
> Ah! Soon he'll prove divine
> This weighty truth, on ADDER lurks.

Dealing with evil, and especially the evils of drink, was one of the Palmers' particular concerns. They were insistent on the evils of drink as being a major hindrance to the work of revival. Phoebe herself was a major temperance campaigner. At Poole in Dorset, when they commenced services in September 1860, it was brought to their notice that the Circuit Steward and Sabbath School Superintendent owned the largest number of liquor establishments in the region. To the Palmers this was the sin of Achan, and they immediately confronted the Circuit Minister. The Spirit-dealer, on being challenged over the issue, preferred to resign than renounce the liquor traffic. Phoebe Palmer reflected that 'in this occurrence I was beginning to hear the death-knell of our revival services in England'.[48] However, on the evening the gentlemen withdrew, 'twenty souls were born in to the Kingdom, besides several who received the sanctifying seal'.[49] By the end of the Poole Campaign 'not less than three hundred, it is believed ... made joyful witness of God's saving mercy'.[50]

Later the same year Phoebe found the work at Banbury was 'checked' and that 'she was too sadly wrung with anguish to sleep'. The cause of this, she eventually discovered, was the presence of 'a brewer, one of the most prominent men on the official board of that church, being a class leader and Sabbath school superintendent'. For that reason the revival came to an end. A similar instance of liquor causing a hindrance to revival services occurred at Windsor in January 1861. Here the Wesleyan Chapel was being used as a vault for spirituous liquor. This became apparent when an intoxicated drayman made an excessive noise rolling the barrels into the vault during the service. When the Palmers protested the Superintendent asked the circuit steward to clear the premises. Following his compliance great blessing flowed. Phoebe wrote: 'This victory, and the subsequent conquest we witnessed while at Windsor, was well worth the voyage over the Atlantic.'[51] At times it seemed as though Mrs Palmer almost made abstinence from alcohol a condition of receiving sanctification. This certainly was the case when she wrote of a certain local preacher in England who

---

48 Palmer, *Four Years*, p. 327.
49 Palmer, *Four Years*, p. 328.
50 Palmer, *Four Years*, p. 332.
51 Palmer, *Four Years*, p. 410.

wrestled to receive the blessing. She reflected: 'Now if I should tell our brethren in America what this Christian brother in England struggled so long and hard over, before he could get his offering on the altar, they would be amazed. It was the habit of using wine, beer, and brandy; not to excess ... but, as it is said, moderately.'[52]

Holiness was the Palmers' constant and persistent theme. Of their time in Newcastle Phoebe wrote: 'World-loving and worldly professors are apprehending as never before, that the God of the Scriptures means just what he says, when He enjoins separation from the world. "Come out from among them and be ye separate, saith the Lord, and touch not the unclean thing" has become an obvious and experimental realisation.'[53] On some occasions the nature of this separation appeared to have descended to the level of trivialities with Phoebe declaring 'that jewelry and costly array are being renounced and we are having a revival, not only of power, but primitive principles'.[54]

Among those who were lastingly impacted by Phoebe's preaching was Frances Willard who had spent time at Oberlin while her father studied there. She described how when the Palmers held a series of meetings in her home church, she responded to the invitation to enter into 'the higher Christian life'. She recalled that her consecration was at first hindered by her simple bits of jewelry but eventually 'great peace came to my soul'. Frances eventually dedicated her life to the Temperance cause which was so close to the heart of the holiness movement.[55]

Prayer meetings were a frequent aspect of the Palmers' campaigns but, at Charlestown, Phoebe instituted a believing meeting. Many had reached a point where they 'believed' God was ready to fulfill his promises to them. They therefore came to claim God's blessing in faith. Phoebe wrote to her sister, 'What extraordinary demonstrations to the power of faith followed.'[56]

The Role of Women in the Church

Revival is essentially a protest against the deadening orthodoxy of establishment religion. It therefore is often associated with radicalism, and in particular with other movements which are both religious and social forms of protest. Some of these kinds of issues surfaced in Phoebe's life and ministry, among them the role of women. At a time when most people considered it wrong for a woman to speak in church or indeed at any gatherings where men were present, Phoebe actively spoke herself and campaigned for the right of other women to do the same. One of her major books was *Promise of the Father*; or *A Neglected*

---

52 Palmer, *Four Years*, p. 691.
53 *The Revivalist*, 1859, p. 186.
54 *The Revivalist*, 1859, p. 187.
55 Information derived from Dayton, '"Your Daughters Shall Prophesy"', p. 77.
56 Wheatley, *The Life and Letters*, p. 342.

Specialty of the Last Days which was first published in 1859.[57] It was written to assert the call and right of women to speak in public. She maintained that the promise of the Father in Joel 2:28 was that in the latter days, the Spirit would be poured out on the daughters as well as the sons. The gift of prophecy, she pointed out, was given to both men and women in the last days. She also emphasized that prophets were appointed to preach (Nehemiah 6:7).[58] She discussed the fact that Joel 2:26 says 'daughters shall prophesy' in relation to the apostle Paul's command to women to 'keep silence' in church. This instruction could not, she wrote, refer to all women because he gives instructions to them to cover their heads when prophesying in church. The injunction in 1 Corinthians 15:34 'let your women keep silence ... let them ask their husbands at home' could only, she asserted, refer to married women.[59] Possibly, she suggests, they were interrupting the services. Phoebe demonstrated the inconsistent thinking of those who imposed restrictions on women preaching but allowed them to sing, pray and respond to liturgies. She cited in support of her argument the example of some of Wesley's early female preachers such as Sarah Millet who was afterwards Mrs Boyce.[60] To her Wesley gave the right hand of fellowship and the full right to preach in the connection. That said, it should be noted that at the time of the Palmers' coming to England the English Wesleyan Conference in its efforts to eschew radicalism had become increasingly opposed to the idea of women preaching. For this reason, Phoebe's forthright presence in their circuits represented a strong threat to the status quo such that, in 1860, both she and her husband were forbidden as lay evangelists to use their pulpits.[61] At that time the Wesleyan parent body was undergoing a reaction against women preachers and were no doubt particularly worried by Phoebe's growing influence.

If her influence on the attitudes of Wesleyan Methodist preachers was limited, that was not the case where Catherine Booth, the wife of William Booth a Methodist New Connexion minister and later co-founder of the Salvation Army, was concerned. After hearing Mrs Palmer speak in a revival service at Gateshead, Catherine Booth was dismayed to come across a pamphlet which rejected her right to preach on scriptural grounds. She wrote a trenchant reply and then on Sunday 8 October 1860 she put her words into action. Walking to the front as her husband was concluding she told him that she desired to speak. Later when her husband was unable to speak owing to an illness she took on his appointments throughout the circuit. William himself soon became thoroughly convinced both of the equality of women and of their right to preach. Thus began an influence which later extended throughout the Salvation Army in which women were treated as equal with men in all aspects of the work. Indeed

---

57 Palmer, *Promise of the Father*.
58 Palmer, *Promise of the Father*, p. 42.
59 Palmer, *Promise of the Father*, p. 47.
60 Palmer, *Promise of the Father*, pp. 116–17.
61 Kent, *Holding the Fort*, p. 127.

one of her daughters was later to become the General of the Army.[62] Catherine's fame as 'The Woman Preacher' was destined to continue for another 28 years. In the early years of their marriage Catherine devoted much time to bringing up her eight children. From the very beginning she instilled into them the principle of the equality between the sexes. She wrote: 'I have tried to grind it into my boys that their sisters were just as intelligent and capable as themselves. Jesus Christ's principles were to put woman on the same platform as men, although I am sorry to say His apostles did not always act upon it.'[63] When Catherine died at the age of 61 the population of England mourned and 50,000 paid their respects as she lay in state. William declared that she was indeed the Salvation Army Mother. 'Other religious movements organizations cannot be said to have a Mother; their guides are and authorities are all Fathers .... Woman has taken her place with man in the new kingdom ...'[64]

Visiting Prisoners, the Poor and the Sick

Mrs Palmer was often to be found when not engaged in revival meetings distributing tracts among the poor. However, she was not concerned only for their spiritual well-being. On 17 September 1844, for example, she recorded a visit in her diary to a poor family to whom she promised a coat. Phoebe Palmer was a frequent visitor to the New York prison known as The Tombs. Here she spoke comfort and the Christian message to the female convicts. She was sometimes accompanied by Sarah Lankford and Mrs Upham. On 15 June 1851 she recorded, 'Held a meeting with the female prisoners at the City Prison'. Again on 22 February 1857 she noted, 'This afternoon we held a meeting with the female prisoners of the City Tombs. Several of the prisoners were affected in tears.'

Anti-Slavery

Phoebe Palmer was a strong abolitionist. With Abraham Lincoln, she held that 'if slavery be not wrong, nothing is wrong'. Nor could she anticipate 'the preservation of American nationality and its glorious institutions, independently of that grand act of simple righteousness, – the emancipation of the coloured millions held in helpless cruel bondage'.[65] There are a number of entries in Phoebe's journal and letters concerning anti-slavery. For instance the following entry is found in her correspondence in 1846. 'Last night I attended a missionary

---

62 See R. Sandall, *The History of the Salvation Army* (Thomas Nelson and Sons, 1947), Vol. 1, pp. 8–9. See also R. Collier, *The General Next to God* (Collins, 1966), p. 40.

63 F. De L. Booth-Tucker, *The Life of Catherine Booth* (Revell, 1892), Vol. 1, p. 348 cited Dayton, '"Your Daughters Shall Prophesy"', p. 76.

64 Booth-Tucker, *The Life of Catherine Booth*, Vol. 2, p. 644.

65 Wheatley, *The Life and Letters*, p. 599.

meeting, which was called for the purpose of raising funds for the sustainment of the recaptured slaves.' She goes on to relate that 1,150 were raised. 'The money,' she writes, 'seemed to be given in the beauty of holiness.'[66]

Benevolent and Mission Societies

In addition to her concerns for the slave, the prisoner and the sick, Phoebe also involved herself in the work of benevolent and missionary societies. In her journal for 29 October 1847 we find her attending the New York Female Assistance Society for the Relief and Religious Instruction of the Sick Poor. She agreed to write the report of the meeting. In her journal for 17 October 1847 Phoebe mentions that The Benevolent Society of Allen Street Methodist Episcopal Church has met in her parlors for the past 17 years. In November 1847 Phoebe was elected corresponding secretary of the New York Female Assistance Society. Phoebe also worked for the Home for the Friendless Institution and provided more than one deserted orphan with a comfortable home.[67]

Phoebe Palmer involved herself in the Methodist Episcopal Home Mission Society and church-planting activities. Additionally, she believed the Lord was going to remove the veil from the Jewish eyes and she worked hard with others to establish a mission to New York's 40,000 Jews. Largely through her efforts the Jewish Mission began its work in August 1855.[68] The Palmers also interested themselves in missions in Palestine and China.

The Impact of the Palmers

The Palmers were a remarkable couple who were devoted to one another, lived out high-standards and gave themselves unstintingly to the work of God. They were perhaps other worldly and somewhat withdrawn from the lower echelons of society. Nevertheless, they were people of great compassion and social concern who were ready to enter the prison and the anti-liquor crusade.

Phoebe Palmer was an early riser who gave herself to prayer and writing. Following in the steps of Wesley, an ordered life with careful administration was an important part of her spirituality. On one occasion she wrote, 'punctuality in my engagements with God, is necessary to my advancement ...'[69] She was diligent in attending her class meeting and sought 'to serve the Lord, in domestic orderings'.[70] In dress she was somewhat austere believing that 'gravity' should distinguish the Christian lady.[71] She made her children a

---

66 Wheatley, *The Life and Letters*, p. 218.
67 Wheatley, *The Life and Letters*, p. 219.
68 Wheatley, *The Life and Letters*, p. 229.
69 Wheatley, *The Life and Letters*, p. 153.
70 Wheatley, *The Life and Letters*, p. 153.
71 Wheatley, *The Life and Letters*, p. 605.

priority and did not venture out on long trips away from home until they were at an age to fend for themselves.

Richard Wheatley in his biography of Phoebe Palmer summarized her life as follows:

> Always accompanied by her husband, she went on to serve Christ, and she wanted no higher right than this, the grandest right ever given to man or woman – the right to commend the Lord Jesus Christ to a dying world. Modestly and in Christian consecration, she went forth to serve God.

> 'Twenty five thousand souls saved under the instrumentality of Phoebe Palmer! What a record for earth and heaven! What an array for the judgment day.' What a doxology for the one hundred and forty four thousand! What a mountain of coronets flung down at the feet of Jesus.[72]

Phoebe Palmer was undoubtedly a woman of substance on both sides of the Atlantic. She was one of the most effective holiness revivalists of the nineteenth century proclaiming entire sanctification. She was the voice of women to churches that had suppressed their contribution and not least in her own Wesleyan Methodist tradition. Not only was she a gifted and able preacher who, along with her husband, was a constant crowd-puller to all classes, she wrote a definitive and influential book to make the case. Among holiness leaders Phoebe was prominent advocate of women's rights, the anti-slavery cause and the temperance movement. In England and Wales alone the Palmers made a significant impact on the lives of 20,000 men and women most of whom were attached in varying degrees to churches in Wesleyan Methodist circuits.[73] But their influence spread well beyond this, encouraging many Methodist ministers and other evangelical clergy, impacting the life and work of many circuits as well as adding weight to the temperance cause and inspiring Christian leaders such as William and Catherine Booth.

---

72 Wheatley, *The Life and Letters*, p. 633.
73 See table below which has been compiled from Phoebe's account of the time she and her husband spent in the British Isles.

Table showing the numbers of individuals 'justified' and 'sanctified' during the visit to England and Wales by Dr Walter and Mrs Phoebe Palmer 1859–63

Place	'Justified'	'Sanctified'
Bowden nr Manchester	13	
Newcastle-on-Tyne	1,300	
Sunderland	2,100 'seekers'	200
North Shields	4,345 'names given in'	
Carlisle	400	
Penrith	700 'received good'	
Gateshead	500–600	
Houghton-le-Spring	No figures	
Tynemouth	100 'blessed'	
Isle of Wight	600	
Poole	300 'witnesses of grace'	
Stroud	250 'pardon or purity'	
Lynn	300 'recipients of grace'	
Leamington	300 'recipients of mercy'	
Banbury	547 'into the kingdom'	
Maidenhead	200 'obtained pardon'	112
Great Grimsby	400 'justified or sanctified'	
Macclesfield	321 'receiving pardon'	85
Boston	200 'recipients of grace'	
Darlington	400 'obtained pardon'	
Barnard Castle	303 'obtained pardon'	
Berwick-on-Tweed	No figures	
Liverpool	600 'seeking mercy'	
Madeley	900 'among the saved'	

continued

Place	'Justified'	'Sanctified'
Bridgend	109 'seekers'	
Cowbridge	150 'seekers'	
Cardiff	750 'found pardon'	
Merthyr Tydvil	194 'newly pardoned'	30
Abergavenny	250 'gathered to Jesus'	
Aberdare	106 'justified'	26
Blaneau	100 'found forgiveness'	
Douglas Isle of Man	No figures	
Leeds	200 'obtained pardon'	
Runcorn	100 'born into kingdom'	
Walsall	300 'added to the Lord'	
Wolverhampton	100 'recipients of grace'	
Birmingham	343 'received pardon'	37 'witness of the spirit'
Manchester	500 'into the kingdom'	100 'sanctified'
Southport *	150	
Edgeworth*	50	
Louth*	575	
	18,556	

Source: P. Palmer, *Four Years in the Old World: Comprising the Travels, Incidents and Evangelistic Labours of Dr and Mrs Palmer in England, Ireland, Scotland and Wales* (Walter C. Palmer Junior, 1869), pp. 26–690.

* Estimated on the basis of Phoebe's comments: Southport – 'nightly the altar is surrounded'; Edgeworth – 'Some professed to receive pardon'; Louth – 'three weeks and two days with between 20 and 30 receiving justifying grace'.

CHAPTER 7

Dwight L. Moody and Urban Revivalism

Dwight Lyman Moody was born on 5 February 1837 the son of Edwin Moody and Betsy Holden. His father who was a rural construction worker died when Moody was only four years old. Of Betsy's seven children the oldest at that time was only 13. The sorrow and hardship of those early years had driven Betsy to trust in Christ as her Saviour and she took the children to the local Unitarian church. Moody loved his mother and said that there were few things he wouldn't have done for her!

His first experience of full-time employment was working for his uncle, Sam Holton, in a Boston shoe shop. During this time he joined Mount Vernon Orthodox Congregational Church. Here he was placed in Mr Edward Kimball's Sunday school class. W.H. Daniels who knew Moody personally later recalled:

> One day Mr Kimball called upon him at his place of business; and putting his hand on his shoulder, inquired if he would not give his heart to Christ. That question awakened him. He began to seek the Saviour in earnest, and in a little while he felt assurance and pardon for his sins and his acceptance as a child of God.[1]

At the church's monthly communion in 1855 Moody was received into full fellowship. Soon after this time he began to be more zealous and striking out west he went to work in the boot and shoe shop belonging to Mr Charles and Augustus Wiswall in Lake Street, Chicago.

Christian Work in Chicago

Shortly after his arrival in the city Moody began attending First Methodist Church. Here he found good fellowship and began to work for their Mission Band. Throughout his life Moody had a great love of children and his love of fun enabled him to enjoy their company. It was no surprise in 1857 that he started a mission of his own in a deserted saloon in North Side Market. About this time Moody said to his old friend, Mr Reynolds of Peoria, Illinois: 'Reynolds I have no education, but I love the Lord Jesus Christ, and I want

---

1 W.H. Daniels, *D.L. Moody and His Work* (American Publishing Company, 1875), p. 22.

to do something for Him; I want you to pray for me.'[2] Moody's North Street Mission had among its scholars 'the daughters of prostitutes and keepers of brothels' many of whom he managed to send away to places of safety.

Among Moody's supporters at the Mission was John V. Farwell, who gave generously. On one occasion, Farwell, who was a person of influence, heard Abraham Lincoln was in the city campaigning in the presidential election. He visited Lincoln's hotel and succeeded in securing a promise from his wife that her husband would visit Moody's school the following Sunday. Lincoln duly obliged and, for the first and only time in his life, made a Sunday school address. Moody's kids were wild with enthusiasm and listened keenly as Lincoln told them 'they were in the right place learning the right things'. 'What they learned out of the Bible', he said, 'would certainly be of use if they practised it.'

Following the Revival of 1857–8 Moody began to take a strong interest in the Young Men's Christian Association (YMCA). He saw it as the most effective way of reaching out to the young men of the city. He began to attend their prayer times when his work permitted. He became more and more involved, and in 1860 he gave up his work as a commercial traveller in order to give himself to full-time working at his own North Market Mission and the YMCA. Bidding goodbye to his business, he said to his friend Mr Jacobs, 'I have decided to give God all my time.' On being asked by his friend how he was going to live, Moody replied, 'God will provide for me, if he wishes to keep me on, and I shall keep on till I am obliged to stop.'

The YMCA recognized Moody's abilities and appointed him, 'chairman of the visiting committee to the Sick and Strangers'. Under Moody's leadership the YMCA, like the North Market Mission, became a free, popular institution which extended its influences to all classes of society. The report of the first year of the committee's work under Moody's chairmanship gave the number of families visited as 554 and the amount of money given to charity as $2,350. Moody encouraged women to join the Association as auxiliary members as early as May 1861. Dorsett wrote, 'To Moody's mind Jesus had died for women as absolutely as he had died for men.'[3]

Moody's work at his North Market Mission also prospered and in 1863 'a commodious chapel with tower and spire' was erected not very far from the old mission at a cost of $20,000, most of which was collected by Moody himself. The church was a success and many converts from the Mission joined him there. The church which was independent operated on Congregational principles and had its own doctrinal basis of faith. The YMCA also grew rapidly in America with 242 institutions in the mid-1860s. The Chicago branch prospered and on 29 September 1867 a new building was erected on Madison Street

---

2 Daniels, *D.L. Moody*, p. 36.
3 L.W. Dorsett, *A Passion for Souls: The Life of D.L. Moody* (Moody Press, 1997), p. 87.

between Clarke and La Salle Streets. Moody in his closing address at the dedication proposed that the building be named Farwell Hall in honour of its chief benefactor.

Moody and the Civil War

In 1861 Abraham Lincoln again campaigned for the presidency with the promise to prohibit the extension of slavery in the Union. South Carolina had earlier voted in 1860 to secede from the Union and a month before Lincoln took office seven other states seceded and four more followed forming the 'Confederate States of America'. Lincoln responded by calling for 75,000 three-month volunteers to fight what he believed would be 'a short war, fought quickly'. His call received an overwhelmingly positive response. As things turned out however, the war was anything but short. It was long and costly and more than three hundred thousand men were to lose their lives during what proved to be a bitter five-year struggle.

The 72nd Illinois Regiment was organized and was billeted for some time at Camp Douglas, a makeshift base about three miles from the city. As the war extended many more regiments were based there. As a friend of many of the Illinois volunteers and also the organizer of the YMCA's visitation programme, Moody went to the camp to read Scripture to the men and to preach and pray. For a brief period he was drawn to the idea of becoming a chaplain to the 72nd Regiment but when numerous other soldiers began to be billeted in the camp he felt that he could do more by remaining unattached and so being able to visit any of the regiments. Moody was concerned at the sight of 'thousands of men huddled together, playing cards, drinking whisky and being solicited by prostitutes who were already moving in and encircling the all-male city'.[4]

Moody showed his great talent for organization in this situation. Within a week he had organized the printing and distribution of 3,500 Sunday School Union hymnals and overseen the giving out of thousands of Bibles. Later a tent was erected for each regiment containing religious literature and writing materials to encourage the soldiers in the duty of making contact with their families. Moody also recruited 150 lay people to manage the tents, distribute literature and serve as song leaders and speakers for the meetings. Moody also spent time moving rapidly from regiment to regiment praying, talking and encouraging the men.

One very positive result of Moody's endeavours was a revival among the prisoners, about ten thousand of their number having been taken at Fort Donelson and brought to Camp Douglas which was transformed into a prison. During the course of the war Moody made nine trips to the battlefronts. On his arrival there he often worked round the clock, visiting, praying, exhorting. Others gave the men whisky, brandy and punch. The report of the Army Committee for the year 1865 showed a distribution of 1,537 Bibles, 20,565

---

4 Dorsett, *A Passion for Souls*, p. 89.

New Testaments, 1,000 prayer books, 2,025 hymn books, 24,896 other religious books, 127,545 religious newspapers, and 43,450 pages of tracts, besides 28,400 literary papers and magazines.[5]

Marriage to Emma Revell

Despite his obsession with Christian ministry and visits to the battlefronts, Moody still found time to court and marry Emma Revell, the daughter of a Chicago ship-builder. He met her almost as soon as he arrived in the city. She was a solid Christian girl. Moody wrote in a letter to his mother, 'I do not know anyone that knows her but that likes her.'[6] After her graduation from high school in 1860 Emma taught in Chicago public schools so with Moody's heavy schedule, time together was at a premium. They were married on 28 August 1862 at First Baptist Church in a simple ceremony. Emma's family had suffered economic hardship so that their marriage was necessarily a very plain occasion. Emma introduced her husband to certain social graces and greatly increased his charm and effectiveness as a person. They had two sons, William and Paul and a daughter, Emma. They all married happily with Christian partners.

Emma became Dwight's right hand and travelled with him whenever she could including some of his major trips. She was particularly drawn to distributing food and clothing and caring for the sick and bereaved. Emma was also one of a small minority of women who went out to the battlefronts during the civil war. Along with her husband she visited troops in Kentucky, Tennessee, Mississippi and Alabama in 1863. In the following year she visited General Grant's battered troops at Richmond during their campaign.

Trial by Fire

After the Civil War was over Moody faced a further trial when his YMCA Farwell Hall was burned to the ground on 7 January 1868.[7] In the event no one was hurt and Moody immediately set about raising the necessary funds to rebuild it. The second Farwell Hall was opened on 19 January 1869. Just under two years later the great Chicago fire devastated the city destroying 18,000 buildings with 10,000 made homeless. Moody later reflected that, 'It seemed to me that I had a glimpse in that fire of what the Day of Judgement will be, when I saw the flames rolling down the street twenty or thirty feet high, consuming everything in its march that did not flee.'[8] The fire raged for two days and a large part of the north side of the city was destroyed including Moody's Illinois Street Church, the Second Farwell Hall and the house which he and Emma had

---

5 Daniels, *D.L. Moody*, p. 101.
6 Dorsett, *A Passion for Souls*, p. 103.
7 There is an interesting account of this in *Evangelical Christendom* 2 March 1868 entitled 'Burning of Farwell Hall, Chicago'.
8 C.F. Goss, *Echoes from the Pulpit and Platform* (A.D. Worthington, 1900), p. 174.

been given. Moody immediately threw himself into the work of providing food and shelter for the homeless before journeying to Brooklyn and Philadelphia to raise money to rebuild his ruined church.

Baptism in the Holy Spirit

Two praying ladies in his congregation had been interceding for many months for Moody to be filled with the Holy Spirit. They were particularly concerned for him on account of his punishing schedule. Moody knew of their prayers and welcomed them. It was while Moody was out east raising money for the victims of the Chicago fire that the Pentecost experience for which he had longed came to him as he walked down a New York Street. Moody recalled:

> My heart was not in the work of begging. I was crying all the time that God would fill me with His Spirit. Well, one day, in the city of New York – oh, what a day! – I cannot describe it, I seldom refer to it; it is almost too sacred an experience to name. Paul had an experience of which he never spoke for fourteen years. I can only say that God revealed Himself to me, and I had such an experience of his love that I had to ask Him to stay his hand. I went preaching again. The sermons were not different; I did not present any new truths; and yet hundreds were converted. I would not now be placed back where I was before that blessed experience if you should give me all the world-it would be as the small dust of the balance.[9]

This experience for Moody was so overwhelming that he once told Reuben Torrey that 'he had to ask God to withhold his hand lest he die on the very spot'.[10] Following this experience Moody returned to Chicago to gather Emma and the children and travel to Northfield to rest and wait for the counsel of the Holy Spirit. Throughout his subsequent ministry Moody laid much stress on developing an intensely personal relationship with Christ through the fellowship of the Holy Spirit.

Moody Joins Forces with Ira Sankey

Ira David Sankey (1840–1908) came from Pennsylvania where both his parents were members of the Methodist Episcopal Church. He was a leading voice in day and Sunday schools. Daniels wrote of him, 'He was full of music and sensitive to musical impressions.'[11] Converted during a revival in his home church Sankey served for three months in Lincoln's volunteer army and then

---

9 W.R. Moody, *The Life of Dwight L. Moody by His Son* (Fleming H. Revell, 1900), p. 135.
10 Marsden, *Fundamentalism and the Shaping of American Culture*, p. 78 citing R. Torrey, *Why God Used D.L. Moody* (Kessinger, 2006; first published 1923), p. 57.
11 Daniels, *D.L. Moody*, p. 230.

Dwight L. Moody

returned home to work for his father. At the same time he continued to be in wide demand as a singer. Sankey prayed over his songs and his music as preachers do over their sermons.

Moody first met Sankey at a YMCA conference at Indianapolis and then persuaded him to come with his wife and child and join his work in Chicago. Daniel recorded that Sankey remonstrated saying, 'I cannot leave my business.' Moody's retort was, 'You must give up your business and come to Chicago and work with me.' Early in 1871 Sankey agreed to resign his employment with the treasury department and made the move with his wife and family. From 1873 Sankey was supervising the music ministry of Moody campaigns. In June of that year the Sankeys and the Moodys set sail for what was Moody's third trip to England.

Moody's Campaigns in the British Isles

Moody came to Britain on five separate occasions during which time he preached or held campaigns in major towns and cities. His first visit, which took place between May and July 1867, was for two reasons. He wanted to hear and learn from Charles Spurgeon and George Muller. Also, his young wife had been suffering an attack of asthma and physicians recommended a long sea journey and a change of climate. Moody spoke in Bristol as well as at a number of YMCA meetings in London. During this time he encountered Henry Moorhouse (1840–80) and was significantly influenced by his preaching.[12] From Moorhouse Moody learned to focus the content of his sermons on the love of God and also saw the value of preaching on a theme running through the books of the Bible and not staying on one verse or passage. It was also Moorhouse who first suggested to Sankey that he cross the Atlantic to sing the gospel. 'I remember', he recalled, 'how confidently he expressed his opinion that God would bless my singing there.'[13]

Moody's second trip was a short one which lasted through the summer months of 1872. He spent nearly all his time during that visit preaching in London mostly in Nonconformist chapels. In late July he gave a major address at the Mildmay Conference which brought him into contact with hundreds of Evangelicals across England and which resulted in his being invited to return in 1873. Moody was deeply impressed by the Church of England clergyman, William Pennefather. He was struck by his holiness of life and the value of Christian conferences such as Mildmay, which he later replicated in America.

In June 1873 Moody embarked on his third visit to England arriving with his wife and family and the Sankeys at Liverpool. Moody was somewhat disconcerted to find that William Pennefather and two others who had invited him had all died. However Henry Moorhouse was there to greet the two families when they came ashore and they found their way to York where he was supported by the Baptist preacher, F.B. Meyer. The meetings got off to a slow start but by the end of their time there audiences reached a thousand. After his time in York Moody went on to Sunderland at the invitation of the Revd Arthur Rees, an open-communion Baptist. Whilst he was in the town Moody spoke at the YMCA meeting following which a visitor found 'the young men were speaking in tongues and prophesying'.[14] Moorhouse assisted the two evangelists at Newcastle and at Darlington taking a leading part in their first all-day meeting.[15] It was at Edinburgh and London however that Moody was most successful. At the close of the Edinburgh campaign it was reported that 1,400 people had professed conversion.[16] During the course of 1874 Moody held services in Manchester, Liverpool and Sheffield and was then in Birmingham in January 1875 where he held crowds of three to four thousand in rapt attention. *The Birmingham Post* reported that on the very first day of Moody's campaign

---

12 Moorhouse later travelled out to America in the autumn of 1867 and worked together with Moody in to Chicago. He again visited Chicago in August 1869 and stayed with Moody preaching for a couple of months at the YMCA's Farewell Hall. See J. MacPherson, *Henry Moorhouse the English Evangelist* (Morgan and Scott, undated), pp. 65 and 71.
13 MacPherson, *Henry Moorhouse*, p. 73.
14 Daniels, *D.L. Moody*, p. 248.
15 Daniels, *D.L. Moody*, p. 73.
16 Moody, *The Life of Dwight L. Moody*, p. 190.

in the town there were large crowds in the street an hour before the service began and 'that on the doors being opened the hall was rapidly filled to overflowing'.[17] The following day the same paper noted that at the evening meeting on the following day, 'Many thousands took their place at least an hour before the time announced for the opening of the service and they waited with the utmost patience.'[18]

In London, where Moody and Sankey operated from February to July 1875, four centres were chosen as preaching places: the Agricultural Hall at Islington in North London seating 13,700 persons with standing room for four to five thousand more; Bow Road Hall in the East End with 10,000 seats; the Royal Opera House in the West End; and the Victoria Theatre in the South. William R. Moody wrote of his father's campaigning in London, 'Nothing is clearer than that London has been remarkably stirred by the labours of these two evangelists.'[19] William also stated that at the London Mission a total of 285 meetings were held and were attended by 2,530,000 people. The total cost of the mission was £28,396. 19s. 6d. nearly all of which was subscribed before the close of the meetings. George Davis estimated that 100,000 people were won for Christ during the entire two-year campaign.[20] Others such as W.G. McCloughlin suggested figures that were considerably lower.[21]

Moody's third visit reinvigorated the British churches. He didn't work for any particular church or denomination. For this reason people of every branch of Christendom attended his meetings, and pastors and ministers were inspired once more to engage in evangelism. Church of England clergy, particularly in London, were once again encouraged by the revival services. While most of the Anglican clergy who supported Moody were evangelicals, a small number of London ritualist priests also threw in their lot with the cause.[22] According to Kent, Moody made a particular effort to get the support of those he called the 'High-Lows', a group of clergy who held to the evangelical insistence on personal conversion but also stressed the importance of Eucharist.[23] The Revd Hay Aitken, who had been a Church of England vicar in Liverpool, gave up his pastoral charge to become an evangelist. Aitken, like his father, Robert Aitken of Pendeen, was a popular preacher who combined his evangelicalism with

---

17 *The Birmingham Post*, January 1875.
18 *The Birmingham Post*, 19 January 1875.
19 *The Birmingham Post*, 19 January 1875, p. 285.
20 G. Davis, *Dwight L. Moody The Man and His Mission* (K.T. Boland, 1900), p. 108.
21 McLouglin, *Modern Revivalism*, pp. 200–1.
22 Kent, *Holding the Fort*, pp. 139–41 is of the view that most as far as most London ritualists were concerned Moody 'came too late'. For them 'Moody paid little attention to the doctrine of the church in what he said. Moody, indeed, often implied that infant baptism was more of a snare than a sacrament; he disapproved of auricular confession, which he thought was beyond the Protestant pale.'
23 Kent, *Holding the Fort*, p. 139.

certain High Church practices.[24] According to his biographer, F.B. Meyer, the distinguished Baptist minister, 'never forgot that he learned from Moody the art of winning men and women for Christ'.[25]

Moody's straight-forward, non-academic and practical way of teaching and explaining the Bible touched people's hearts. His humour and homely illustrations brought its message to life and helped thousands to see the relevance of Christianity. It was reported that during the time of Moody's meetings in Great Britain, the Bagster Publishing House could hardly keep pace with the demand for Bibles which he created.[26] F.B. Meyer (1847–1929), the Baptist minister from York, stated that 'no-one has given a greater impulse to Bible study than Mr Moody'.[27]

Moody's Appeal

It is the case that Moody and Sankey had greater appeal to the middle classes of society. Also, in some cities, such as Edinburgh for example, there was a higher proportion of women converts. Nevertheless, Moody attracted many from the upper classes. He gave afternoon Bible readings at the Queen's Opera House in the Haymarket which drew the wealthy and influential in large numbers. A witness reported that the roads in the vicinity were 'literally blocked with carriages of the aristocratic and plutocratic of the land'.[28] *The Record* reported that the 60 meetings held at the Opera House during the London Mission of 1875 drew an audience of 330,000 people.[29] During the London meetings Moody even preached to the boys of Eton College in a garden close to the school with a 150 boys and 4 masters in attendance. The occasion provoked hostility in High Church circles and even resulted in disaffected comments in the House of Lords.[30] Moody's ability to attract the support of the upper classes was important because the influence and financial backing of wealthy laymen such as Admiral Fishbourne (1811–87), Lord Radstock (1833–1913), Lord Cairns (1819–85), Lord Shaftesbury and W.F. Cowper-Temple (1811–88) was a vital ingredient in his success.

John Kent cited the comments of John Moorhouse who wrote from his vicarage that 'the great mass of godless working class have not yet been touched by American revivalists'.[31] He went on to suggest that Moody and

---

24 Kent, *Holding the Fort*, p. 140.
25 W.Y. Fullerton, *F.B. Meyer: A Biography* (Marshall, Morgan and Scott, second edition undated), pp. 32–3.
26 Moody, *The Life of Dwight L. Moody*, p. 148.
27 Moody, *The Life of Dwight L. Moody*, p. 148.
28 J.C. Pollock, *Moody without Sankey: A Biographical Portrait* (Hodder and Stoughton, 1963), p. 143.
29 *The Record*, 23 April 1875.
30 *The Times*, 22 June 1875.
31 Kent, *Holding the Fort*, p. 208.

Sankey failed to touch the working classes and that they really only engaged with the 'evangelical sub-culture' of the day.[32] James Findlay endorsed this view writing that 'in Scotland the soberest assessments, prepared by officials of churches generally sympathetic with Moody's work, spelled out his clear failure to reach the unchurched'.[33] Findlay went on to suggest that 'Moody himself was disappointed at the ineffectiveness of his revival in London to reach the unchurched poor' and that this was part of the reason why he founded the Training Institution in Chicago on his return home.[34] That said however, it is clear that when Moody was holding services in areas where the poor were located in large numbers his preaching and style was clearly effective. The Revd Thomas Richardson, of St Benet's Church in Stepney, reported that the effect of Moody and Sankey's meetings in the East End had been to make his church and congregation 'enlarge the place of their tent, and stretch forth the curtains of their habitation'. He went on to say that

> ... he had no doubt but that thousands of souls would be recorded in their various chapels and churches all over London by next year. His district visitors had sent in to him formal returns, showing that of 1,008 families in his parish, 672, or two families out of every three, had attended the services at Bow-road Hall .... He had something to say about the influence of the movement on the dock labourers. He had received testimony from several of the large docks that the men did not swear so much since Messrs Moody and Sankey came; praise God for that. Besides, drinking was not so prevalent among the dockmen, and that was the kind of work that the world believed in. He had been privileged to attend every service in Bow-road Hall, and he would thank God to all eternity for it .... He had had the privilege of conversing personally with 450 anxious souls; his wife had spoken to 150, and his curate had spoken to 100. There were 700 souls whose names and addresses they knew, and to whom they had written. Formerly, he had an after-meeting once a month; now he had one every Sunday evening, and not a Sunday passed without some souls being gathered in. The direct results of the meetings were seen in his church, his wife's Bible-class, his young men's meetings, and among his district visitors.[35]

---

32 Kent, *Holding the Fort*, pp. 356–68. See especially p. 363.
33 J.F. Findlay, *Dwight L. Moody American Evangelist 1837–1899* (Chicago Press, 1969), p. 173.
34 Findlay, *Dwight L. Moody*, p. 174. W.G. McLoughlin, *Revivals, Awakenings, and Reform* (University of Chicago Press, 1980), p. 144 also endorsed this view. He wrote that 'Moody had to admit that his revivals did not reach the poor in the cities.'
35 E.J. Goodspeed, *A Full History of the Wonderful Career of Moody and Sankey in Great Britain and America* (Concord, 1876), pp. 207–8.

John Coffee in his study of Moody and Sankey's mission to Britain 1873–5 interpreted the evidence differently,[36] as did John Pollock.[37] He cited *The Times* of June 1875 which reported that 'it is an error to say that they have not reached the lower strata of the life of London and of our large towns generally. It is no opinion but a fact that they have done so.'[38] Coffee also noted two other reports which testified to Moody and Sankey's ability to appeal to the poor. A special service for the unchurched which the two evangelists held in Sheffield was 'unmistakenly composed of the class for which the service was intended'.[39] At another in Liverpool, 'Rough ill-clad working men were there, and in the motley assemblage were sailors, dock labourers, and horny handed artisans, whom it was presumed had never been reached by a clergyman or minister.'[40] W.H. Daniels, who knew Moody personally, endorses Coffee's view with reports of his impact on the shipyards of Glasgow. Here he received a request signed by five hundred 'working men' to come and visit them during their noon lunch break. Moody and Sankey preached and sang for half an hour of their three-quarters of an hour lunch break. A large portion of the work force of 2,000 gathered every day for 20 minutes of prayer for some weeks and members of the revival services choir went and sang to the men twice a week for the first two months. In Birmingham Daniels reported that 'artisans in the manufactures crowded to the meetings in large numbers'.[41] Bishop Thorold of Rochester attended one of Moody's meetings at New Cross on 18 February 1884 and found the hall, which held 5,200, was packed.[42]

In London the revival meetings created a fresh burst of enthusiasm for Christian songs with errand boys reportedly whistling Sankey's tunes and barrel organs sounding out 'Hold the Fort' instead of 'Pop goes the Weasel'. Sankey's hymns were great favourites with many agricultural labourers whose union marches were accompanied along the streets by songs like 'God Speed the Plough' and 'God save Joseph Arch' sung to the tunes of *Sacred Songs and Solos*.[43]. The British series of *Sacred Songs and Solos* eventually sold more than 8 million copies world-wide. They were particularly suited to the

---

36 See J. Coffee, 'Democracy and Popular Religion: Moody and Sankey's Mission to Britain 1873–1875' in E.F. Biagini (ed.), *Citizens in Community* (Cambridge University Press, 1996), pp. 93–119.
37 Pollock, *Moody without Sankey*, p. 211. Pollock wrote: 'Despite this plutocratic base Moody effectively reached the lower classes.'
38 Pollock, *Moody without Sankey*, citing *The Times*, 23 June 1875.
39 Pollock, *Moody without Sankey*, citing *Sheffield Independent*, 1 January 1875.
40 Pollock, *Moody without Sankey*, citing *Nonconformist*, 17 February 1875, p. 1.
41 Daniels, *D.L. Moody*, p. 343.
42 C.H. Simpkinson, *The Life and Work of Bishop Thorold* (Isbister, 1896), p. 164.
43 Scotland, *Methodism and the Revolt of the Field*, pp. 104–5. For further evidence of Sankey's hymns among farm labourers see J.W. Robertson, *The Day Before Yesterday: Memories of an Uneducated Man* (Methuen, 1951), p. 92.

working masses because their short choruses were easily memorised by those unable to read. William Gladstone, who was leader of the Liberal opposition at the time of the London Crusade, thanked God that, 'I have lived to see the day when He should bless his church on earth with the gift of a man able to preach the gospel of Christ as we have just heard it preached.'[44] Archbishop Tait was somewhat guarded about the work of the two evangelists and whilst he rejoiced 'that the present movement is conducted on so great a scale with such apparent success', he remained 'apprehensive' about 'the after meetings for confession of sin and for guidance of conscience'. In what was a lengthy letter which he penned to Lord Cairns on 18 May 1875 he also noted 'that the great majority of those who have frequented these services hitherto have been the ordinary worshippers in churches and chapels, and that comparatively few from the neglected masses of society have been reached'.[45]

Accurate statistics of the numbers of converts are always hard to establish and Moody made things difficult on this score because he didn't make a serious effort to find out the numbers of those who professed faith in Christ. That said, there were some indicators of the success of the two evangelists. For example, after the meetings in Birmingham 2,000 applied for tickets in order to attend a special converts' meeting, with 1,400 professing faith in Christ and 600 still seeking. A Sunderland-based Methodist minister wrote to *The Christian* in 1881 informing readers that all the main branches of Methodism in the area had experienced significant growth in their circuit membership in 1876–7. The Wesleyan returns showed an increase of 24,227, the Primitive Methodists of 11,298 and the United Methodists 4,345.[46]

Later Years

Moody and Sankey came to the British Isles on two further occasions from 1881–4 and more briefly from November 1891 to November 1892. During his fourth visit he travelled to Scotland and Ireland, and conducted an extended campaign in London during which it is estimated that he spoke to over two million people. Anthony Thorold, the evangelical bishop of Rochester, was a welcoming supporter on their arrival in London. He attended one of their meetings and found Moody's address about copying Christ had 'rough power in it'.[47] Moody also spent a week preaching in both Oxford and Cambridge which

---

44 Pollock, *Moody without Sankey*, p. 140.
45 R. Davidson, and W. Benham, *Life of Archibald Cambell Tait* (MacMillan, 1891), pp. 507–10.
46 P.B. Morgan, 'A Study of the Work of American Revivalists in Britain from 1874–1914' (B.Litt. thesis, Oxford, 1961), p. 61.
47 Simpkinson, *The Life and Work of Bishop Thorold*, p. 164. Thorold had been a little disappointed at some aspects of Moody's visit in 1875, see Morgan, 'A Study of the Work of American Revivalists', p. 63, but warmed to Moody on the occasion of his second visit and entertained him to breakfast on 24 February 1884 – see p. 164.

subsequently resulted in a number of recent graduates offering themselves for the foreign mission field. They included Charles Studd, the England cricket captain.[48] On his last visit Moody went to Rome and the Holy Land but held a short campaign at the Metropolitan Tabernacle whose long-standing pastor had recently died.

On returning to his homeland Moody was acclaimed an international figure went to his childhood home at Northfield, Massachusetts. There he established an office from which he organized revival campaigns in some of America's major towns and cities. Moody and his family enjoyed the rural setting and found that the countryside provided a welcome retreat from the urban campaigns.

Revival and Revivalism

Moody was without doubt in the category of those who saw revival as a largely human endeavour. By careful planning and the right procedures he was of the view that a revival could be scheduled to begin at a particular venue. Moody saw revival as essentially large numbers of individuals accepting Christ's forgiveness through the cross and entering into personal relationship with Him. In keeping with some of his predecessors he regarded 'full consecration' as an important aspect of this relationship. Revival times will see the emergence of Christians who are wholly given and committed to God. Moody therefore stands as a 'revivalist' along with Finney, Caughey and the Palmers who saw revival not primarily as 'a surprising work of God' but rather an occasion that could be fostered, planned and promoted at a given time and place. That said, Moody avoided the hype and excitement that had often featured in the meetings of his predecessors such as Dow, Finney and Caughey. *The Times* of 1 December 1874 carried a report that 'emotion' as it had been known in the revivals of 1859 was absent from his meetings.

Moody taught a version of Pre-Millennialism which had become a feature of Evangelicalism on both sides of the Atlantic through the writings of John Nelson Darby and others. According to Kent, Moody came under Darby's direct influence 'from at least 1872, and always preached on the Second Coming'.[49] Darby and Moody certainly had contact with each other, both in England and the United States. On several occasions Moody invited Darby to speak at his meetings but Darby always declined because he could not share Moody's

---

48 See J.C. Pollock, *A Cambridge Movement* (John Murray, 1953), pp. 54–89 and N. Grubb, *C.T. Studd Cricketer and Pioneer* (Religious Tract Society, 1935), pp. 11–16.

49 Kent, *Holding the Fort*, p. 137. See also E.R. Sandeen, *The Roots of Fundamentalism* (University of Chicago, 1970). See also L.E. Dixon, 'The Importance of J.N. Darby and the Brethren Movement in the History of the Conservative Theology', *The Christian Brethren Review*, 1990, Vol. 41.

Arminian view of salvation.⁵⁰ He stated on a number of occasions that his conviction that Christ's return was imminent motivated him to wholehearted service and commitment. Moody also felt the inherent pessimism of Pre-Millennialism gave an added incentive to promote a Christian counter culture in British and American society.⁵¹ Moody's experience of the Baptism in the Holy Spirit revolutionised his Christian life and reinforced this desire. It led to his teaching a version of holiness that emphasized victorious Christian living. Indeed Moody often spoke of the importance of power for service. Apart from his stress on Pre-millennialism and the final estates of heaven and hell, Moody displayed a general lack of theology. To someone who told him that they didn't believe in his theology Moody replied, 'I didn't know I had any'!⁵²

Revival Methods

Preaching

Moody employed a number of distinctive methods in his campaigns. First and foremost his preaching had several marked features. His addresses and talks contrasted with many Evangelicals in both England and America who tended to follow the old style of text, doctrine and application.⁵³ Most often he preached on topics or themes and rather than staying on one passage or verse he would often expound a number of key texts from different books of the Bible on his chosen theme or topic. Moody was also particularly effective with his Bible characters such as the Good Samaritan and Daniel or 'Dan'l' as he liked to pronounce it. Moody's use of language was plain and colloquial, and he was always on a level with the man in the street. He used short sentences and rugged Anglo-Saxon words of everyday life.⁵⁴ Lord Shaftesbury 'thanked God publicly that Mr Moody had not been educated at Oxford for he had a wonderful power of getting to the hearts of men, and while the common people hear him gladly, many persons of high station have been greatly struck with the marvellous simplicity of his preaching'. Lord Shaftesbury added that the Lord Chancellor of England a short time before had said to him: 'the simplicity of that man's preaching, the clear manner in which he sets forth salvation by Christ, is to me the most striking and the most delightful thing I ever knew in my life'.⁵⁵

Moody was a fluent speaker who used a minimum of notes and for the most part spoke extemporaneously. He used a variety of speaking techniques

---

50 H.A. Ironside, *Historical Sketch of the Brethren Movement* (Zondervan, 1993), p. 81.
51 H.D. Foos, 'Moody, Dwight Lyman', in M. Couch, *Dictionary of Premillennial Theology* (Kregel, 1996), p. 273.
52 R. Hofstadter, *Anti-intellectualism in American Life* (Knopf, 1964), p. 108.
53 S. Sizer, *Gospel Hymns and Social Religion* (Ark Publishing, 1979), pp. 118–19.
54 See E.L. Pell, *Dwight L. Moody*, p. 521.
55 Moody, *The Life of Dwight L. Moody*, p. 217.

including satire, ridicule and humour. His preaching was also anecdotal. He would announce a particular point or truth and then would drive it home with a well-chosen anecdote or story. Coffee commented that he had the gift of telling stories with great vividness.[56] John Kent observed that what stood out in the addresses that he used in England in 1875 was 'the huge number of anecdotes, contemporary in character, and not the number of Biblical references'.[57] He also made good use of humour, his son commenting that 'he was not afraid to laugh and often made his audiences laugh in church'.[58] This was in stark contrast to the majority of ministers on both sides of the Atlantic who were increasingly trained to give critical sermons. These often had little application to the practical issues of life; Iain Murray wrote: 'His strength was in his spirit, his Sunday School simplicity and his 'superabundant anecdotes.'[59]

Moody's theology was straight-forward and orthodox as he laid before his hearers the simple choice between heaven and hell. The content of his addresses always focused on the loving Heavenly Father and the God of love, although on occasion he could portray hell in vivid terms. One writer was of the view that Moody outshone his competitors by putting the soft pedal on hell. In this emphasis Moody was in tune with the age in which many Protestant laity were retreating from the doctrines of hell and eternal punishment. Rather than believing the final estate of the wicked in terms of everlasting flames some were beginning to think of it as simply exclusion from the presence of God. On occasion Moody spoke of hell in terms of the break-up of the human family and heaven as the great centre of reunion, and he began to put the responsibility on the one who rejected salvation rather than on God. In essence therefore Moody's message was the gospel of God's fatherly love rather than the terrors of a Christ-less eternity. In explaining salvation Moody emphasized the substitutionary atonement and the resurrection of Jesus. The sins which Moody most often referred to in his addresses were largely personal such as drunkenness, the lusts of the body and over indulgence. He always impressed on his converts the importance of fostering a deep personal relationship with Jesus through the Holy Spirit. He also urged on his hearers the importance of knowing the power of the Holy Spirit for service.

In terms of lifestyle there is an emphasis on separateness in Moody's preaching particularly in regards to Sabbath breaking by such activities as boating, fishing and excursions requiring public transport. Moody also spoke out strongly against drunkenness, and hymns such as 'Hark the Temperance Bells are Ringing' and 'Out of Darkness into Light' were sung.[60] Moody, as a

---

56 Coffee, 'Democracy and Popular Religion', p. 102.
57 Kent, *Holding the Fort*, p. 170.
58 Kent, *Holding the Fort*, p. 197.
59 Murray, *Revival and Revivalism*, p. 401.
60 See I.D. Sankey, *Sacred Songs and Solos* (Marshall, Morgan and Scott, revised and enlarged edition, undated), No. 700 'Hark! The temperance bells are ringing' and No. 702 'Out of Darkness into Light' (temperance hymn) tune by Ira D. Sankey.

number of writers have pointed out, shared the widespread evangelical emphasis on the home as the place of stability which is why he often underlined the importance of the domestic sphere in his preaching. As far as Moody was concerned a solid home life would provide the answer to social ills of poverty and drunkenness.

Timing was of the essence, and Moody's sermons and addresses were of suitable length. One woman who heard Moody preach many times noted that 'he had the good judgement to cut his sermon to twenty five or thirty minutes if the crowd was large and the meeting long'.[61] Moody was also flexible as was illustrated on the first day of his Birmingham campaign on 17 January 1875. After the congregation had failed to enter into two of the hymns he had chosen he brought in 'the old hymn, "Guide me, Oh Thou Great Jehovah" in the place of the next one. This was sung 'with vigour'.[62]

Confidence in the Bible

Against the background of Darwinianism and the growing impact of Biblical criticism, many thoughtful Christians on both sides of the Atlantic were beginning to have doubts about the inspiration of the Bible. If its early history could no longer be trusted perhaps some of what was written in the New Testament was in doubt. Moody's straightforward use and application of the Bible to every-day living in his preaching, teaching and writing gave many a new sense of confidence. It is clear that Moody believed the Bible to be infallible and like the fundamentalists of his age always followed the most literal interpretation of the text and believed wholeheartedly in the universal nature of Noah's flood. He had no time for Biblical criticism and once remarked, 'What is the point of telling people there are two Isaiahs when most of them don't even know there was one!'[63]

Music and Song

Although Moody was not himself musical he recognized the vital and spiritual importance of music. Ira Sankey joined Moody as his musical director in 1872 and it was often said that 'Moody preached the gospel and Sankey sang it.' One who heard him stated: 'Mr Sankey possesses a voice of great volume, and he manages it with much skill though it has not been properly educated. His utterance is remarkably distinct, and he is able by himself to fill with vocal sound a building in which from 10,000 to 15,000 people are congregated.'[64] Sankey could thus deliver a message through song and lift the spirits of

---

61 Dorsett, *A Passion for Souls*, p. 184.
62 *The Birmingham Post*, 18 January 1875.
63 J. Harries, *G. Campbell Morgan* (Fleming H. Revell, 1930), p. 160.
64 *The Birmingham Daily Post*, 15 January 1875.

a congregation. Many of the songs that he sang began as solos, each with a chorus which could easily be memorised by the masses of his hearers who could not read.[65] A number of Sankey's songs presented a simple contrast between lost and wandering sinners lost in their sinfulness and the tender love and compassion of Christ. Others had a prodigal theme which urged the sinner, 'Come home, Come Home, you are weary at heart'. Sandra Sizer rightly emphasized the emphasis on intimacy in Moody's songs. The focus is not the distant creator God but Jesus who is loving and kind, charming and beautiful and who enfolds the sinner in his arms.[66] Among the most popular melodies were 'Jesus of Nazareth Passeth By', 'Hold the Fort' and 'There were Ninety and Nine that Safely Lay'. The 'Ninety and Nine' tells of the Saviour's love as he makes his bloodstained way through the thickets and deserts to rescue the lost sheep. The famous 'Holding the Fort' was based on an incident from the Civil War but still presenting the contrast between a lost world and the power of Jesus to save. Like William Booth, Sankey used the melodies of the music hall. His tunes were catchy and could be picked up easily so that people left the meetings humming the tunes in their minds or under their breath. Many of the melodies became household refrains in every place that Moody and Sankey went to and, as has been noted, were sung at trade-union meetings and other public gatherings. John Kent underlined the fact that the picture of heaven as the ideal home to which believers come or return, appealed particularly to women rather than men, although those with themes of weariness, disease and healing had a more universal appeal.[67]

It became customary for Moody's meetings to begin with half an hour of congregational singing mixed in with solos by Sankey. Indeed one of his great contributions to revivalism was to develop the massed choir. He understood the attraction and the power of many voices. The massed choir proved to be the vital means to captivate people in song in large halls that held audiences 10,000 and more. In fact what Sankey initiated became the key to success for several generations to come. Whilst it was undoubtedly the case that the majority of hymns that were used at the great revival meetings were gospel and testimonial in character, Sankey's collection also contained a number of classic hymns penned by the likes of Martin Luther, Charles Wesley, William Cowper, Reginald Heber, Horatius Bonar (a Free Church of Scotland minister), and some of the translations of the Anglo-Catholic ritualist, John Mason Neale.[68] Observers noted the great power that emanated from the singing at Moody and

---

65 See Pollock, *Moody without Sankey*, p. 143.
66 Sizer, *Gospel Hymns*, pp. 33–5.
67 Kent, *Holding the Fort*, p. 225.
68 Sandra Sizer's comment (*Gospel Hymns*, p. 130) that 'doctrinal hymns of the sort found in Watts's collections are virtually absent from the gospel hymns' is substantially the case, though it should be noted that the Gospel section (Nos 355–499) does include one by W. Cowper, J.M. Neale, J. Newton and W. Walsham How and two by H. Bonar and C. Wesley.

Sankey's meetings. *The Birmingham Daily Post* reported that at the evening meeting in the Bingley Hall on 18 January 1875, 'the Old Hundredth was sung with the utmost fervour' and 'with remarkable effect' and 'such a volume of harmony as perhaps has never before been heard in Bingley Hall'.[69] At the peak of his campaigning Moody was selling 250,000 songbooks a month. Commenting on the enduring quality of Sankey's music John Kent commented that *Sacred Songs and Solos* remained an active symbol of the revival long after the printed volumes of Moody's sermons and addresses had been wholly forgotten.'[70]

Prayer

For Moody prayer gatherings were a vital ingredient in all his revival campaigns. Shortly before Moody began his London campaign in March 1875 a letter from him had been published in *The Christian* in which he urged the establishment of noonday prayer meetings all over the country. As Moody's organization became more developed they were organized in every town or city both before Moody's arrival and during his campaign. Moody regarded the noonday prayer meetings as a vital part of his mission strategy. They were attended for the most part by businessmen and others who could spare the time during their lunch breaks. He saw these occasions as an opportunity for women to participate in the work. Large numbers participated in Moody's prayer meetings. Between two and three thousand were reported at Manchester and a similar number in Birmingham. Some of the Liverpool meetings attracted between four and five thousand.[71] Moody revolutionised the traditional evangelical prayer meeting. People were urged to sit close together and the prayers were interspersed with lively singing of new songs. Another feature was the recitation of key biblical texts that were designed to create an environment of faith. Moody's stress was always on brevity. Again and again he stressed that prayers must be short. On one occasion when he was enduring a rather sluggish prayer time, he banged his hands on the table and said: 'Gentlemen some men's prayers need to be cut in the middle and set on fire at both ends!' At another meeting in London in 1884, a young doctor, Wilfred T. Grenfell, was attracted by Moody shutting down a clergyman's tedious prayer with the words, 'While our brother is finishing his prayer we will sing number 75.' Grenfell, who was impressed, later went out as a medical missionary to Labrador. Moody also urged that people's prayers be practical: 'There is no use in asking God to do things you can do yourself.'

---

69 *The Birmingham Daily Post*, 19 January 1875.
70 Kent, *Holding the Fort*, p. 154.
71 *Narrative of Messrs Moody and Sankey's Labors in Great Britain and Ireland* (Supplementary Issue 4), pp. 97–8.

Sacred Songs and Solos contained a section of hymns and songs for use at prayer meetings a number of which had been set to music by Sankey himself.[72] Also included were hymns by individuals such as Bishop Edward Bickersteth, Charles Wesley and Fanny Crosby. One can imagine that songs such as 'What A Friend we have in Jesus' with its chorus of 'take it to the Lord in prayer' must have added a strong note of fervency to the proceedings. R.W. Dale vividly recalled the impact of one of Moody's prayer meetings in the winter of 1875. 'A prayer meeting with an address, at eight o'clock on a damp cold January morning, was hardly the kind of thing – let me say it frankly – that I should generally regard as attractive; but I enjoyed it heartily; it seemed one of the happiest meetings I had ever attended; there was warmth and there was sunlight in it.'[73]

The Inquiry Room

Moody had a real capacity to help men and women make a personal commitment of their lives to Christ. He did not however share Finney's tactic of the anxious bench whereby converts and those under conviction were brought to the front of the meeting. He possibly was of the opinion that too much emotional pressure was being put on individuals to make such a decision. It was not therefore his general practice to give a final plea for converts to get up out of their seats and move to the area near the preaching platform. He felt that forcing penitents to allow their feelings to be seen by the rest of the congregation was to violate their integrity. When inviting his audiences to partake in what he termed 'instant salvation' or the decision to come to Christ, Moody therefore asked people to go out of the building to a separate inquiry room. There he began what he styled an 'after meeting' in which trained helpers assisted the inquirers to clarify the decision they were making.

In order to bring his hearers to the inquiry room Moody usually adopted the following procedure. First, he created an atmosphere in which his hearers could all be still and consider their position before God. Then he would challenge them to make a public confession by standing up, following which they would be invited to the inquiry room. Thus at Birmingham for example, he ended his address on 18 January 1875 by begging all present to join in silent prayer. Then after a brief period Sankey sang to great effect

> Come home! Come home you who are weary in heart;
> For the way has been dark, and so lonely and wild;
> Oh! prodigal child, come home;
> Oh come home.

---

72 Sankey, *Sacred Songs and Solos*. See Nos 303–33.
73 A.W. Dale, *Life of R.W. Dale of Birmingham* (Hodder and Stoughton, 1898), p. 318.

Following this Moody urged them to join in silent prayer with heads bowed, after which he invited all who wished to be prayed for and to be on the Lord's side to stand up fearlessly. Then while another hymn was sung all who had stood were asked to make their way to the inquiry room.[74]

He began this practice in England at Newcastle his goal being to make 'personal contact' with inquirers. He usually gave a short talk and then his helpers went individually to talk with those who had come into the room. Sometimes songs were sung in the 'After-Meetings' such as No. 335 'Why not Tonight?', No. 348 'Why Waitest Thou?' with music by Sankey. Heated debate or questioning was not allowed on these occasions. The only people Moody engaged with were those who wanted to become Christians. At Newcastle it was reported that 'Mr Moody speaks to the inquirers with an open Bible in his hands, fixing them down to the Word of God, and anchoring their souls on the living rock of Holy Scripture.' The same writer went on to relate that 'he gets them on their knees in prayer; and I have seen them rising from his side by twos and threes, wiping their eyes, and smiling through their tears, confessing Christ'.[75]

Moody evidently on occasion encountered criticism for his use of the Inquiry Room usually from those who doubted immediate conversion. To them Moody's response was to hold up examples such as the man with leprosy who was made immediately clean.[76] During his campaign in Birmingham in January 1875, Moody took time at a midday meeting to justify his practice. He stressed that the inquiry room was in fact no novelty or innovation and quoted a number of texts to show that 'persons in the time of Christ and his apostles were in the habit of making inquiries'. He showed for example, 'how Christ's disciples went to Him, saying, "Declare unto us the parable of the tares in the field" and how Christ received them kindly, and complied with their request. He believed that if more enquiry meetings were held now-a-days people would not be drifting towards the Church of Rome.'[77]

Moody himself often wandered among the inquirers to see what progress was being made. Dorsett rightly emphasized that Moody's inquiry meetings were a most important aspect of the meetings. R.W. Dale of Birmingham reflected that 'without the after-meeting, the preaching would not have accomplished one fifth of its results'.[78] Moody's ability at securing instant conversion was a major aspect of his effectiveness. It was probably because he was so effective at it that he incurred so little criticism on this score. It was in

---

74 *The Birmingham Daily Post*, 19 January 1875.
75 *Narrative of Messrs Moody and Sankey's Labors in Great Britain and Ireland*, p. 14.
76 *The Birmingham Daily Post*, 19 January 1875.
77 *The Birmingham Daily Post*, 23 January 1875.
78 Dale, *The Life of R.W. Dale of Birmingham*, p. 319.

consequence of this fact that Iain Murray observed that 'from the 1870s "decisionist evangelism" became a permanent part of the British scene'.[79]

All Day Meetings

These were only held perhaps once or twice during a campaign. They were of course very demanding on Moody himself. They were however 'novel' and attracted a great deal of attention. W.H. Daniels detailed one such meeting at York.[80] First there was an hour of confession and prayer; second an hour for praise; third a promise meeting which consisted of promises in their own experiences; fourth a witness meeting which was a succession of public confessions of Christ by young converts; fifth a Bible lecture by Mr Moody; and finally a communion service, conducted by Mr Moody and four ministers who were present in the Presbyterian style. Two such all-day meetings were also held at Newcastle.[81]

Publicity

Following in the steps of his predecessors Moody recognized the value of publicity. This was an aspect of his work in which he became increasingly adept. He seemed to have a particular gift in persuading the secular and religious press to report his meetings in other towns and cities. This helped to create both interest and anticipation. Thomas Cree, who was in charge of the arrangements for Moody's Philadelphia meetings, estimated that over fifty thousand handbills were distributed to the public each week of the campaign.[82] Before the London meetings in 1873, thousands of copies of *The Christian* which reported Moody's missions in Scotland and Ireland and the large manufacturing cities of the north of England, were circulated among the ministers of London. Moody asked for the sum of £2,000 so that copies of the paper could be sent to ministers all over England.[83] At the time of Moody's London campaign the secularist *National Reformer* complained of the 'large posters, seven feet broad, the patrols of sandwich men and the unlimited advertising'.[84] Moody was particularly keen on house-to-house visiting in conjunction with his campaigns. Thus at Liverpool for example in 1875, a concerted effort was made to visit every house during the time when meetings were being held. The parochial-boundary difficulties were overcome by using

---

79 Murray, *Revival and Revivalism*, p. 404.
80 Daniels, *D.L. Moody*, p. 243.
81 Daniels, *D.L. Moody*, p. 263.
82 Findlay, *Dwight L. Moody*, p. 199.
83 See Kent, *Holding the Fort*, p. 136.
84 *National Reformer* 13 June 1875, p. 378 cited Coffee, 'Democracy and Popular Religion', p. 99.

only lay people in both the organization and the visiting.[85] Similarly in North London the Revd R.C. Billing organized a large scale visitation programme in preparation for Moody's visit which included following up inquirers after the campaign was concluded.[86]

His Interdenominational Sympathies

Moody was adamant that there should be no divisions in the church. Christians should present a united front and they shouldn't pick holes in one another's theology. Moody always tried to work with local ministers and clergy. He was humble and recognized it wasn't just his work, but that God was working through him. Moody refused invitations to come and speak or hold campaigns unless the support of local clergy and lay leaders was guaranteed beforehand. Moody sought to honour and recognize local clergy and gave them a place on the platform. Not only did Moody choose not to put down other theologies including Calvinism, he actively despised sectarianism and spoke against it in his sermons, maintaining it to be a barrier to revival. His conviction was 'Christ loved all men and so should we.'[87] In London Moody spoke in secular buildings from the start, a move which dispelled any thought that he might be favouring one particular denomination, and which made it easier for those who had no church attachment to attend. When Moody accepted the invitation of the Revd Arthur Rees, a local Baptist minister, he insisted on holding the meetings in the Victoria Hall to avoid sectarian divisions.[88] The invitation to Moody to come to Liverpool in November 1874 was given by 86 clergymen and ministers. In the account of the Albert Hall meeting in Sheffield, it is notable that ministers of all denominations within the town joined the meeting and that at the end of the gathering the 'vast assemblage' of up to three thousand were 'engaged in silent prayer. It was an impressive scene'.[89]

Before the commencement of Moody's 1875 London campaign a Preliminary Meeting of Ministers was held on Friday 5 February in the Freemasons Hall attended by 'nearly two thousand persons representing all the evangelical churches ... and there was beside a contingent from the ritualistic clergy'.[90] At a farewell gathering in London of the seven hundred and odd ministers who were present there were 188 belonging to the Church of England, 154 Congregationalists, 85 Baptists, 81 Wesleyan Methodists, 39 Presbyterians, 8 foreign pastors, 8 United Methodists, 7 Primitive Methodists, 3 Plymouth Brethren, 2 Countess of Huntingdon's Connection, 2 Society of Friends, 3 Free Church of England, 1 Bible Christian and

---

85 *The Christian*, 18 March 1875.
86 *The Christian*, 25 March 1875.
87 E.L. Pell, *Dwight L. Moody His Life, His Work, His Words* (B.F. Johnson Publishing, 1900), p. 539.
88 Daniels, *D.L. Moody*, pp. 246–7.
89 Pollock, *Moody without Sankey*, p. 60.
90 Moody, *The Life of Dwight L. Moody*, p. 203.

upwards of 20 whose allegiance was not known. These figures, which were taken from an official statement supplied at the meeting, demonstrate the catholic and non-sectarian character of Moody and Sankey and their ability to work with a wide range of theologies and backgrounds. It was this ability which contributed in large measure to their success.

The Poor

Coming himself from a relatively modest background Moody was always mindful of the poor. He frequently saw to it that where possible meetings were held nearer to the places of the people who were unlikely to travel to them. He worked with the poor, collected for the poor and spoke the language of the poor. His son noted that his father made deliberate efforts to go the 'crowded districts' of London, where the poor could easily attend.[91] During his four-month period in London in 1875 for a time Moody ran two meetings per evening, one in Bow in the East End, and another in the Haymarket, thereby in one day preaching to audiences that represented both ends of the continuum of British Society.[92]

In his earlier years Moody shared the general evangelical emphasis on charity, as was witnessed by his concern for the soldiers of the Civil War and the victims of the great Chicago fire. Of those early days he remarked on more than one occasion, 'When I was at work for the City Relief Society before the fire I used to go to a poor sinner with the Bible in one hand and a loaf of bread in the other .... My idea was that I could open a poor man's heart by giving him a load of wood ... but I soon found that he wasn't any more interested in the Gospel on that account.'[93] But by the 1870s and 1880s he changed his tune along with many others. According to Marsden, Moody dropped direct social involvement for the same reason that he avoided controversial theology, namely that they both deflected him from his primary concern which was evangelism.[94] Moody, along with Spurgeon and others, remained compassionate to the poor but regarded evangelism as his first and primary concern. That said, we need to take note of the fact that temperance work became increasingly important in Moody's second mission to Britain. *The Methodist Recorder* of 28 May 1875 reported that on the Thursday night Sankey had given out temperance as the subject. Whilst he was in London in 1882 temperance meetings were held every Saturday evening in the hall at Wandsworth and at Southampton a Blue Ribbon meeting accompanied the work of Moody and Sankey.[95]

---

91 Moody, *The Life of Dwight L. Moody*, p. 271.
92 Moody, *The Life of Dwight L. Moody*, p. 271.
93 See D.L. Moody, *Echoes from the Pulpit and Platform* (A.D. Worthington, 1900), p. 31 cited by Marsden, *Fundamentalism and American Culture*, pp. 36–7.
94 Marsden, *Fundamentalism and American Culture*, p. 37.
95 *The Christian*, 7 December 1882.

Style and Lifestyle

Moody proved an appealing figure in both Britain and America. At a time when people in London were reacting against ritualism and priestcraft he presented himself as a smartly dressed layman. He had an air of the businessman's efficiency about him which was particularly appealing to both the lower middle-classes and to the aristocracy. The Revd Lyman Abbott, writing shortly before Moody's death in 1899, recalled his impression of Moody in the guise of a businessman: 'As he stood on the platform he looked like a business man; he dressed like a business man; he took the meeting in hand as a business man would ...'[96] *The Spectator* of March 1875 remarked that 'Messrs Moody and Sankey appear business-like, amiable, at heart modest, and thoroughly sincere men.' Moody's style and manner was altogether calmer than that of his predecessors such as Lorenzo Dow, Charles Finney or James Caughey. There was no hysterical enthusiasm, holy shout or people falling to the ground in large numbers.

Moody's Impact

Moody and Sankey introduced revivalism in both America and Britain on the scale of big business and initiated what was in effect a new era of mass evangelism. Without question Moody 'awakened' an enormous number of people on both sides of the Atlantic. His revival services touched all levels of society including the unskilled and manual workers, re-invigorated church life, inspired evangelism and impacted the missionary movement. Indeed in 1889 Moody established *The Bible Institute for Home and Foreign Missions* in Chicago. Moody's campaigns, which were built on a foundation of prayer and the inquiry room, brought a fresh burst of song and music into church life. The songs of Philip Bliss and Fanny Crosby became popular in churches and Sunday schools frequented by ordinary citizens of America and the British Isles. By the Second World War 90 million copies of Sankey's *Sacred Songs and Solos* had been sold by British publishers alone. Hymns such as those of P.P. Bliss and Fanny Crosby that were favourites in the revival of 1873–5 remained popular at evangelical gatherings 80 years later. Moody and Sankey opened the way for the development of mass evangelism that was to follow in the twentieth century. Their interdenominational approach, extensive use of publicity, meticulous organization and advance preparation of local churches established a pattern of urban revivalism which was to follow and last for the greater part of the twentieth century. As a result of Moody's endeavours evangelistic work became increasingly professionalized. The generation which followed Moody all felt it was necessary to have a singer to work with them. Moody also endorsed those Evangelicals who sought to work with the poor. He was concerned for

---

96 Marsden, *Fundamentalism and American Culture*, p. 32 citing D.L. Moody, *Echoes from Pulpit and Platform* (A.D. Worthington, 1900), p. 31.

the education of the poor. In 1879 he opened a preparatory school for girls and shortly afterwards one for boys in the town of Gill, Connecticut. Marsden summed up Moody's influence by stating that

> Scarcely a leader in American Protestantism in the next generation, it seemed, had not at some time been influenced by Moody. He was a transitional figure in an age of rapid change, yet he helped to make some characteristics of that age lasting parts of the revivalist tradition.[97]

---

97 Marsden, *Fundamentalism and American Culture*, p. 33.

CHAPTER 8

Edward Payson Hammond and Children's Revivalism

Early Years

Edward Payson Hammond was born in Ellington, a quiet valley town in Connecticut, on 1 September 1831 but passed his boyhood days in Vermont. His parents Elijah and Esther Griswold Hammond were firm believers and he was nurtured in the Christian faith. At the age of 17 he was impacted by a powerful revival at Southington where he attended school. He went on to attend Williams College where he was noted for his zeal in spreading the gospel among his fellow students. One of his tutors, Professor Chadbourne, later recalled 'the zeal that stirred his heart when a Freshman'.[1] He received his BA degree in 1858 and an MA in 1861. In 1858 Edward who had planned to be a missionary entered on a two-year course of study at Union Theological Seminary in New York. He then went on to complete his studies at the Free Church Theological College in Edinburgh during which time he received a clear call from God to become a children's evangelist. He had worked in New York during the great revival of 1859 of which he was a staunch defender. He wrote that 'the Revival is not a failure, but a glorious triumph over the powers of darkness. You have only to read the books that have been published in America giving reliable accounts of the glorious results of the work, to be convinced that the Revival in anything but a failure.'[2]

Whilst engaged in his studies at Edinburgh Edward began to feel it 'necessary for my soul that I should be engaged in some kind of evangelistic work'.[3] He sought through the help of the college authorities to find a sphere of work at precisely the time that the declining congregation in Musselburgh were asking for a pastor to supply their pulpit. Young Hammond at once agreed to go down and preach at their Sunday services. Within a very short space of time a visitor to the church found the vestry 'quite full of children' and was deeply impressed at the way in which Hammond adapted himself to the children and 'talked as well to their understanding as to their hearts'. The observer couldn't help but notice 'the number of young lads, ragged-looking collier lads, fisher

---

1 P.C. Headley, *The Reaper and the Harvest: scenes in connection with the work of the Holy Spirit in the Life and Labours of the Rev E. Payson Hammond* (Marshall, Morgan and Scott, undated), p. 42.
2 Headley, *The Reaper and the Harvest*, p. 49.
3 Headley, *The Reaper and the Harvest*, p. 54.

lads and that class of young men ... who seemed ... almost beyond the reach of evangelistic efforts'.[4] The whole company was engaged in vibrant singing after which they went down on their knees and joined together in prayer for one another and for those who were mourning over their sins. Hammond worked on studying by day and preaching each night amid the excitement of a revival. He soon introduced American melodies and his manner of conducting the meetings was 'bright and sharp'.[5]

Such was Edward Hammond's success that the church soon extended a call to him to become their permanent pastor. However his heart was set on evangelism and he shortly afterwards accepted an invitation from six churches and five ministers of Haddington to hold a series of meetings there. For a week meetings were held in different churches and the old cathedral which seated 500 people, where John Knox had preached, was filled. Soon after this assignment had been completed Edward travelled south to the Suffolk coast of England and held a series of meetings at Lowestoft and other nearby villages. Here he tried both to awaken the people to the reality of Christ and salvation and at the same time to promote a better observance of the Sabbath. The latter objective was of particular concern in the neighbourhood because many of the fishermen were taking their boats out on the day of rest and worship. One surviving account advertised: 'On Wednesday last, the 18th, a full meeting was held at the National School-room, Gorleston, for the purpose of promoting the better observance of the Lord's Day, and especially among the owners, masters, and men, of the fishing boats in that village. Among those present were ... the Revd E.P. Hammond from New York.'[6] The report went on that

> Mr Hammond was introduced and commenced speaking of what had already been done in the adjoining towns. In Lowestoft and vicinity large public meetings had been held, attended by the most influential of the residents and by many of the boat-owners and fishermen; and pledges were now being circulated there, and had been signed in large numbers. In Southwold all of the boat-owners and fishermen had given their pledges against Saturday night and Sunday fishing. In Pakefield and Kessingland there was almost a universal feeling in its favour. In Kessingland especially they were anxious for both nights' fishing to be given up. The only excuse he found offered for Sunday fishing was that others practised it .... Mr H. spoke of the physical argument in favour of making the Sabbath a day of rest after the toils of the week, even as the night is for the rest after the labours of the day. This was the divine plan, and those

---

4 Headley, *The Reaper and the Harvest*, p. 55.
5 Headley, *The Reaper and the Harvest*, p. 62.
6 Headley, *The Reaper and the Harvest*, pp. 78–9.

Revd Edward Payson Hammond

who infringed the laws of nature, and especially of the decalogue, will sooner or later find themselves the losers.[7]

Hammond went on his address to give an account of the recent revivals which he had witnessed in America, Ireland and Scotland and indicated the ways in which they had contributed to a better observance of the Sabbath. He ended with an interesting story of a weather-beaten battleship he had once observed being towed into New York harbour, its rudder gone, sails tattered and torn. What would you have thought, he asked the congregation, if the officers had immediately ordered the battered vessel back out to sea? Such inhuman conduct we all condemn and are we not even more guilty if we refuse our fishermen the rest and privileges of the Sabbath?

Despite the vigour and enthusiasm with which Mr Hammond pursued the Sabbath cause on this occasion he seems to have had subsequent doubts about the wisdom of it. He wrote of his time in Suffolk: 'It was a mistake trying to combine the two things. Had I devoted my whole energies to the revival of religion and the conversion of souls, I think I would, though indirectly, have done more for the promotion of the better observance of the Sabbath.'[8] Whilst it was the case that a number of holiness revivalists pursued the Sabbath day agenda as part of their revival strategy, it ceased to be a major focal aspect of Hammond's revival strategy.

---

7 Headley, *The Reaper and the Harvest*, p. 79.
8 Headley, *The Reaper and the Harvest*, p. 78.

Following his time in South-East England, Hammond returned to Scotland and visited Huntly and spoke at two days of open-air meetings which had been organized by the Duchess of Gordon, who had expended the equivalent of $2,000 in putting on free trains to bring people to and from the meetings. *The British Herald* reported that 'A great work of grace has been going on for a considerable period in different parts of some of the northern counties of Scotland, particularly in Aberdeenshire and Bamffshire.'[9] In November 1860, Edward Hammond was invited to Tillicoultry where the Lord 'owned his labours, and he spent a precious week with us'. The meetings, which were held at the Popular Institute Hall, grew in numbers until 1,400 were present at the last occasion. A Glasgow newspaper noted that at each evening at the close of the address there was a separate second gathering called 'The Inquiry Meeting' and that towards the end of the week two or three hundred attended it. Most who did so wanted to commit their lives to Christ while a few were either curious or wanted to mock the proceedings. These inquiry meetings later became an integral part of Hammond's revival services and were adapted for the needs of his children's campaigns.

After Tillicoultry similar meetings were held in the vicinity of Glasgow. At Motherwell and Wishaw, in the great coal region of Scotland there were 'rich displays of the Holy Spirit's victorious might' as strong men 'bowed before his presence, and declared, in the great congregation, what God had wrought in their behalf'.[10] The *Edinburgh Mercury* reported 'the intense religious anxiety manifested by the multitude' at the close of the meeting in the public school at Wishaw with about three hundred remaining for the inquirers meeting. Both 'the poor and illiterate' and 'men and women of education and superior circumstances' had been impacted. The men were dealt with by themselves in one room and women on their own in another room. One observer stated that 'he had seen nothing like the religious revival he had then witnessed ... and could not but thank God from the bottom of his heart, for the indefatigable labours of his brother, Mr Hammond, through whom this great awakening had taken place. Mr H., he believed, was specially fitted for breaking up the fallow ground, and commencing a series of revival meetings'.[11]

One of the places that Hammond visited after Wishaw was the small town of Anann in Southern Scotland where he arrived on 12 January 1861 and stayed for two weeks. Ebenezer Young, the pastor of Independent Congregational Church in Anan, reported that the youth 'have been abundantly blessed' and that it seemed to him 'as if all the young men were converted'. The same writer observed that 'Very blessed has been the work among the children, and especially among such as had been under Sabbath school instruction,'[12] More

---

9 Cited Headley, *The Reaper and the Harvest*, p. 81.
10 Headley, *The Reaper and the Harvest*, p. 94
11 Headley, *The Reaper and the Harvest*, p. 95.
12 Headley, *The Reaper and the Harvest*, p. 107.

than a year later he still vividly recalled 'the enormously crowded meetings' with the United Presbyterian Church, the largest place of worship in town, 'filled to overflowing' and 'the country for many miles around deeply awakened'.[13] Sometimes the meetings had to held in two churches at once with Mr Hammond speaking first at one and then at the other. On a number of occasions the inquiry meetings lasted till after two in the morning.[14] A number of positive results were seen to stem from Hammond's campaign. There were many conversions with 'the professed converts holding out well'. Among those who were taking 'deep interest in religion' since the revival were 'a vast number of young men, many of them energetic and active, and some of them persons of influence'.[15] The intemperate had been reformed with many now 'clothed and in their right minds'[16] and 'the children of God have had their faith greatly strengthened'.[17] Later in January Hammond went on to Dumfries where the work of revival was seen 'with a fervor even greater than was witnessed at Annan'. *The Dumfries Standard* of 30 January reporting that long before the service on the Sunday evening 'the large and spacious church' in which the Revd Dr Wood ministers was 'crowded in every part, while hundreds were pressing around the door eager to obtain entrance, but could not'. In consequence the Congregational chapel was opened and a second service held. Many, according to the local paper, 'suffered great mental anguish from the discovery of their sin against the God of love. The tears were flowing plentifully while ... others found peace to their troubled conscience.'[18]

After his time in Scotland, Edward Hammond went briefly to London before going to Liverpool where he boarded the *Great Eastern* for Canada. In the nation's capital he preached in St James's Hall, his discourse lasting for nearly an hour 'in a strain that was peculiar, remarkable, and exceedingly fitted to be useful'. It was, said the report in *The British Standard,* 'stamped by godly simplicity'.[19]

Hammond returned to the British Isles with his new wife for a brief visit in 1867 preaching in both Scotland and London. Following a short spell in Edinburgh Hammond received an invitation from the Revd William Reid and the former lawyer turned Evangelist, Gordon Furlong, to go to Carlisle. This was followed by three weeks in Cardiff where the meetings, which were in the city's largest hall, were filled to capacity and 'hundreds of all ages professed conversion'.[20] Weston-Super-Mare was Hammond's next assignment. The main inspiration had come from the Revd Dr R.G. Walker and Lord Cavan of the

---

13 Headley, *The Reaper and the Harvest*, p. 113.
14 Headley, *The Reaper and the Harvest*, p. 113.
15 Headley, *The Reaper and the Harvest*, p. 114.
16 Headley, *The Reaper and the Harvest*, p. 115.
17 Headley, *The Reaper and the Harvest*, p. 115.
18 Headley, *The Reaper and the Harvest*, p. 119.
19 Headley, *The Reaper and the Harvest*, p. 197.
20 Headley, *The Reaper and the Harvest*, p. 446.

Church of England but all the churches united behind them.[21] Before he left the area Edward Hammond responded to an invitation from George Muller to hold services at his orphanage in Ashley Down where there were 1,150 orphans. Hammond made use of the inquiry room, and many children were deeply affected and responded to the call to make a personal commitment. Hammond wrote, 'I think it would be safe to say that at the close of my address nearly all of that great gathering were bathed in tears, although there had been no special appeals to their feelings, only a simple proclamation of the gospel.'[22]

London and the Children's Special Service Mission

Shortly after this Hammond was invited by the Hon. and the Revd Baptist Noel[23] and others to come to London to hold a series of union services in the nation's capital. It was a campaign that lasted for 16 weeks and led to the founding of what became known as the Children's Special Service Mission. The meetings with children were marked by a deep repentance with many boys and girls weeping with conviction over their sins. Hammond also held meetings for young women at Noel's church. Many 'sobbed aloud with a deep conviction of God's presence'. Among those 'the scores of youthful mourners' were children of five and six years of age.[24] Meetings were also held twice a week at Surrey Chapel where Newman Hall was pastor. At the close of the first meeting Newman Hall invited any children and others who were spiritually anxious to come to the schoolroom. There an observer reported a solemn scene with 'very many children sorrowfully weeping'.[25] Later that day they had a tea meeting at John Street Chapel for children and youths who believed they had been brought to Christ through Mr Hammond's meetings. It was attended by 350 children and 70 adults. Baptist Noel also took the opportunity to address the teachers and office-bearers and urged them not to hinder the work 'by standing aloof from it'.[26] His words bore fruit with many Sunday school teachers and other members of the chapel engaging in the work of speaking to inquirers and counselling those who were anxious. The John Street meetings continued on a twice-weekly basis with one hundred to a hundred and fifty children in attendance.[27] Meetings were also held at Greenwich organized by the Revd

---

21 Hammond, *The Conversion of Children*, p. 17.
22 E.P. Hammond, *Early Conversion* (Paternoster and Alabaster, undated), p. 105.
23 Baptist Wriothesley Noel (1798–1873) was educated at Westminster School and Trinity College, Cambridge, took Anglican orders and became the evangelical incumbent of St John's Chapel, Bedford Row, London. He became a Baptist in 1848 and ministered at John Street Baptist Chapel, London 1849–68.
24 Headley, *The Reaper and the Harvest*, p. 455.
25 Headley, *The Reaper and the Harvest*, p. 456. See also J.C. Pollock, *The Good Seed* (Hodder and Stoughton, 1959), p. 17.
26 Headley, *The Reaper and the Harvest*, p. 457.
27 Headley, *The Reaper and the Harvest*, p. 464.

Benjamin Davis. At one of the meetings at Maize Hill, Hammond asked all who had found Jesus to go into the vestry and none were allowed in who did not really believe they had come to Christ. On that occasion, 110 children were found to have made a personal commitment and experienced peace with God.

One of the most significant aspects of Hammond's labours in London was a series of children's meetings at the Metropolitan Tabernacle. On the Sunday morning service immediately preceding them, Charles Spurgeon preached a sermon in which he urged the people to pray for great blessing and do all they could to assist Mr Hammond in the work. In the afternoon the tabernacle was crowded with an audience of no less than six thousand to listen to Hammond's earnest address. Although it was primarily a service for children many adults were also present. A marked feature of the meeting was that every single child had a leaflet containing hymns reprinted from Hammond's *Hymns of Salvation*. Many of the children had evidently practised the hymns beforehand since the whole audience knew them and sang them in a most moving manner. At the close of gathering two inquiry meetings were held, one in the lecture hall and one in the tabernacle. One of those involved in those meetings estimated that 'from two thousand to three thousand were convicted of sin and brought to Christ'.[28]

As these meetings progressed Hammond was concerned to pass on his method to others in England. A number of men including Samuel Spiers, Tom Bond Bishop, Samuel Tyler, R. Westwall and others took up the work. Spiers in particular warmed to Hammond's emphasis on love rather than fear and was much taken with his anecdotes and melodic hymns especially the one with a haunting refrain, 'Yes, Jesus loves me, The Bible tells me so'. Spiers later stated that if he had heard preaching of the kind that Edward Payson Hammond gave he would have given his heart to Christ at least ten years earlier. Whilst many Sunday school teachers sought to distance themselves from Hammond's approach, thinking that young children were not capable of understanding the finer points of creedal Christianity, Spiers came to the view that these special services were exactly what was needed to bridge the gap between the often rather dull Sunday school meetings and the child expressing personal faith in Christ.

When Hammond went on to continue his London campaign south of the Thames, Spiers felt that his special services needed to continue. He discussed the matter with his friend the artist, Thomas John Hughes, who agreed to offer his house for the first such meeting if Spiers would invite the children and run the service.[29] Shortly before eight o'clock in the evening of 2 June 1867 14 children arrived and were greeted by Mrs Hughes. Spiers sang and taught them hymns with memorable choruses and told them Bible stories in a way that made

---

28 Hammond, *Early Conversion*, p. 19.
29 T.B. Bond, *T.B.B. of the C.S.S.M A Memoir of Tom Bond Bishop, for Fifty-three Years Honorary Secretary of the Children's Special Service Mission* (Children's Special Service Mission, 1923), p. 41.

friendship with Jesus seem real. Each subsequent week the children were back with more of their friends such that by the autumn it was clear that the experiment was a success. At the committee meeting held on 1 August 1868 the secretary gave a brief review of the first year's activities. It included the following lines:

> On Sat eve July 13th 1867 some children / about seventeen / were taken to the Rev E.P. Hammond's services for children at St John's Chapel, and again on the following Sat Eve July 20th. On the latter occasion it was felt most important to continue the happy influence that had been received, several of the children having professed to have found the Saviour and others in deep anxiety. The friends interested resolved that an inquiry meeting should be held every Sunday evening for half an hour at the close of ordinary public worship. The children were accordingly invited and the first inquiry meeting was held on July 21st at 309 Essex Road at 8.00 pm. fifteen children being present.[30]

As numbers increased a committee was formed and a local schoolroom was hired for £12 a year on the corner of Church Road Islington on 8 December 1867 with 65 children.[31] It was then that the name Children's Special Service Mission was made public. The first Annual Report listed the Mission's objectives.

> The Mission was established for carrying on Special Sunday and Week Evening services for the young. Also to assist those interested in the religious training and salvation of the young in the opening and establishment of similar services. It is an Evangelising Mission, without regard to denominations. Children connected with about twenty different churches, chapels, and Sunday Schools have been in the habit of attending the Central Mission Services at Islington. Any friends interested in the work are invited to visit these Services which are now held at St Jude's Elementary Schools, King Henry's Walk, Balls Pond Road, Islington.[32]

Such was the continuing progress of these meetings that in March the following year they hit a further problem over the renting of the hall. The Revd William Pennefather, the vicar of nearby St Jude's Mildmay Park, heard of their predicament and suggested that Spiers join his Children's Special Service Mission with a similar smaller venture in his church school which he offered rent free.[33] Tom Bishop ran a similar venture south of the river at Blackfriars and decided to affiliate it with Spiers. From that point the CSSM ceased to be

---

30 *Minutes of the Children's Special Service Mission*, 1 August 1868, Scripture Union Archives.
31 Pollock. *The Good Seed*, p. 21.
32 *First Annual Report of the Children's Special Service Mission*, 1867, p. 2.
33 *First Annual Report of the Children's Special Service Mission*, 1867, p. 21. See also Bond, T.B., *T.B.B. of the C.S.S.M.*, p. 43.

local organization. From its inception it was also interdenominational and enjoyed the active support of both churchmen and Nonconformists. A letter from Tom Bishop penned in October 1877 shows how the work had progressed over the next decade. 'It would require a treatise', he wrote, 'to write fully on the work we have had in this country during the last few years among the children.' He went on to thank Hammond as the one who was 'the first mover in the work' and 'gave us the first impulse'. Among other things he stated that they were making it their practice to take down the names of all who came to the conversational meetings, with age and Sunday school details, sending them on to the superintendent of each Sunday school. Bishop continued in praise of Spiers' writing: 'Mr Spiers has a Christian instruction class of more than two hundred and fifty. At his central services in London these were converted as children, but now are growing up. But of course his great work is in visiting different towns.'[34]

Work in America

On his return to America Hammond soon received invitations to minister in different places. Among them was Boston where after the first few evenings the congregation gathered in such numbers that it was found necessary to open a large audience room and 'from that time to the present, the lower floor has been filled almost uninterruptedly, and in several instances it has been packed full – galleries, organ loft, and aisles'. The topics of Hammond's addresses were described as 'those which are often thought old and threadbare; the City of Refuge, the Prodigal Son, the love of Christ for lost sinners, their danger of endless punishment, and such as these'.[35] From Boston Hammond went on to Portland, Maine, where 'an unusual solemnity pervaded the meetings, and especially was this the case in the inquiry meetings'.[36] In the autumn of 1861 he went on to Bethel, a small town near the White Mountains, where, according to *The Christian Mirror*, 'God was pouring out His Spirit.' In the spring of 1862 Hammond was in the City of Lewiston in Maine and his campaign resulted in 'the greatest outpouring of the Spirit, perhaps ... for years' during which 'it is believed, five hundred persons were hopefully converted'.[37] In the autumn of 1862 Edward Hammond held services in Montreal 'where as many as fifteen hundred sought an interest in the prayers of God's people, and large numbers were converted'.[38]

In the spring of 1864 prompted by warm invitations from D.L. Moody, Hammond began services in the First Congregational Church of Chicago. There he worked together with Moody who was present at nearly all the meetings and

---

34 Headley, *The Reaper and the Harvest*, p. 460.
35 Headley, *The Reaper and the Harvest*, p. 217.
36 Headley, *The Reaper and the Harvest*, p. 226.
37 Headley, *The Reaper and the Harvest*, p. 262.
38 Headley, *The Reaper and the Harvest*, p. 300.

took extensive notes from Hammond's addresses. A correspondent of *The New York Times* estimated the number of conversions at 'nearly or quite a thousand'. This was followed in 1865 by a glorious work in Detroit, Michigan, where as many as five thousand were present.

On 24 May 1866 Edward was married to Miss Eliza Overton in Towanda, PA, and soon afterwards started with his new wife on an extended tour through Scotland and England, as noted above, and France, Italy, Egypt and Palestine. He held services in Jerusalem and Beirut during which he was assisted by Bishop Samuel Gobat[39] of the Episcopal Church. He then returned early in 1868 to his old family home in Vernon, Connecticut. Campaigns then followed in Cincinnati where according to the local paper 'the numbers who united with the various churches in and around the city were found to aggregate about five thousand'.[40] In the six years that followed Hammond laboured in a number of major American cities culminating in St Louis where he began working in January 1874.

Invited by 18 ministers from the city his endeavours resulted in the addition of over five thousand members to the different churches and in the organization of the Evangelical Alliance of St Louis, which comprised of clergymen of all denominations, who united to prosecute evangelistic work. They covenanted to 'bind ourselves together as a band of brothers, combining our Christian forces as a unit, presenting an unbroken front against intemperance, infidelity, and unbelief, laying aside all local preferences, and in a grand union effort on one common platform to do all we can to bring sinners to Christ, to the living Saviour'.[41] The same pastors adopted a paper in which they set out what they considered to be the marks of a genuine revival: 'the union of services, the conversion of children, the deep stillness and solemnity of inquiry meetings, free from all objectionable extravagances, the effect of gospel singing, the clearness of preaching, and its thoroughly sound doctrinal tone, and the closer bond of union created between all the ministers of the gospel'.[42] In 1874 he also made a missionary tour as far north as Alaska, reaching that territory before any other missionary. In 1875 he had remarkable successes in Washington and the Cumberland Valley resulting in 'a revival throughout all the towns of the valley'. A report spoke of 'this most gracious awakening' which resulted in 'a general reformation of the morals of the community, a better observation of the Christian Sabbath, and a strong check upon the vices of intemperance, and licentiousness'.[43] Hammond was not above using sensational means to attract people to his meetings. At San Francisco, for example, he rode through the

---

39 See G.R. Balleine, *A History of the Evangelical Party in the Church of England* (Longman, Green, 1933), p. 259. Gobat was appointed Bishop of Jerusalem in 1845.
40 Balleine, *A History of the Evangelical Party*, p. 303.
41 Balleine, *A History of the Evangelical Party*, p. 304.
42 Balleine, *A History of the Evangelical Party*, p. 304.
43 Balleine, *A History of the Evangelical Party*, p. 306.

streets on a white pony followed by a wagon with an organ playing gospel hymns. At Oakland, California, he had a special tent pavilion constructed capable of holding 4,500 people.[44]

Hammond's Revival Methods

Hammond had many endearing personal attributes. Ebenezer Young who had observed him at first hand, wrote that 'of his peculiar qualifications for an Evangelist, I place in the foreground his humble, child-like confidence in the Lord'. Hammond stayed for a time in Young's manse and he was struck by Hammond's 'peculiar sweetness of temper or disposition'. He is 'a man to be loved who loves everybody'. Young also observed that he was 'full of zeal, but by no means too zealous'. He 'believed God's promises implicitly expecting Him to keep them'.[45] He recalled that Hammond frequently quoted with excellent effect the prophet Jeremiah's words: 'Call unto me, and I will answer thee, and shew thee great and mighty things which thou knowest not.'[46] Those who heard him delighted in his almost boyish exuberance and his mixture of joyfulness and seriousness. As one who heard him put it, 'He brings a dash of Christian sunlight and breath of free Christian courage and hope with every sermon.'[47]

Hammond was by nature a humble man. He did not seek the limelight and often spoke of himself as 'a shepherd's dog' for the reason that he saw his major task as that of assisting the shepherds of the flock coaxing some of the stray sheep into the fold. Those who knew him well were of the view that he constantly sought to hide behind the shadow of the cross. Hammond was not one to engage in boisterous proclamation or protracted emotional appeals. Rather he was one who burned with the presence of Christ and presented his plain Protestant and evangelical gospel with blazing sincerity and everyday relevance.

Union Meetings

From his earliest days as a revivalist in Scotland Edward Hammond always worked where there was a united invitation on the part of the local churches. He called these campaigns 'Union Meetings' because all or a majority of the local churches were working together in cooperation with him. At Bath for example, where Hammond held a campaign in January and February 1862 the Central Church, the two Methodist churches, the Baptist, and the Free-will Baptist all shared in the work, some of them 'had large accessions to their numbers'.[48] Hammond was of a humble and teachable disposition and always honoured and

---

44 McLoughlin, *Modern Revivalism*, p. 156.
45 McLoughlin, *Modern Revivalism*, p. 115.
46 McLoughlin, *Modern Revivalism*, p. 115.
47 McLoughlin, *Modern Revivalism*, p. 308.
48 McLoughlin, *Modern Revivalism*, p. 248.

encouraged all the local ministers. He was always ready to seek their advice and guidance on any matter connected with his campaigns.

Clearly preaching was one of Edward Hammond's great gifts. He preached the orthodox evangelical, creedal faith. The Revd J.O. Fiske, the pastor of Winter Street Church in Bath, wrote of Hammond's time in the town: 'It has been a revival of the straightforward, unflinching, abundant preaching of the old-fashioned truths of God's word.' Hammond, he stated, 'preached nothing but what all faithful ministers of the gospel have always preached'.[49] Central to Hammond's theology was the doctrine of the substitutionary atonement. According to a contemporary report of his preaching

> The substance of his sermons is ruin through sin and present redemption through Christ, who was 'wounded for our transgressions, and bruised for our iniquities'. The substitution of Christ in the sinner's place; the full satisfaction to Divine justice; the full justification of the sinner in God's sight on account of the Saviour's work, and the believer's privilege to live ever in the light of conscious acceptance with God, are the notes that he is never weary of ringing in people's ears.[50]

A report in *The Dumfries Standard* stated that 'Mr Hammond never preaches essays, or deals in the elaborate or transcendental; he wants to make religion a thing of ordinary life – the great business of every day.'[51] The same article noted that many of his illustrations 'have a strong human interest' and that he spoke with great earnestness always making 'a powerful impression on his audience'.[52] Following his campaign in Indiana a report in one of the local papers stated that 'his power of illustration is remarkable. He is eminently successful in picturing before his audience whatever scene he is trying to impress on their minds.'[53] Hammond also had a particular gift of being able to portray Jesus as 'a heavenly friend' and being able to enthuse his hearers about 'the joyfulness of Christ's service'.[54]

Hammond clearly had the gift of being able to produce good anecdotes and stories. A Mr G. Kirkham, who heard one of his Sunday addresses to young men, reported his illustrations 'were chiefly gathered from his observations while travelling, and were remarkably appropriate, and forcibly told'.[55]

Although Hammond was altogether different from James Caughey, he was quite prepared, if in his opinion the situation required it, to make use of shock tactics. On one occasion he related the story of a wealthy young New York

---

49 Letter from the Revd J.O. Fiske, cited McLoughlin, *Modern Revivalism*, p. 248.
50 McLoughlin, *Modern Revivalism*, p. 307.
51 McLoughlin, *Modern Revivalism*, p. 117.
52 McLoughlin, *Modern Revivalism*, p. 117.
53 McLoughlin, *Modern Revivalism*, p. 307.
54 McLoughlin, *Modern Revivalism*, p. 307.
55 McLoughlin, *Modern Revivalism*, p. 451.

debutante. The Spirit of God had been striving with her and she became very concerned for her soul. However, her father, a godless individual was worried over his very pretty young daughter 'moping and talking about religion' and resolved to get her married to a rich man. He provided her with rich dress and valuable jewels so that she could enter into the city's fashionable assembly and eventually she gave in to his wishes. But in less than two weeks she had taken a severe cold and died. 'And you, young women here', Hammond said in his sermon, 'are you going to ally yourselves with worldly young men? ... Has He not said, "Be ye not unequally yoked together with unbelievers: for what fellowship hath righteousness with unrighteousness? And what communion hath light with darkness?"'[56] On one occasion Hammond presented a fairly graphic portrayal of hell which he drew from a visit he made to the smoking top of Mount Vesuvius. 'While looking down into the seething abyss three German students ventured too near the edge and were plunged into the red-hot lava to rise no more.' Hammond noted that a 'profane sailor' who 'had always tried to think there was no such place as hell' remarked that 'all this makes me feel there may be'![57]

Pressure for Decisions

There is no doubt that Hammond had the gift of bringing his hearers to the point of decision. Sometimes as he stood at the church door he would urge those who were on the point of departing to go back into the building to make their peace with God. There were also times when he put considerable emotional pressure on the congregation to make a decision at the end of his address. At the close of one of his meetings in Bethel he said: 'Those who are Christians may rise and sing. Those who are not Christians may remain on their seats. Now, if any of you who are not Christians rise, *you will tell a lie.* If any of you who are Christians remain in your seats *you will tell a lie.*'[58] In these circumstances one can well imagine the pressure under which some of the unconverted might feel to rise in order not to declare themselves as unbelievers. Happily on that occasion one unbeliever who was walking out at the end of the meeting 'very angry' was suddenly taken with the thought that 'God drew the line before Hammond did' and he went instead into the inquiry meeting where he resolved 'to give up all for Christ'.[59]

Hammond made great use of the inquiry meeting. For example, at the close of one of his sermons at Dumfries in January 1861, he invited 'the anxious' to remain for conversation 'pressing those who wished to be saved and those who hoped to be saved at some future time, to remain to be conversed with on the

---

56 McLoughlin, *Modern Revivalism*, p. 157.
57 E.P. Hamond, *The Better Life and How to Find It* (Morgan and Chase, undated), pp. 70–1.
58 Headley, *The Reaper of the Harvest*, p. 239.
59 Headley, *The Reaper of the Harvest*, p. 239.

momentous inquiry, "What must I do to be saved?".' Some had to wait more than two hours before they were able to engage in personal conversation.[60] *Harvest of the Years* which tells the story of Hammond's revival endeavours, includes a lengthy piece from the editor of *The Wynd Journal* on the value of Hammond's emphasis on the inquiry room. 'The Inquiry meeting', he contended, 'is the real line of battle in the campaign from which men and women go away either with their consciences awakened or their hearts renewed.' He also pointed out that in many instances people have no place of private retirement in their homes and nor do they have any Christian counsellors there. In any event they are afraid to move from the place where they have been brought under conviction of their sins. The writer of the journal article felt that there should be no difficulty in providing beforehand a number of judicious Christian counsellors who could be ready to undertake spiritual conversations with inquirers.

On the occasion of his first meetings in Boston shortly after his return from England, *The Congregationalist* reported that 'The great and peculiar feature of the movement is found in the inquiry meetings that follow the preaching.' There all Christians who are willing to converse and pray with anxious sinners are invited to go with them into the lecture room. After a few short addresses and prayers the meeting became informal and social allowing the inquirers to raise questions and discuss issues freely.[61] At the inquiry meetings at Portland, Maine it was reported that 'a verse of a hymn was occasionally sung' and 'now and then a word of warning and of encouragement, and occasionally a short prayer was offered for some special case of inquiry, or for the presence of the Divine Spirit'.[62] Hammond was noted for his tact in bringing Christians and inquirers together.

Edward Hammond set great store by singing and his young congregations often sang for an hour before he spoke to them. Some of his critics felt that this was too much but Hammond's view was that God had been pleased to perfect praise out of the mouths of babes and sucklings. Miss Etta Campbell, the author of 'Jesus of Nazareth Passeth By', wrote that the children at Hammond's meetings are taught 'to sing with the spirit and the understanding. The simple, stirring hymns are suited to their capacities and are clearly explained until they understand every word. They know what they are singing, and it is no dull exercise.'[63]

Like his contemporary, Dwight L. Moody, Hammond set much store on gatherings for prayer. In his hugely popular book, *Early Conversion*, Hammond stated that for campaigns such as he was organizing 'there must be unceasing, persistent prayer'. For that reason, he wrote, 'in nearly all the places where I have held meetings these forty years I have started a daily prayer-meeting'.[64]

---

60 *The Dumfries Standard*, 30 January 1861 cited Headley, *The Reaper of the Harvest*, p. 119.
61 Headley, *The Reaper of the Harvest*, p. 217.
62 Headley, *The Reaper of the Harvest*, p. 226.
63 Hammond, *Early Conversion*, p. 43.
64 Hammond, *Early Conversion*, p. 64.

During his four-week campaign in the American town of Bath a prayer meeting was held at two o'clock every day. They were continued for four months, well after the time when Hammond had moved on. The Revd J.O. Fiske, the pastor of Winter Street Church, in a report to the *Christian Mirror* stated that 'Almost all the evangelical ministers of the city attended those meetings, and were exceedingly devoted to them.'[65]

The Work with Children

Right from his earliest days at Musselburgh in Scotland Hammond had shown a particular concern for children and children's evangelism. 'Let those who suppose children must arrive at maturity before they can become Christians', he wrote, ' look carefully into the New Testament for light on the subject. They will find that there is no class of believers so particularly mentioned by our Lord as children.'[66] At Boston, Hammond held gatherings for young converts at the same time as the adult group came together to pray for the main evening meeting. At Bath from the very first Edward Hammond gave particular attention to meetings for children with meetings on Wednesday afternoons and at other times. A correspondent of *The Christian Mirror* reported that:

> ... one of the best features of Mr Hammond's labours among us was his unintermitted skilful and believing zeal for the conversion of children. Quite a number of these lambs of the flock we hope have been passed from death into life, and a few of them between the ages of twelve and seventeen years, have been received into our church. No meetings that I have ever attended have been more delightful and solemn, than some of these children's meetings. [67]

While in Maine Hammond received an invitation from the pastors of the various churches to preach in the city of Lewiston. During his time there he preached to the children in Pine Street Chapel on the Sunday afternoon and 'many children were wrought upon, many of whom have since expressed hope'.[68] During his first visit to London the children were enthralled. As J.C. Pollock put it, 'Hammond saw things through their eyes and spoke as child to child, without condescension and yet with such simple clarity that every point was plain.'[69]

Following his campaign in London in the spring of 1867 Hammond returned home to America in the spring of 1868. The following year he went to Cincinnati and held a six-week campaign in the Presbyterian Church beginning with a series of children's meetings. It was reported that 'a large number of

---

65 Headley, *The Reaper and the Harvest*, p. 246.
66 Hammond, *The Conversion of Children*, p. 29.
67 *The Christian Mirror* cited by Headley, *The Reaper and the Harvest*, p. 247.
68 Headley, *The Reaper and the Harvest*, p. 263.
69 Pollock, *The Good Seed*, p. 16.

young people gave evidence of having been truly converted'.[70] Following Hammond's campaign in Indiana one of the religious papers stated that 'the criticism that might be founded on his too great urgency in bringing to an announcement of a decision for Christ is largely shorn of its strength by the undoubted fact that he is as careful to make them intelligent as he is to make them decided. He gives them a reason for the hope he would have them entertain.'[71] Hammond always made a particular point of warning children against making a profession of their faith in Christ for which they couldn't give a simple scriptural reason. It was Hammond's pioneering work with children that was his particular contribution to nineteenth-century revivalism in both America and the British Isles. As one writer put it:

> The church will, perhaps, advance by increasing experiences to better methods than have yet been adopted. But the essential idea that supports work among children, both in Sunday-schools and revival meetings, that little ones can be soundly converted; that the law of spiritual growth from very feeble beginnings may be emphasised in religious life, and children be trained up in the Church, rather than recovered to it after a prolonged wandering, is one that will throw heavenly radiance on all the future life of the church.[72]

Hammond was of the opinion that children as young as four and five years of age were quite capable of making a definite decision to follow Christ. During his campaign at Weston-Super-Mare in 1868 he invited any young child who wanted to make a commitment of their life to Christ to do so and to give testimony to the fact by coming up onto the platform. Before they could take that step Hammond required them to first give a clear reason for their new-found faith either to the local parish priest, the Revd R.G. Walker, or to Lord Cavan. He was quite shocked to find a small boy of just four years of age on the platform and worried at what local people might feel about this. On hearing how the little fellow had prayed and was in obvious earnest he asked for God's forgiveness for his fear of man and for doubting the child.[73]

The Independent commenting on Hammond's ministry in Rochester, New York State, in 1863 stated that he had 'a pre-eminent gift of being able to interest children in Christian truth'.[74] The reasons for this, the paper maintained was 'his earnest love for Jesus and for souls, his aptness of illustration, his power of language and personal magnetism' which all combined to give him a

---

70 Headley, *The Reaper and the Harvest*, p. 303.
71 Headley, *The Reaper and the Harvest*, p. 307.
72 Headley, *The Reaper and the Harvest*, p. 309.
73 E.P. Hammond, *The Conversion of Children* (Marshall, Morgan and Scott, undated), pp. 17–18.
74 Headley, *The Reaper and the Harvest*, p. 339.

singular hold on the minds of children.[75] It should also be noted that Hammond was strongly of the view that the quickest way to reach adults with the gospel was often through the children. For this reason he often began his campaigns with meetings for children.[76]

The Personal Question

When conducting Children's meetings Hammond quite often went along the aisles asking individual children if they loved Jesus.[77] The procedure seems inquisitional but, by all accounts, Hammond's gentle disposition enabled him to awaken hundreds of children to their need of Christ without seeming to exert excessive emotional pressure to bear on their young lives. The Revd George Boardman, the pastor of First Baptist Church in Rochester, reported that Hammond's use of this procedure in his city campaign had produced wonderful results with seventy persons of a young age joining his congregation. A Christian worker who was present at one of his London meetings observed that he prayed at the close of his address and then, 'while a hymn was being sung, went in among the young men, speaking to them one by one, briefly and pointedly'.[78]

The Use of Hymns and Songs

Hammond, who was himself a musician, set great store on singing. It was reported that at some of the London meetings Hammond let the children 'sing for nearly an hour one after another of the sweet "Hymns of Salvation", by which hearts are softened and prepared for the beautiful gospel of God'.[79] There is no doubt that this procedure was felt to have 'impressed them deeply with the love of Jesus'. That said however, contemporary critics would doubtless counter that extended periods of singing of this length would create passive states of consciousness which made them unable to resist the call to commitment. At the beginning of Hammond's fourth week of meetings at John Street Chapel the service was planned for half past six but many of the children came well before time because they wanted to sing some his hymns and tunes from his own *Hymns of Salvation*. At the end of the meeting that followed, it was estimated that 'there could not have been less than three or four hundred children who bowed their heads and wept, feeling deeply their sin in never having loved the so precious a Saviour'.[80] During each week of the campaign two meetings for

---

75 Headley, *The Reaper and the Harvest*, p. 339.
76 Hammond, *The Conversion of Children*, p. 112.
77 See Headley, *The Reaper and the Harvest*, p. 381.
78 Headley, *The Reaper and the Harvest*, p. 451.
79 Headley, *The Reaper and the Harvest*, p. 452.
80 Headley, *The Reaper and the Harvest*, p. 463.

children were also held in Surrey Chapel at which it was reported 'there was a good deal of singing using Mr Hammond's beautiful hymns and tunes'.[81]

Hammond made the same full use of the inquiry room at his children's meetings as he did at his adult campaigns. He began this practice with children largely as a result of the meetings that he held in 1868 at the Revd Baptist Noel's church in London. On the very first Sunday when 'the church was crowded in every part' he stated that it was not too much to say that 'hundreds were bathed in tears'.[82] This led him to put it to Noel that they should call out those who had made a profession of faith into a side room, and then after they had received careful questioning to ensure they understood their decision, be allowed to come up on the platform where their parents could see that they 'are not ashamed to confess Christ'.[83] At one of his early London meetings 'two hundred and fifty children came into the vestry at Mr Hammond's request' with a few older Christians standing at the door to see that only those who professed to have believed on Jesus entered the room.[84]

The Covenant

An important part of Hammond's strategy for helping children to maintain their commitment to Christ was his adoption of what he called the 'Covenant Book'. Hammond related in *The Conversion of Sinners* that he was early prompted to this means by Miss M.E. Winslow of Brooklyn, a teacher at the Brooklyn Institute. She wrote to him that when a person was able to give a reason for the hope that is within them, it seems 'most proper that he should be able "to subscribe with his hand unto the Lord", and thus enter a covenant with Him who said, "I will make an everlasting covenant with them that I will not turn away from them .... They shall not depart from me."'.[85] After his meeting with Miss Winslow, Hammond made use of the covenant in almost all the places in which he laboured. In Chicago he recalled 'one thousand and seventy-five persons in three different localities signed a covenant in May 1899'.[86] He set out the mechanics of this in his publication entitled *The Conversion of Children*. A well-known or responsible person is selected by the pastor or minister to examine each child who professes conversion and to allow them, if they choose, to put their names to the following statement: 'I, the undersigned, hope I have found Jesus, to be my precious Saviour; and I promise, with His help, to live as His loving child and faithful servant all my life.' Hammond based this covenant on Jeremiah 50:5 'They shall ask the way to Zion with their faces thitherward, saying, Come let us join ourselves to the Lord in a perpetual covenant that shall not be forgotten.'

---

81 Headley, *The Reaper and the Harvest*, p. 464.
82 Hammond, *The Conversion of Children*, p. 40.
83 Hammond, *The Conversion of Children*, p. 41.
84 Headley, *The Reaper and the Harvest*, p. 453.
85 Hammond, *The Conversion of Children*, p. 147.
86 Hammond, *Early Conversion*, p. 214.

Although Hammond also used the covenant with adults, he found it particularly effective with children and young people. A Dr R.E. Cole carried out a survey which included the ages of those who signed the 'Covenant Book' during the first three weeks of Hammond's campaign at Oakland, California.

Ages	
5–10	109
10–15	372
15–20	283
20–30	68
30–40	29
40–50	16
50–60	11
Over 60	4
Not given	158[87]

One advantage of the covenant which Hammond foresaw was that children who didn't go on to join a church and become regular members could still register their commitment. The simple act of signing led many to feel that they were committed to the Christian cause and must not in consequence go back on their decision to follow Christ.[88] The covenant card was kept by the signer but the convert's name was recorded in a special book.

Summing up what he considered to be the key to successful work with children Hammond emphasized the following. The evangelist must 'first possess and cultivate a deep love for children'. Secondly he or she must bring before each child the great fact that 'Jesus loved each one of them and died a cruel death on the cross in their stead.' These great facts, he stresses must be illustrated by simple stories that children can readily understand. Great stress must be laid on the doctrine of substitution, 'a doctrine which children as young as five and six years of age can readily understand'.[89] Hammond was also at pains to stress that 'simplicity should be sought by those who gain the attention of children and win them to Christ'.[90] Hammond was also adamant that children needed regular spiritual feeding. He quoted Lorenzo Dow who used to say that a good farmer would always put the hay so low in the racks that even little lambs should could get some of it. In the same way Hammond stressed that spiritual nourishment should be dealt out to children in a way that would enable them to grow and mature in the faith.[91]

---

87 Headley, *The Reaper and the Harvest*, p. 495. See also Hammond, *Early Conversion*, p. 17.
88 Hammond, *The Conversion of Children*, p. 148.
89 Hammond, *The Conversion of Children*, pp. 63–5.
90 Hammond, *The Conversion of Children*, p. 69.
91 Hammond, *The Conversion of Children*, p. 95.

Hammond's Tracts and Books

A significant part of Hammond's work with children were the many tracts which he wrote and printed in large quantities. In North America they were published by Drummond's Tract Depot in Stirling, New Brunswick. They were also printed in London by S.W. Partridge and Co. and sold in packets of 15. Each tract which was a little under a thousand words measured 4 inches by 2.5 inches so that it would slip easily into a child's pocket. At the top of the front page were the overarching words 'Trust in Jesus' with the title at the foot. Between the two titles most of the British tracts carried a picture of a different bird on a tree branch or flowering shrub and one can imagine that some children also enjoyed collecting the tracts for that reason. There were 32 in total and most were on salvation themes with captions such as 'He came to seek and to save the Lost' (No. 1), 'I have redeemed thee' (No. 2), 'He died on the Cross for thee' (No. 6), 'He loved us and gave himself for us' (No. 11), 'He will guide you to heaven (No. 18), 'He will change your heart' (No. 23), 'He will make you happy even in death' (No. 31) and 'He loves you' (No. 32).[92] In places some of the tracts have a hint of Hannah More's style. Thus number 4 begins with 'Why Nellie loves Jesus' and number 16 'Believe his Word' introduces us to Charlie, a little boy from New England, whose mother was on the point of death and had only one thing to give him, her Bible. He promised her that 'he would read it every day and trust with all his heart in the precious saviour who bled and died on the cross for us'. Charlie of course was faithful and lived by the book and so 'he has now gone to meet his dear mother in Heaven'. There is no doubt that these tracts which were distributed in hundreds of thousands were immensely popular and proved to be a very effective means of disseminating basic evangelical truths to young children.

As well as producing tracts, Hammond also wrote a number of books for children. These included *The Better Life, Jesus the Lamb of God, Jesus' Lambs* and *Gathered Lambs*. The latter volume exemplifies Hammond's straightforward style of writing which was always designed to touch the hearts of children for Christ with simple anecdotes and stories from his own experience. The following short paragraph typifies the way in which Hammond aimed to capture the attention of his young readers.

> There was a poor 'charity scholar' in London who, after she was converted, used to attend all my meetings, and often walked four or five miles day after day to get to them. One day she had to walk six miles; and so she got no dinner. My wife asked her if she was hungry. 'Oh no', said she; 'the meetings feed me'. She meant that she got so much good to her soul in them that she had rather lose her dinner than the meetings.

---

92 For detailed information of all Hammond's tracts, see *Hammond Collection* in the Bodleian Library, Ms Bod 100g 85(i).

> Do you think this poor little girl was one of Jesus' 'GATHERED LAMBS'? 'Oh yes', do I hear you say? – but I am not quite sure that I am one now.[93]

Hammond went on in the remaining part of the chapter to urge children not to drift away from the Christian faith but to follow the example of the London charity girl and keep attending Christian meetings.

An Assessment of Hammond's Labours

There is no doubt that Hammond was a remarkably effective evangelist whose importance has been somewhat overlooked. In America his work was so effective 'among adults of all classes'[94] that the work among children was considered to be of secondary importance. Indeed one estimate suggested that 'not fewer than forty thousand genuine converts' had resulted from his labours in the United States and Canada.[95] At the time of Hammond's London services in 1868 D.L. Moody was paying his first visit to the nation's capital. On being asked for his opinion of Hammond's influence Moody replied that he believed that up to that time 'there could not be less than fifty thousand in the churches in the United States and Canada who had been converted in his meetings.'[96]

That said, Hammond clearly felt that his ministry to children was of major significance. It was this area of ministry that engaged much of his thinking and it was on this subject that he wrote most. He was particularly encouraged to discover that his work among children was an enduring one. In the autumn of 1869, a year after he had held meetings for children in London, he returned to Baptist Noel's church. At the close of his first meeting he asked that all the children present who had made a commitment to Christ the previous year to come up on the platform. A number nearly as large as before ascended the platform.[97] Writing in *The Conversion of Children* he noted:

> I have frequently visited places, and found those who years ago were converted when children, grown up to be men and women; and what is more, I have found them earnest Christians, and ready to testify that when those children's meetings were held in their town or city, they experienced the forgiveness of their sins and a change of heart, and then began the new life which is by faith in the son of God, 'who loved us and gave Himself for us'.[98]

---

93 E.P. Hammond, *Gathered Lambs* (Marshall, Morgan and Scott, undated), p. 64.
94 Headley, *The Reaper and the Harvest*, p. 451.
95 Headley, *The Reaper and the Harvest*, p. 451.
96 Headley, *The Reaper and the Harvest*, p. 467.
97 Hammond, *The Conversion of Children*, p. 42.
98 Hammond, *The Conversion of Children*, p. 38.

The Revd J.B. Currens wrote that 'after being with Hammond in three tours of Nebraska, in which 3,000 children came to the Saviour, and talking and praying with hundreds myself, I cannot but believe that the work is just as genuine and lasting as that of any of the Evangelists who labour for adults'.[99] Something of the measure of Hammond's influence as a children's revivalist among children can be gathered from the fact that the first edition of his book *Early Conversion* sold 98,000 copies.[100]

Whilst Hammond will be chiefly remembered in the British Isles for his work among children, his influence was by no means confined to that sphere. William Booth, the founder of the Salvation Army, surprised him by relating that it was through his prompting that he had given up his role as a Methodist minister and taken up work as a freelance evangelist. Booth told him that in 1861 he had asked him whether he should trust the Lord for support and go forward and work as a full-time evangelist and that the encouragement that Hammond gave enabled him to take the decision.[101]

Hammond was an immensely hard-working individual. Dr C.E. Babb wrote of his time in San Jose, California:

> Mr Hammond is working indefatigably. He is endearing himself to multitudes by his simplicity and godly sincerity, his burning love for Christ and for the souls of men. He conducts the morning prayer-meeting, expounding the Scriptures and talking to inquirers. He goes to Santa Clara in the afternoon and holds a children's meeting; he then goes to jail to talk and pray with the prisoners. He is busy all the time, and the wonder is that even his stalwart frame can endure a pressure so constant and so great.[102]

Another observer of his work in California wrote, 'I suppose I shall not exceed the truth in stating that since arriving in San Francisco, Mr Hammond has held one hundred services and spoken to fully one hundred thousand people.'[103]

Hammond's straightforward message attracted men and women from all sections of society. A report following his meetings at Terre Haute in Indiana stated that 'all classes, from the most respectable to the most abandoned, have been reached'.[104] Dr Fowler, the pastor of the First Presbyterian Church in Utica, reported that Hammond's labours in the city 'embraced all classes – young men sceptics, and scoffers'.[105]

---

99 Hammond, *Early Conversion*, preface, p. i.
100 Hammond, *Early Conversion*, p. i.
101 Headley, *The Reaper and the Harvest*, p. 468.
102 Headley, *The Reaper and the Harvest*, p. 478.
103 Headley, *The Reaper and the Harvest*, p. 488.
104 Headley, *The Reaper and the Harvest*, p. 306.
105 Headley, *The Reaper and the Harvest*, p. 338.

CHAPTER 9

Amanda Berry Smith and Holiness and Singing Revivalism

Early Years

Amanda Smith was one of five children born in slavery to Mariam and Samuel Berry at Long Green in the state of Maryland on 23 January 1837. Her parents worked on adjoining farms each having good masters. Sam Berry's master died young and he became a much-trusted servant of his widow buying and selling produce in the Baltimore markets once or twice each week. In consequence of his faithfulness she allowed him to buy himself out of slavery. He toiled long additional hours of work in order to purchase the freedom of his wife and children. He also testified how the Lord helped him in this when his wife's young mistress decided out of curiosity to attend 'an old-fashioned red-hot Methodist Camp Meeting'. Amanda related how as they sat the spirit of the Lord took hold of the young mistress and she was mightily convicted and wonderfully converted 'in the old-fashioned way; the shouting hallelujah way'.[1] Although she died tragically shortly afterwards having contracted typhoid fever she made a deathbed request that Samuel should have Mariam and the children. So it proved and in later times Amanda often said to people, 'I have a right to shout more than some folks; I have been bought twice, and set free twice, and so I feel I have a good right to shout. Hallelujah!'[2]

Amanda was nurtured in an atmosphere of piety, both her parents were strong Christians and she recalled that her grandmother was a woman of great faith and prayer. Both her parents could read and always on Sunday mornings her father would gather the children together and read the Bible to them. In later years Amanda recalled that he never sat down to a meal, however sparse, without asking God's blessing before eating. Every night her mother would call all the children together and ensure that they said their prayers before going to sleep. Amanda had a very brief period of schooling which lasted only six weeks when she was eight years old. The school was run by the daughter of a Methodist minister who lived opposite to her mother. Notwithstanding this very

---

1 Smith, *Amanda Smith*, p. 8: 'All of the book is Amanda Smith's own writing, except a few paragraphs by the editors who have briefly summed up her work in India by introducing Bishop Thoburn's appraisal of her two years spent there.' See Foreword. The first edition *An Autobiography: Mrs Amanda Smith The Colored Evangelist* was published in Chicago in 1893.
2 Smith, *Amanda Smith*, p. 10.

brief encounter with school, Amanda taught herself to read by cutting large letters out of newspapers that her father brought home. Amanda did not return to school again until she was 13 years old. She and her brother then had to walk five miles each way and so missed several of the lessons that the majority white children who lived close by were able to access with relative ease.

At this time Amanda was living about 13 miles from York on the Baltimore and York Turnpike with a widow by the name of Mrs Latimer and her five children. During her first spring a revival broke out at the Albright church in which scores of people were converted. It lasted for many weeks and although 'no coloured persons' went up to be prayed for Amanda was captivated by the proceedings. One night during the revival Miss Mary Bloser, the daughter of a well-known Christian man in the region, was speaking to individual members of the congregation. She came to Amanda, 'the only coloured girl present', when she was sitting at the back by the church door. With tears and entreaties Mary Bloser asked her to go forward to the front of the church. Amanda recalled that 'she knelt beside her with her arm around her and prayed for me. O, how she prayed! I was ignorant, but I prayed as best I could.'[3] This was the moment of Amanda's conversion. She wrote of it as follows:

> The meeting closed I went to get up, but found I could not stand. They took hold of me and stood me up on my feet. My strength seemed to come to me, but I was frightened. I was afraid to step. I seemed so light. In my heart was peace, but I did not know how to exercise faith as I should. I went home and resolved I would be the Lord's and live for Him.[4]

Amanda joined the church and became an active member of the class led by Joshua Ludrick whom she liked on account of his lung power. 'You could hear him pray half a mile away when he would get properly stirred.'[5] Amanda's parents also joined his class in order to encourage her and to save her going out alone at night.

John Lowe, Amanda's father's landlord, was a strong anti-slave campaigner and he allowed him to do what he could in secret to help poor slaves escape from the south. The family home was one of the main stations of the Under Ground Railroad and after a full day's ploughing Sam Berry often spent the greater part of a night helping poor slaves, perhaps a mother and child, find a place of security.

Marriage and Conversion

In September 1854 Amanda married her first husband, Calvin Devine. Her father did not stand against the marriage but felt that she was rather young.

---

3 Smith, *Amanda Smith*, p. 15.
4 Smith, *Amanda Smith*, p. 15.
5 Smith, *Amanda Smith*, p. 15.

Amanda, who was somewhat headstrong at the time, was taken in by his charm and his ability 'to talk on the subject of religion very sensibly at times'. Sadly, he was prone to strong drink which would often get the better of him causing him to be profane and unreasonable. The year after her marriage Amanda, who had drifted somewhat from her earlier profession of faith in Christ, became very ill. The doctors who were treating her said that they could do no more for her which caused her father to pray earnestly. However, during the afternoon of the next day Amanda had what she described as 'a kind of trance or vision' in which there were many thousands of people and she was preaching to them from a very high stand from the words; 'And if I be lifted up, I will draw all men unto me.' 'O, how I preached', she recalled, 'and the people were slain right and left.'[6] When the vision, which lasted for about two hours, was over Amanda was, to the astonishment of her doctors, decidedly better and she resolved to pray and lead a Christian life. After her recovery she was still in a state of doubt and confusion, and called out in desperation, 'O Lord, if Thou wilt help me I will believe in Thee.' In the act of her praying, God did as she asked and she recorded, 'O, the peace and joy that flooded my soul.' She continued but her attendance at a watch night service in a local Baptist church brought more peace to her soul. Finally on 17 March 1856 she went down into the basement of the house where she worked and cried out to the Lord 'to have mercy on my soul'.[7]

> The burden rolled away; I felt it when it left me, and a flood of light and joy swept through my soul such as I had never known before. I said, 'Why, Lord, I do believe this is just what I have been asking for', and down came another flood of light and peace.
>
> Then I sprang to my feet, all around was light, I was new. I looked at my hands, they looked new; I took hold of myself and said, 'Why I am new all over' .... The change was so real and so thorough that I have often said that if I had been as black as ink or as green as grass or as white as snow, I would not have been frightened.[8]

From this moment on Amanda never had any further doubts as to her conversion. 'God', she wrote, 'helped me and He settled it once for all.'[9]

Following this affirmation of her conversion Amanda went to live in Columbia, Pennsylvania, during which time the Civil War broke out and her husband enlisted and went south with the army but never returned. Some time after his death Amanda became acquainted with a local preacher by the name of James Smith who had a daughter of 18 years of age by a previous marriage. Her

---

6 Smith, *Amanda Smith*, p. 23.
7 Smith, *Amanda Smith*, p. 27.
8 Smith, *Amanda Smith*, pp. 27–8.
9 Smith, *Amanda Smith*, p. 29.

daughter was about nine years old at the time. Amanda had great hopes of setting up a Christian home thereby serving God more effectively. James also said that he supported her in her desire to become an evangelist and told Amanda that he was preparing to offer himself to Conference as an itinerant preacher. Amanda mused about how nice it would be to work alongside him and for them to be spoken of as 'Revd Mr and Mrs Smith'. As things turned out her husband proved to be a major disappointment and failed to take up itinerant work, admitting that he had been dishonest over the matter. In 1865 he took a position at Leland's Hotel in New York where his membership with the Masons and the Odd Fellows provided him with many contacts. Amanda herself joined a new Masonic Society called the 'Heroines of Jericho' which was only open to wives of Master Masons such as her husband was. She remained a member until 1868 'when God opened my eyes to see the folly of all this and taught me how to trust in Him. I came out of every one of them'.[10]

Sanctification

Amanda's life with her second husband James was often stressful and she felt herself to be bullied, controlled and mistreated by him. Over the course of many months she began to seek the blessing of sanctification which she first had learned from 'Mother Jones' while she laboured at her washtub. Mrs Jones had told her that her husband had treated her badly until God had sanctified her soul and given her enduring grace. In the event Amanda's search for sanctification proved a long one. The situation began to change when one day when she was cleaning she distinctly heard a voice say, 'On Sunday morning go to Green Street Church and hear John Inskip.' '"Yes, Lord", I said, "I will."'[11] Despite considerable inner turmoil in which 'the enemy seemed to approach me again fiercely' she went on. In later life she never forgot that September morning in 1868 and the thrill of hearing Brother Inskip pray as she ascended the steps into the building. Inskip, as it happened, preached on the topic of sanctification and explained that the blessing of purity like that of pardon could be received by faith and if by faith, why not at that moment? In what seemed to Amanda a flash as quick as the tinkling of an eye she felt the touch of God 'from the crown of my head to the soles of my feet'.[12] She felt the urge to shout out but restrained herself fearing that the many whites in the congregation would be offended. However when she went to stand up at the end of the service she found herself unable to stand on her feet. Her head 'seemed a river of waters and my eyes a fountain of tears' as she struggled with a trembling grip to take hold of the pew in front of her and stand up. As she did so the congregation struck up the last verse of the hymn,

---

10 Smith, *Amanda Smith*, p. 33.
11 Smith, *Amanda Smith*, p. 38.
12 Smith, *Amanda Smith*, p. 43.

> Oh! bear my longing heart to Him,
> Who bled and died for me.
> Whose blood now cleanseth from all sin,
> And give me victory.

As they sang those words 'Whose blood now cleanseth' a wave of glory swept over her soul and she shouted, 'glory to Jesus' and Brother Inskip responded with 'Amen, glory to God'. Amanda described her experience as 'a done moment' in which 'I felt something part and roll down and cover me like a great cloak' and 'a mighty peace and power took possession of me!'[13] This was also a liberating moment for Amanda. She had always had a fear of white people 'not that they intended her harm but simply because they were white, and were there, and I was black and was here' but in her special moment she distinctly heard the words as though from the north-east corner of the church: 'There is neither Jew nor Greek, there is neither bond nor free, there is neither male nor female, for ye are all one in Christ Jesus.'[14]

Call to Public Preaching

Since her coming to New York Amanda had spent whatever spare time she could find 'working among my own people, and our coloured churches'[15] though she often also visited white Methodist churches. One day in November 1869 as she was praying she had a strong impression that she must leave New York and go out. She asked the Lord to show her where and 'clear and plain the word came, "Salem".' She asked for confirmation and the same word, 'Salem', came again with renewed intensity. In consequence she began to make plans to follow her calling. She went to Philadelphia and left her daughter, Mazie, with her grandfather. She arrived at Salem just at the time of the Quarterly Meeting and Brother Holland who was presiding asked Amanda to tell her story to the Sunday morning congregation. She did so basing her very first message on Acts 9:2, 'Have you received the Holy Ghost since ye believed?'[16] That same evening, following a short address from Brother Holland, she was invited to 'exhort' the congregation. Every part of the building including the galleries were packed but she recalled, 'the Lord gave me great liberty in speaking' and 'the Holy Ghost fell on the people and we had a wonderful time'.[17] Following this success she was appointed to preach on the following Thursday night. She was convinced that the Lord would have her speak on the subject of sanctification despite discouraging warnings from Sister Curtis with whom she was staying. Notwithstanding this, Amanda, who began her address with trembling, felt the Spirit of God come

---

13 Smith, *Amanda Smith*, p. 44.
14 Smith, *Amanda Smith*, p. 45.
15 Smith, *Amanda Smith*, p. 82.
16 Smith, *Amanda Smith*, p. 88.
17 Smith, *Amanda Smith*, p. 88.

upon her mightily. It proved to be an evening not easily forgotten for 'the Lord convicted sinners and backsliders and believers for holiness, and when I asked people to come to the altar, it was filled in a little while from the gallery and all parts of the house' and a revival broke out, and spread for 20 miles around. She went on 'for two weeks, day and night' and she often stayed in the church until one or two in the morning.[18] Amanda recalled those events in the following lines:

> Oh! what a time it was. It went from the coloured people to the white people. Sometimes we would go into the church at seven o'clock in the evening. I could not preach. The whole lower floor would be covered with seekers – old men, young men, old women, young women, boys and girls. Oh! glory to God! How He put his seal on this first work to encourage my heart and establish my faith, that he indeed had chosen, and ordained and sent me. I do not know as I have ever seen anything equal that first seal that God gave to his work at Salem. Some of the young men who were converted are in the ministry.[19]

Camp Meetings

In July 1870 Amanda Smith attended her first camp meeting at Oakington in Maryland. There she heard testimonies and preaching on holiness such as she had never heard before. She herself was able to share her own experience 'of how I found the great salvation' at the Sunday morning 'love feast'.[20] After this she attended the camp meeting at Sing Sing and was then invited to be a worker at Round Lake and Wesley Grove camp meetings. On these occasions and at Kennebunk Camp meeting Amanda was in reality serving her apprenticeship as she gained vital experience in leading meetings, exhorting and public singing.

Call to England

In July 1878 Amanda left her daughter Mazie in Baltimore and went to England. She related that God made it 'so clear' and 'put it in my conscience so real and so deep, that I could no more doubt that he wanted me to go to England than I could doubt my own existence'.[21] She had planned to stay only three months but as things turned out she was away from her homeland for over 12 years.[22] She explained her unexpectedly long stay in the 'old country' in the following lines:

---

18 Smith, *Amanda Smith*, p. 90.
19 Smith, *Amanda Smith*, p. 90.
20 Smith, *Amanda Smith*, p. 100.
21 Smith, *Amanda Smith*, p. 140.
22 Smith, *Amanda Smith*, p. 137.

Amanda Berry Smith

After I had been in England about three months, the Lord made it very clear to me that I was to remain longer; so I thought three months longer; but when six months had passed, my way seemed shut to come home, but open to remain. Now, people say, 'But how was that?' That is just what I say; for I am just as sure that God was in it, as I am of my own existence. It is one of God's inexplicable dealings. I wrote and sent money home to my daughter, and had made all arrangements for her for two years.[23]

Before Amanda took ship to England she had received a letter from her friends Mr and Mrs Johnson telling her about the Keswick Convention for the deepening of spiritual life. She later noted that Keswick meetings were similar to the camp meetings which she had experienced in her homeland. When she came ashore at Liverpool she immediately set out for Keswick following Mrs Johnson's instructions. The Johnsons had spoken of her to their circle of friends and Amanda related that everyone seemed to be anticipating her arrival. On the first morning she was introduced to Canon Harford-Battersby whom she described as a very

---

23 Smith, *Amanda Smith*, p. 137.

holy man and was asked to lead the after meeting. She expressed her anxiety that she would not be able to do things in the British way and was told, 'just to go right on in my own way, just as I was accustomed to do in America, and that they would stand by and assist in anything I wished to do'.[24] At this her very first meeting in England she asked those who wanted personal conversion and prayer to stand, and 'a great number arose all over the tent'.[25] She then asked all the Keswick workers to go round and speak and pray with the seekers.[26] Years later Mr George Grubb recalled how Mrs Amanda Smith had stood on the platform and related how the Lord met her one day as she stood at her washtub, setting her apart for Himself, and filling her with His Holy Spirit, adding in her quaint style, 'When my Lord does a thing, He always does it handsome.'[27]

Whilst at Keswick Amanda met with some women from Liverpool who were members of Christ Church Everton where the Revd Hay Aitken was formerly rector. They invited her to come to Liverpool to hold some meetings. A Mrs Stephen Menzies of Eggleston Hills just outside Liverpool arranged for her to hold meetings in a large hall. A few days later Canon Evan Hopkins presented her with a letter from Lord Mount Temple inviting her to the August Convention at his home at Broadlands. Although warned by Mrs Boardman and others that the teaching was deep and might confuse her straightforward thinking Amanda was convinced that it was right for her to attend. In the event however she didn't make it to Broadlands that year as she received a telegram from Mrs Menzies stating that the meetings were already advertised at Eggleston Hills with large placards that announced 'Amanda Smith, *the converted slave girl*, will sing and hold gospel meetings in Victoria Hall'.[28] Amanda therefore fulfilled her engagement, before going on in September to Galashields in Scotland where she spoke to a mixed congregation of men and women from the Presbyterian Church. Every night the hall which held about three hundred was crowded.[29]

Amanda did get to attend the Broadlands Conference in the summer of the following year, 1879. Lord Mount Temple and Lady Beechman and a number of others came to Mr Charlton's East End Mission one night during the time that she was holding meetings there and gave her a second personal invitation. She was blest as a result of her time there and believed that she for her part was a blessing to many who were present. Amanda recalled how Lord Mount Temple personally escorted her to lunch. Taking her by the arm he announced, 'We will lead the way' and then took her to the dinner table and seated her at his right amid a throng of English dignitaries. During the convention Amanda held a Gospel Meeting with a Mr E. Clifford. She shared something of her own

---

24 Smith, *Amanda Smith*, p. 149.
25 Smith, *Amanda Smith*, p. 149.
26 C.G. Moore (ed.), *Amanda Smith: An Autobiography* (Hodder and Stoughton, 1894), p. 158.
27 Sloan, *These Sixty Years*, p. 75.
28 Sloan, *These Sixty Years*, p. 151.
29 See Moore, *Amanda Smith*, pp. 161–3.

experience of how God both converted and sanctified her heart. As she spoke 'the power of the Spirit seemed to come mightily upon all the people. Oh, what a stir; they wept and sobbed, and one woman was so baptized that she cried out and could not restrain herself ... [the] work was very real in many hearts.'[30]

Earlier in August 1879 Amanda had preached in Darlington and, after Broadlands had ended, she took engagements in Doncaster and then in Perth where she held meetings for a week at a place where they weren't used to the idea of women addressing men. At the last service on a Sunday 'a hundred stood up for prayers, mostly men with tears running down their faces, and trembling as they stood'.[31] Before leaving for India in the autumn of 1879 Amanda took a period of rest in Eastbourne and then travelled north to fulfil a week-long engagement speaking in Aberdeen.

India, Africa and a Return to England

Amanda's contacts in England and America helped to open up the way to India, a country whose conditions deeply disturbed her. She left England for India in the autumn of 1879 and remained there for two years. She had inherited her parents' deep concern for the spiritual needs of Africa and at the close of 1881 she set sail for Monrovia. She remained there until 1889 returning to England in November of that year with Bob, a native boy she had adopted in 1887. After travelling and doing evangelistic work for some months in the British Isles she returned to America in September 1890 eventually settling in Chicago where she raised funds to open an orphanage home for American African children. She opened a home at Harvey, Illinois in 1899. Her fundraising was substantial and enabled her to operate a school along with the home without government assistance.[32]

Revival Methodology

Amanda Berry Smith clearly understood revival to be at least in part a human endeavour. She often spoke of 'going to work in revival meetings'.[33] Her meat and drink was to see souls coming to Christ. The stock in trade of her preaching was simplicity and homely illustrations. She was noted for her quaint expressions and warm-hearted appeals.

As a Methodist, Amanda Berry Smith was always ready to emphasize the role and importance of the Holy Spirit in the life of the believer. She wrote in later years that 'the witness of God's Spirit to my conversion has been what has

---

30 Moore, *Amanda Smith*, p. 152.
31 Moore, *Amanda Smith*, pp. 167–8.
32 See D.C. Bartlett and L.A. McClellan, 'The Final Ministry of Amanda Berry Smith. An Orphanage in Harvey, Illinois 1895–1918', *Illinois Heritage*, Vol. 1, No. 2, pp. 20–5. See also, J. Gilbert, *Perfect Cities: Chicago's Utopias of 1893* (University of Chicago Press, 1991).
33 Smith, *Amanda Smith*, p. 51.

held me amid the storms of temptation and trial that I have passed through. O what an anchor it has been at time of storm!'[34] Later she had a similar witness following her experience of sanctification in September 1868. Hers was a remarkable experience and she recognized that not everyone would share it. What she did stress however was that it is every person's privilege to have a clear and distinct witness of the Spirit to both justification and sanctification.[35]

Full Salvation

For Amanda Smith justification by faith alone fell short of full Christian experience. 'Full salvation' was the added blessing of holiness or sanctification which Amanda sometimes referred to as a 'pearl of great price' or 'the blessing'. She described the difference between these two experiences of justification and sanctification as akin to the difference between the moon and the sun. The moon is beautiful and many times she read and sewed by its light. But the light of the sun is infinitely greater and penetrates into every dark corner. If there is even a nail hole in a door or a crack the sunlight penetrates it. There were, she said, deep recesses in my heart that the moonlight as it were did not reveal, but 'when the great sunlight of sanctification came, it seemed almost to eclipse the moonlight of justification'.[36] In this Amanda Smith was part of a growing holiness revivalism that emerged in both England and America in the second half of the nineteenth century.

While in New York City Amanda associated herself with Phoebe Palmer's Tuesday meetings for holiness[37] although she had of course received sanctification at an earlier point at Mr Inskip's church. She was also a close friend of Hannah Whitall Smith and acquainted with her husband, Robert.[38] Much of her time in New York was spent in holding what she termed 'consecration meetings' for women. At these occasions she would often invite those who wanted a clean heart to go forward to the front of the meeting and kneel down.[39] For Amanda such steps of faith included a pledge to give up the use of tobacco which she described as 'a filthy habit' and a commitment to temperance. It was probably for this reason that she became active in 'The Woman's Christian Temperance Union' from 1875 and again in her later years when she returned to America in 1890. She was one of the few African American women to play a prominent part in the activities of the Union. *The Union Signal*, the WCTU's national periodical, carried a number of reports of her meetings in the 1890s.

---

34 Bartlett, 'The Final Ministry of Amanda Berry Smith', p. 29.
35 Smith, *Amanda Smith*, p. 49.
36 Smith, *Amanda Smith*, p. 67.
37 Smith, *Amanda Smith*, pp. 74 and 117.
38 Smith, *Amanda Smith*, p. 119.
39 Smith, *Amanda Smith*, p. 115.

In conducting revival meetings she came increasingly to see the importance of obeying the promptings of the Holy Spirit. She described how on one occasion she was prompted to lift up her right hand but resisted the impulse to do so. She recognized her disobedience immediately afterwards and resolved that on future occasions she would be obedient to such impulses. Shortly afterwards she found herself at another meeting and felt again the spirit of God say, 'Lift your right hand. She did so and immediately 'the power of the Spirit fell on the people and the whole congregation'. 'There were', she continued, '"Amens", and "Amens", and sobs and weeping and "Praise the Lord", heard all over the house. Many were led out of prison by this simple act of obedience to God.'[40]

Singing

Amanda Smith had a powerful gift of singing and in consequence she was often invited to sing at camp meetings, and sometimes sang at meetings she was conducting, before she exhorted her congregations or started a prayer meeting. Looking back on the early 1870s Amanda recalled that 'in those days I used to sing a great deal, and somehow the Lord always seemed to bless my singing'.[41] At that time the 'Winnowed Hymns' were very popular and Amanda knew a number of them very well. On one occasion during a camp meeting in the small community of Sing Sing she was invited to step up onto the stump and sing to a crowd of about four hundred. After she had sung one or two favourites, one of which was the very familiar

> All I want, all I want,
> Is a little more faith in Jesus.

She testified, '... my heart grew warm, and the power of the Spirit rested upon me, and many of the people wept, and seemed deeply moved and interested, as they had never been before. And God, I believe, blessed that meeting at that big stump on the old Sing Sing Camp Ground.'[42] When Amanda invited people to come forward to receive sanctification she frequently put her beautiful voice to good use singing melodies such as 'All I want is a little more faith in Jesus'.[43] She was invited to sing that same song at the American Methodist Episcopal Church Annual Conference in 1870 and did so to great effect with 'the preachers getting happy and the people weeping and shouting 'Amen' and 'Praise the Lord!'.[44]

Amanda's gift of singing was a key aspect of her revival work and meetings. Charles Price and Ian Randall in their history of the Keswick Convention noted that 'a gospel singer, Amanda Smith, who was at Broadlands and who was known

---

40 Bartlett, 'The Final Ministry of Amanda Berry Smith', p. 60.
41 Bartlett, 'The Final Ministry of Amanda Berry Smith', p. 117.
42 Bartlett, 'The Final Ministry of Amanda Berry Smith', p. 107.
43 Bartlett, 'The Final Ministry of Amanda Berry Smith', p. 116.
44 Bartlett, 'The Final Ministry of Amanda Berry Smith', p. 125.

for such powerful songs as "I am a child of the King", later sang as Keswick'.[45] Bishop James Thoburn, who was for many years head of the American Methodist Episcopal Church in India, described his first experience of being present at a gathering during the Epworth Heights camp meeting near Cincinnati. He remembered that for most of the day the meeting had not been very successful and that 'a spirit of depression rested upon many of the leaders'. Then suddenly 'the coloured sister' broke out with 'a triumphant song'. He found himself startled at the change in the meeting and 'at once absorbed with interest in the song and the singer'. He described Amanda's remarkable gift in the following paragraph:

> Something like a hallowed glow seemed to rest upon the dark face before me, and I felt in a second that she was possessed of a rare degree of spiritual power. That invisible something which we are accustomed to call power, and which is never possessed by any Christian believer except as one of the fruits of the indwelling Spirit of God, was hers in a remarkable degree.[46]

Although Amanda 'believed that the days of miracles are not past' and often prayed for the sick in their private homes and saw them healed, she doesn't appear to have prayed for the sick in her public meetings. She wrote: 'God has healed without the use of means of any kind, as well as with; and why he does not now heal every case as He used to do, I do not think I have any right to say is because of a lack of faith on the part of some poor, weak child of God; and so consign them to perdition.'[47]

Like Zilpha Elaw before her, Amanda does not appear to have been a liberated woman in the domestic sphere at least in her earlier days. At the time when she worked night and day to support her second husband by taking in washing she found that 'he was a man of those poor unfortunate dispositions that is hard to satisfy'.[48] That said, away from the domestic sphere, Amanda Berry Smith became a powerful figure in the holiness movement in America where she spoke at many camp meetings. In England, her influence touched both the holiness conference at Keswick and the Broadlands meetings organized by Lord Mount Temple. Although it is beyond the scope of this book, it is worthy of note that she inherited her parents concern for the needs of Africa and worked in Liberia from 1881-9, mostly with Methodist Missionaries, organizing temperance societies and concerning herself with the needs of children. On her return to America she continued to preach and endeavoured to establish an orphanage for black children. Her reputation as an evangelist enabled her to open up greater opportunities for women to minister in the American Methodist churches.

---

45 C. Price and I. Randall, *Transforming Keswick* (OM Publishing, 2000), p. 149.
46 Smith, *Amanda Smith*, p. 154.
47 Smith, *Amanda Smith*, p. 65.
48 Smith, *Amanda Smith*, p. 37.

CHAPTER 10

Robert and Hannah Pearsall Smith and 'Higher Life' Revivalism

Early Years to 1865

Hannah Whitall Smith (1832–1911) and her husband Robert Pearsall Smith (1827–99) were a Quaker couple whose teaching on the 'Higher Life' had a remarkable impact on the evangelical world on both sides of the Atlantic. In England it was primarily their teaching which played a major part in the founding of the Keswick Convention. They were both accomplished writers and Hannah's book, *The Christian's Secret of a Happy Life* was first published in 1875 and is still read today. The Pearsall Smiths played out their public roles in two different nineteenth-century worlds. Up until 1875 theirs was the world of evangelical revivals and camp meetings but during the later Victorian era, when they settled in England, they became part of the intellectual elite who doubted orthodox Christianity and advocated radical and socialist ideas. Robert Pearsall Smith seems to have turned away from Christianity altogether and, although Hannah remained a mainstream believer to the end of her days, she saw and expressed her faith very differently. The Smiths' daughter Mary left her first husband, Frank Costelloe, and went to Italy to study art with Bernard Berenson. Their daughter Alys was the first wife of the philosopher Bertrand Russell, and their son Logan became a lecturer at Oxford University. It is however their role as evangelical revivalists that is the focus of this chapter.

Their Quaker Upbringing

Both Hannah and Robert were born into notable Quaker families in the Philadelphia New Jersey area. Robert's family on his father's side went back to James Logan, a staunch Quaker of Colonial Pennsylvania and personal secretary of William Penn. His father John Jay Smith and his mother Rachel Pearsall, of Flushing, Long Island, were both birthright Quakers. John Smith was a printer and publisher who also held the position of librarian of the Philadelphia public library. This was an honorary and hereditary position given to the Smiths in recognition of the very valuable Loganian collection which James Logan had given to the library company.

Hannah Tatum Whitall was the daughter of John Michel Whitall and Mary Tatum. Both were birthright Quakers. Her family was able to live in very comfortable circumstances from the highly profitable Whitall Tatum glass plants in southern New Jersey. From the adoption of the name Whitall Tatum

Company in 1858 to the company's merger with the Armstrong Cork Company in the 1930s, Whitall Tatum was a name to be reckoned with in the American glass industry.

Hannah describes her upbringing in her book entitled *The Unselfishness of God and How I Discovered It: A Spiritual Autobiography*, which was first published in 1903. Her childhood was a time of great happiness and security. She wrote in a few terse sentences, 'I was born in Philadelphia, Pennsylvania, in the year 1832. My parents were strict Quakers, and until my marriage at nineteen, I knew nothing of any other religion. I had an absolutely happy childhood and girlhood.'[1]

Hannah's life was regulated in all its aspects by the practices of the Friends. 'Every word and thought and action of our lives was steeped in Quakerism', she recalled. Although she was later to leave the Meeting for a period, her parents' faith provided her with a secure basis. 'Daily I thank God', she wrote, 'that it was such a righteous and enabling influence.'[2] Although strict in some aspects the Whitall household was a place of love and happiness. As she looked back on the early years as a septuagenarian Hannah wrote, 'But the chiefest charm of my life was that I possessed the most delightful father and mother that ever lived.'[3]

Hannah relates how like all good members of the Friends she was taught to listen and obey the voice of God in her soul. To the Quakers this was 'the true light which lighteth every man that cometh into the world'. This light if followed seriously would teach its subjects all that was necessary and be their divine guide.

Hannah Tatum Whitall married Robert Pearsall Smith in June 1851. She was 19 and he was 24. He was in every way a desirable suitor, handsome, gifted and, above all, according to his son, Logan, 'a magnificent salesman'.[4] Hannah, who had only months previously been dreaming of becoming a preacher and going to England,[5] was swept off her feet. In the spring of 1851 he is recorded as having picked a bouquet of flowers from the garden of the small house in Germantown, Pennsylvania, which was to be their future home, and attached the following lines: 'Mayest thou live to enjoy many beautiful flowers there as my bride, my friend, my congenial companion and ardently loved (may I say it, Wife?).'[6]

The early years of their marriage were a happy period of their life together. They were both close to their families. Robert was absorbed in the work of the

---

1 H.W. Smith, *The Unselfishness of God and How I Discovered It: A Spiritual Autobiography* (Fleming H. Revell, 1903), p. 20.
2 Smith, *The Unselfishness of God*, p. 37.
3 Smith, *The Unselfishness of God*, p. 26.
4 P.L. Smith, *Unforgotten Years* (Little, Brown, 1939), p. 33.
5 M. Henry, *The Secret Life of Hannah Whitall Smith* (Zondervan, 1984), p. 24.
6 Smith, *Archive Journal of H.W.S., Volume VII December 30, 1857* cited Henry, *The Secret Life of Hannah Whitall Smith*, p. 5.

Hannah Pearsall Smith about the time of her marriage

family publishing business. He became a map publisher of some note. Eventually however, he joined the Whitall-Tatum firm, often travelling long distances as a company sales representative. His son, Logan, wrote of his business dealings.

> He was, above all, a magnificent salesman, and travelling all over the U.S., and offering the firm's wares to the chemists of the rapidly expanding Republic, he exercised upon these apothecaries the gifts of his persuasion and blandishment, almost of hypnotization.[7]

In 1865 Smith was appointed to the position of resident manager of the Whitall-Tatum works at Millville, New Jersey. Hannah was understandably anxious about the change from the pleasant environment of Germantown to the drab mill town in southern New Jersey. As things turned out however the move would alter the course of the couple's future life. It was through the influence of Methodist factory workers at the Millville plant that both Hannah and Robert learned the doctrine of entire sanctification and the Spirit-filled life.

---

7 Smith, *Unforgotten Years*, p. 33.

Discovering the 'Higher Christian Life'

Personal Faith and Baptism

With the passing of their first few years of marriage Hannah and Robert began to feel a deadness in the Quaker Society in which they had both been nurtured. Logan Smith, their son, later wrote: 'My parents, dissatisfied with what they considered the spiritual deadness of Quaker doctrine, welcomed the new outburst in America of revivalism, into which they plunged as into a great flood of life-giving water.'[8] Early in the year 1858 Hannah who related 'no plan of salvation, or any such thing as "justification by faith" was even heard among us', had her first real encounter with 'some very orthodox Christians'.[9] They were Methodists. As a result she came to have a personal faith in Christ. She wrote in her diary.

> August 30, 1858. I am resting now simply on God's own record as the foundation of my hope. He says Jesus Christ is His well-beloved Son, and I believe it .... He is my Saviour, not only my helper, and in His finished work I rest. Even my hard heart of unbelief can no longer refrain from crying out, 'Lord, I believe. Help Thou my unbelief?'.[10]

Hannah now found her life transformed as the result of her new-found faith. 'My heart is filled with the exceeding preciousness of Christ. And I am lost in wonder at the realization of His infinite mercy to me, who am so utterly unworthy of the least favour from His hands.'[11] Robert came to share her experience. She and her husband, she says, 'learned thoroughly the blessed truth of justification by faith, and rejoiced in it with great joy'.[12]

The following year in September Robert and Hannah were baptized by immersion in the Baptist church at Pottsville, Pennsylvania, by a German Reform minister.[13] Although they felt at peace about the step which they had taken they were banned from their parents' homes. In a secret letter to her sister, Sally, Hannah spoke of feeling 'like an outcast from my earthly father's house. But not, Oh thanks be to God, not from my heavenly Father's house! And ... I know He is caring for me ...'[14]

The Pearsall Smiths resigned their membership with the Society of Friends, Robert joining the Presbyterians and Hannah attaching herself to the Plymouth

---

8 Smith, *Unforgotten Years*, p. 35.
9 Smith, *The Unselfishness of God*, p. 50.
10 Smith, *The Unselfishness of God*, p. 177.
11 Smith, *The Unselfishness of God*, p. 177.
12 H.W. Smith, *The Record of a Happy Life* (J.B. Lippincott, 1873), p. 37.
13 Henry, *The Secret Life of Hannah Whitall Smith*, pp. 35 and 175.
14 *Letters of H.W.S.*, letter to Sally, 13 October 1859 cited *The Secret Life of Hannah Whitall Smith*, p. 38.

Brethren. She related her deep gratitude to new fellowship in the following lines:

> The disapproval of my own religious society, in these early stages of my new life, threw me very much under the influence of the Plymouth Brethren, who were at that time making quite a stir in Philadelphia, and whose clear doctrines, and especially of the doctrine of 'justification by faith', was particularly congenial to my new way of looking at things. They were great Bible students, and I soon found under their teaching a fascinating interest in Bible Study.[15]

Hannah felt she could 'never be thankful enough' to the Brethren for opening up the Bible for her. 'It was no longer, "How do I feel?" but always, "What does God say?" And He said such delightful things that to find them out became my supreme delight.'[16]

Holiness Camp Meetings

With the passing of time, Hannah gradually began to find some aspects of Brethren teaching hard to accept. In particular, she found herself strongly opposed to what she perceived as their extreme Calvinism. She was aware that their religion 'provided perfectly for my future deliverance, but it did not seem to give me present deliverance'.[17] This set her searching once more and at some point in 1867 she discovered the Methodist teaching that sanctification can be received by faith in the same way that justification is by faith.[18] This new revelation came to Hannah through a young Baptist theological student who was living in her home as a tutor, and a Methodist dressmaker who lived in their town of Millville, New Jersey.[19] From the tutor she learned that the way of victory was by faith, and from the dressmaker, that there was an experience called the "Second Blessing", which brought one into a place of victory.[20]

This spiritually alive dressmaker urged Hannah to come to one of their Saturday night meetings. By attending this group regularly Hannah came to the realization that her Christianity depended too much on her own efforts, resolutions and fervent endeavours to achieve holy living. She realized that 'I alone can do nothing – and if the Lord does not do it all, it will not be done. But when I trust Him, He delivered me from the power of sin as well as from its

---

15 Smith, *Unselfishness of God*, p. 190.
16 Smith, *Unselfishness of God*, p. 193.
17 Smith, *Unselfishness of God*, p. 228.
18 Smith, *Unselfishness of God*, p. 243.
19 Smith, *Record of a Happy Life*, p. 37.
20 Smith, *Record of a Happy Life*, p. 37.

guilt.' She continued, 'I can leave in His care my cares, my temptations, my growth, my service, my daily life, moment by moment.'[21]

By the year 1867 Hannah had come to accept the Methodist teaching that one could be victorious over sin by believing. In her autobiography she cited an extract from her journal of 11 February 1867.

> The present attitude of my soul is that of trusting in the Lord. And I have found it is a practical reality that He does deliver. When temptation comes, if I turn at once to Him, breathing this prayer, 'Lord save me, I cannot save myself from this sin, but Thou canst and will', He never fails me.[22]

Hannah also spoke of her experience in an article in *Guide to Holiness*, July 1867.

> I confessed my own absolute inability to dedicate myself to his service, my powerlessness to submit my will to his, and I cast myself, as it were, headlong into the ocean, of his love, to have all these things accomplished in me by his almighty working. I trusted him utterly and entirely. I took him for my Saviour from the daily power of sin, with as naked a faith as I once took him for my Saviour from its guilt. I believed the truth that he was my practical sanctification as well as my justification ... Jesus became my present Saviour, and my soul did rest at last; such a rest, that no words can describe it, ... rest from all its legal strivings, rest from all its weary conflict, rest from all its bitter failure. The secret of holiness was revealed to me; and that secret was Jesus, ... Jesus, made unto me wisdom and righteousness and sanctification.[23]

Deeply impacted by this experience Hannah persuaded Robert to attend camp meetings held by a Methodist Holiness Group every summer at Manheim, Pennsylvania. They had by this time become particularly interested in the 'second blessing' experience, also called the baptism of the Holy Spirit. Robert attended a prayer gathering before breakfast in one of the large tents for those who were seeking the baptism. Several laid their hands on him and prayed for him to receive the blessing. Robert was deeply stirred by their earnest supplications and found a quiet spot in the adjoining woodland. Hannah recounted his experience in the following lines:

> Suddenly, from head to foot, he had been shaken with what seemed like a magnetic thrill of heavenly delight and floods of glory seemed to pour through him, soul and body, with the inward assurance that this

---

21 Smith, *The Unselfishness of God*, pp. 238–45.
22 Smith, *The Unselfishness of God*, p. 244.
23 H.W. Smith, 'Believing, Resting, Abiding', *Guide to Holiness*, 52, July 1867, p. 23.

was the longed for Baptism of the Holy Spirit. The whole world seemed transformed to him, every leaf and blade of grass quivered with exquisite colour and heaven seemed to open out before him as a blissful possession. Everything looked beautiful to him, for he seemed to see the divine spirit within each one without regard to their outward seemings.[24]

Robert's ecstatic experience lasted for several weeks and was the beginning of what Hannah described as 'a wonderful career of spiritual power and blessing'.

Hannah's experience had been less emotional in character and it left her in her own words 'rather jealous' and feeling that she needed it quite as much as her husband. At various times in 1868 and 1869 Hannah prayed constantly and earnestly for the experience that Robert had had but it proved to be in vain. She experienced no floods of joy or any overwhelming thrill. She never seemed to get out of the region of conviction and into emotion. 'I found myself', she wrote, 'compelled to take all my experiences intellectually and not emotionally.'[25] She found to her surprise and delight that her 'convictions' brought her a more stable and permanent joy than many of her more emotional friends seemed to experience.[26]

The Essence of 'Higher Christian Life' Teaching

The new-found teaching and experience which Hannah and Robert had entered into has been given a variety of names. Hannah wrote:

> This new life I had entered upon has been called by several different names. The Methodists called it, 'The Second Blessing' or 'The Blessing of Sanctification', the Presbyterians called it 'The Higher Life' or 'The Life of Faith', and the Friends called it 'The Life hid with Christ in God'.[27]

For herself Hannah most often called it 'The Higher Christian Life'. In 1874 she published a series of articles under that title in *The Christian's Pathway of Power*, a journal started by her husband in that year. In essence, she taught that the 'Higher Life' is simply 'letting the Lord carry our burdens and manage our affairs, instead of trying to do it ourselves.'[28] When once a believer is doing this, he or she will experience a sweet rest.

In the next issue of the same journal Hannah considered 'The Higher Christian Life' and how it is to be obtained. Her answer was quite simply that it is achieved only by faith, the same faith which brought forgiveness of sins. God has said certain things and faith, Hannah underlined, is believing them.

---

24 Smith, *The Unselfishness of God*, pp. 288–9.
25 Smith, *The Unselfishness of God*, p. 289.
26 Smith, *The Unselfishness of God*, p. 290.
27 Smith, *The Unselfishness of God*, p. 261.
28 *The Christian's Pathway of Power*, Vol. 2, 2 March 1874, p. 38.

> We are saved by faith .... And the faith by which we are to enter this Higher Life is just the same as that which we exercised then, only it lays hold of a different thing. Then we believed Jesus was our Saviour from the guilt of sin, and according to our faith it was unto us. Now we must believe that He is our Saviour from the power of sin, and according to our faith it shall be unto us.[29]

An essential aspect of this trust in Christ for deliverance from the power of sin and life's associated burdens was 'Consecration' or a willingness on the part of a believer 'to commit your case to Him in absolute abandonment'.[30] In the May issue of *The Christian's Pathway of Power*, Hannah wrote of the 'Practical Difficulties in the Way of Entering into "The Higher Christian Life"'. Here she further developed the idea of 'consecration' in terms of 'full surrender'. Christians, she urged, must surrender their 'whole self to His Will' as completely as they can make it. They must ask the Holy Spirit to reveal any hidden rebellion. Once the surrender has been made it must 'never be questioned or recalled'.[31]

Both Robert and Hannah also set out this teaching more fully in book form: Robert in *Holiness Through Faith*, first published in 1870 by A. Randolph in New York and revised for a second edition in 1875 by Marshall Morgan and Scott; and Hannah in *The Christian's Secret of a Happy Life*, first published in 1870 by Revell. Robert laid stress on unbelief as the major obstacle to receiving victory over sin.

> To sinner and saint, alike, upon whatever level, unbelief is the bar, while faith is the channel of God's blessing .... Full faith gives full deliverance; partial faith, partial victory. So much faith, so much deliverance, – no more, no less! If we would live up to the Gospel standard of Christian holiness we must believe up to the Gospel standard of faith. Every complaint of leanness, failure, or sinning is but a confession of want of belief.[32]

In chapter 3 of *The Christian's Secret of a Happy Life* Hannah stated that the chief characteristics of the 'life hid with Christ in God' were 'an entire surrender to the Lord, and a perfect trust in Him, resulting in victory over sin and inward rest of soul'.[33] In a subsequent chapter she described the 'Higher Life' as being like a little child in the Father's house. Just as an infant has no worries in a

---

29 *The Christian's Pathway of Power*, 1 April 1874, p. 46.
30 *The Christian's Pathway of Power*, 1 April 1874, p. 46.
31 *The Christian's Pathway of Power*, 1 May 1874, p. 69.
32 R. Smith, *Holiness Through Faith. Light on the Way to Holiness* (Marshall, Morgan and Scott, 1875), p. 36.
33 H.W. Smith, *The Christian's Secret of a Happy Life* (Zondervan, 1984 edition), p. 37.

caring household and is fed, clothed and loved, so it is for Christian believers who can leave themselves in God's hands and learn to literally be careful for nothing.[34]

In chapter 5 Hannah considered the difficulties of consecration and she developed an altar theology which is very similar to that of Phoebe Palmer. She spoke of everything which is surrendered to Christ as 'holy'. Even an offering 'grudgingly' and 'half-heartedly given' becomes 'holy'. It was not made holy by the state of mind of giver but by the holiness of the Divine receiver. The altar sanctifies the gift and an offering once given, once laid upon the altar belonged to the Lord.[35] Once again Hannah, as did Robert, stressed the crucial importance of faith. The key is always 'to believe that God takes that which you have surrendered, and to reckon that it is his'.[36]

Revival Years 1865–75

Meetings in America

Robert and Hannah's acceptance of sanctification by faith or the 'Higher Christian Life' propelled them both into a period of intense holiness revival activity. During this time they spoke at many of the summer camp meetings of the Methodist sponsored National Camp Meeting Association. They also co-operated with the leaders of the deeper life movements in non–Methodist traditions. Dr Levy, a Baptist, Dr William Boardman, a Presbyterian, and Dr Charles Cullis, an Episcopalian, soon became friends and co-workers. In these years, which immediately followed the ending of the Civil War in which more than six hundred thousand had died, there was a sudden upsurge of desire for holiness and a higher Christian life across America.

Something of the hectic nature of Robert and Hannah's lifestyle can be gauged from one of Hannah's letters addressed to her son, Franklin, and dated 12 March 1871:

> If thee could just be in my shoes for one day, thee would not scold about my not writing! My very head seems ready to come off sometimes. I have a Bible class every morning in the week except on 7th days, and every afternoon a perfect levee (flood) of visitors at home. And then there are no end of things to do besides. Tonight I am expecting every minute Mrs S. and Mrs K and Miss N.M. to tea, and then we are all to go to S. Shipley's to the Merrick Street meeting. So do forgive thy poor mother, dear boy, and comfort thyself with thinking how popular she is![37]

---

34 Smith, *The Christian's Secret*, p. 44.
35 Smith, *The Christian's Secret*, p. 62.
36 Smith, *The Christian's Secret*, p. 66.
37 L.P. Smith, *A Religious Rebel The Letters of H.W.S.* (Nisbet, 1949). Letter to Frank Whitall Smith, 12 March 1871.

Robert's Breakdown

With the relentless round of speaking engagements and the death of their son, Frank, a promising under-graduate student at Princeton University, Robert suffered a nervous breakdown in the autumn of 1872. The whole family took up residence for a time in a large rest home run by a man referred to as Dr Foster. Robert was in a highly distressed state. He was very hurtful and threatening to Hannah saying such things as 'Thee doesn't know how thee hurts me' and 'is thy skin as thick as a rhinoceros?'[38] On one occasion he called on Hannah to 'Pray for me to be delivered from this unbearable torment.'[39]

Hannah was deeply perturbed by Dr Foster passing on to some of his patients, among them her husband, a 'spiritual' discovery he had made. He had learned to experience physical thrills akin to sexual feelings in his prayer times. Robert was certainly influenced by this teaching and it may have contributed to his later crisis in England. Barbara Strachey Halpern, the Smiths great granddaughter, wrote many years later in 1980:

> I do believe that he [Robert] had accepted and was preaching heretical and fanatical doctrines concerning the physical manifestations that should accompany the 'Baptism in the Holy Ghost' which were of a dangerously sexual nature. He and Hannah had fallen under the influence of a Dr Foster who was extremely fanatical – his behaviour and views are described in two of Hannah's papers in Religious Fanaticism, edited by my mother, the Dr R. fanaticism (a pseudonym for Dr Foster) and Miss S's fanaticism (who is also identifiable from the letters).[40]

Around Christmas time 1872 Robert began to calm down. Early in the following year Robert left his job in the glass factory and, supported by his father-in-law, started the holiness journal entitled *The Christian's Pathway of Power*. His physicians believed his breakdown had been brought about by overwork and, after further relapses in February, they recommended a trip abroad where invitations to meetings and speaking engagements would be closed down. So in March 1873 Robert took a steamer to England with the intention of continuing across Europe to Mannedorf in Switzerland. Hannah was therefore profoundly shocked to learn from Robert that, instead of continuing his journey of recovery to central Europe, he had become involved in the Mildmay Conference in England and was teaching and exhorting on the Higher Life in peculiarly effective way.

---

38 Henry, *The Secret Life of Hannah Whitall Smith*, p. 68.
39 Henry, *The Secret Life of Hannah Whitall Smith*, p. 59.
40 Barbara Strachey Halpern to Professor S. Barabas 12 March 1980, Keswick Collection, Wheaton College, Illinois.

Ministry in England and Europe 1873–5

The two-year public ministry which followed in England, Holland, France and Germany was, according to his critic Benjamin Warfield, one of the most spectacular in the history of modern evangelism. His son, Logan Pearsall Smith, later recalled 'immense crowds flocked to his ministrations; his thrilling voice held audiences of thousands in rapt attention'. Soon his reputation as a preacher crossed the Channel.[41] He was invited to Paris where he held many meetings and the wives of the monarchs of Belgium and Holland welcomed him to their countries, and discussed the state of their royal souls with him in private interviews.[42] Logan remembered that 'thousands listened to the doctrines he proclaimed'. And that 'my father's photograph adorned the windows of the London shops'.[43]

Robert and Hannah, who joined him with some of their children in January 1874, were active as speakers and leaders in a series of meetings which led directly to the founding of the Keswick Convention in the summer of 1875. In February 1874 Robert was one of several speakers at a three-day gathering of 'Meetings for Consecration and Power for Service' held at the Hanover Square Rooms. He spoke of 'the mighty movement sweeping over the Churches where the Grace of God had been truly preached, drawing the people of God near to Christ and to each other'.[44]

The Broadlands Conference July 1874

The meeting which really launched the Pearsall Smiths into the English evangelical world was the Conference organized in July 1874 by Mr and Mrs Cowper-Temple, later Lord and Lady Mount Temple, in their beautiful home at 'Broadlands'. About two hundred people attended. Some fifty guests stayed in the mansion itself. A number of under-graduates camped in the park-like estate while others rented rooms in nearby villages. The purpose of the Conference was to 'have a few days of quiet prayer and meditation upon the Scriptural possibilities of the Christian life, as to maintained communion with the Lord and victory over all known sin'.[45] During the six-day Conference Hannah's preaching, as well as Robert's, was much admired.[46] *The Christian's Pathway of Power* reported that 'no description could convey the wonderful sense of the

---

41 Smith, *Unforgotten Years*, p. 57.
42 Smith, *Unforgotten Years*, p. 57.
43 Smith, *Unforgotten Years*, p. 57.
44 *The Christian's Pathway to Power*, 1 April 1874, p. 57.
45 *Account of the Union Meeting for the Promotion of Scriptural Holiness, held at Oxford, August 29 – September 7, 1874,* (H. Revell, 1875), pp. 19–20 give this brief account of the earlier meeting at Broadlands.
46 *The Hampshire Telegraph and the Sussex Chronicle*, 25 July 1874 gives a report of the Broadlands Conference including details of Sunday sermons given in local churches by some of the participants.

presence and power of God which attended those six days of waiting upon the Lord'. The editorial continued that 'something of what it is to "be filled with the Spirit" was realized'.[47]

The Oxford Conference 29 August – 7 September 1874

The Broadlands meetings proved so successful that Robert decided to organize a further meeting at Oxford on 'The Higher Life'. This took place from 29 August to 7 September 1874. The number present was estimated to be between twelve and fifteen hundred with participants coming by rail from Ireland, Scotland, England, Switzerland, Germany and Holland. Among other features there were Bible readings by Hannah Pearsall Smith and 'Consecration Meetings'.

The Oxford Conference was said to be 'the expression of a widely realized need of a more definite consecration to the Lord and trust in His promises'.[48] In the opening meeting at the Town Hall, Robert Pearsall Smith said in his address that 'the Scriptural privilege of the Christian life which we are urging upon Christians has only been named "The Higher Christian" because so few were living it.... Anything short of complete self-surrender, of entire faith in the promises of God, is lower than the Christian life.'[49]

On the second day of the conference, Hannah spoke on 'Law and Grace' and a number of gentlemen attended, although the meeting had been primarily intended for women. Many Christians, she urged, 'try to live their Christian lives under a covenant of works'. They trust Christ for the forgiveness of their sins but when comes to the daily living, 'they feel they could and ought to help'.[50] She went on to stress that it was not a matter of Christians 'working in order to make yourselves right' rather it is letting Christ 'work in you to will and to do of His good pleasure'.[51] 'You received Him by faith', she emphasized, 'you are to walk in Him by faith also.'[52] At the conclusion of her talk the whole congregation bowed in silence for several minutes while Mrs Smith made a prayer of full surrender on her own behalf and on behalf of each member of the congregation.[53]

The influence of the Pearsall Smiths on English Evangelicals was very strong. Following the Oxford Conference, the Revd Alfred Christopher (1814–1913), rector of St Aldate's, Oxford, from 1859 to 1905, spoke of his experience of the power of God. It was so signally manifested 'that I felt as if I had never witnessed this power in visible operation upon Christians before'. He also spoke of 'the calmness and simplicity of the addresses' and 'the absence of excitement'

---

47 *The Christian's Pathway to Power*, 1 August 1874. p. 124.
48 *Account of the Union Meeting*, introductory page.
49 *Account of the Union Meeting*, p. 54.
50 *Account of the Union Meeting*, p. 67.
51 *Account of the Union Meeting*, p. 69.
52 *Account of the Union Meeting*, p. 69.
53 *Account of the Union Meeting*, p. 71.

Robert Pearsall Smith

which made it all the more clear that this was the fruit of God's power and not man's influence.[54] Christopher continued, 'The special manifestation of God's power which most impressed me was the great change wrought in some of the most faithful, diligent and lovable Evangelical clergymen I know.'[55] A measure of the influence of the Pearsall Smiths' teaching can be gauged from the reported comment of a Church of England clergyman who said in 1874: 'Just name a consecration meeting, and the people run together from twenty or thirty miles round.'[56]

Robert Preaches in Europe

Following the Oxford meeting the Smiths returned to the United States in late September. They remained on home soil over the winter period and settled into a routine until Robert sailed for Europe in early March 1875 on a preaching tour. By this point he had become an international speaker whose teachings captivated large audiences. Kaiser Wilhelm had invited him to Berlin and placed the old Garrison church at his disposal. Through his powerful preaching Robert impacted the lives of thousands in German cities. The Philadelphia Press began

---

54 *The Christian's Pathway of Power*, 1 October 1874, p. 177.
55 *The Christian's Pathway of Power*, 1 October 1874, p. 177.
56 *Guide to Holiness*, February 1874. p. 59.

to receive reports of his revival mission in Germany and stated that 'Immense crowds attend the meetings and members of the nobility occupy seats on the platforms.'[57] According to his son, Logan, Robert was reported to have said in triumphant tones, 'All Europe is at my feet.'[58]

The Brighton Convention 28 May –7 June 1875

Within nine months of the great Oxford Conference a still large series of meetings was held at Brighton from 29 May to 7 June 1875. Robert Pearsall Smith who acted as Chairman, advertised the convention in *The Christian's Pathway to Power* and elsewhere[59] reminding people that the Holy Spirit 'is everywhere creating hungerings and thirstings after righteousness, and to a degree scarcely known before'.[60] He urged people to come together at Brighton 'for renunciation of sin and for seeking the presence of the Lord ... confidently believing that God the Holy Spirit, will multiply to us the grace and peace of the September meeting at Oxford'.[61]

People came from many parts of the world to attend. When at one of the meetings, the Chairman asked those from other lands to stand, representatives from 23 countries were found to be present. During the time of the convention D.L. Moody was just concluding his great evangelistic campaign at Covent Garden, London. On the opening day of the Brighton Conference, he said to his audience, 'Let us lift up our hearts to seek earnestly a blessing on the great Convention that is now being held in Brighton, perhaps the most important meeting ever gathered', and he sent the following telegram, 'Moody and 8,000 persons at the closing meeting at the Opera House have specially prayed for the Convention, that great results may follow.' Robert Pearsall Smith, as Brighton Chairman, said, 'Let us ask an answering blessing upon our beloved brother, Mr Moody, a man who walks with God.'[62]

Both Robert and Hannah took a leading part in speaking. Hannah addressed meetings which were attended by men which was thought by some of those present to be scandalous and by others unscriptural. Brighton was a triumph for the Smiths save for one small episode in which a Miss Hattie Hamilton, one of Roberts adoring fans, rushed up to him, threw her arms around him and kissed him at the end of one of the meetings. It didn't seem much at the time but it was to lead to further more serious trouble.

---

57 Henry, *The Secret Life of Hannah Whitall Smith*, pp. 74–5.
58 Smith, *Unforgotten Years*, p. 60.
59 See for example, *The Christian's Pathway to Power*, 1 May 1875.
60 *The Christian's Pathway to Power*, 1 May 1875.
61 *The Christian's Pathway to Power*, 1 May 1875.
62 J.B. Figgis, *Keswick from Within* (Marshall Bros., 1914), p. 34.

The First Keswick Convention and Robert's Fall from Grace June 1875

At the Brighton convention, Canon T.D. Harford-Battersby, vicar of St John's Keswick, and his close friend, Mr Robert Wilson, a Quaker, who had also been particularly blessed by the 'Higher Life' meetings, decided to share their experience by holding a convention at Keswick. They invited some of the leading speakers at Brighton to take part, including Robert and Hannah Pearsall Smith. Robert also agreed to preside.

The Keswick Convention was scheduled to begin on 29 June, just three weeks after the close of the Brighton convention. The invitation was headed 'Union Meetings for the Promotion of Practical Holiness', and Christians from every section of the Church were invited to attend. Hannah who was exhausted decided to take a two-week trip to Switzerland prior to the start of Keswick, while Robert remained in England. Shortly after Hannah left, what was regarded as a scandalous incident involving Robert took place. The precise nature of what happened isn't entirely clear. In substance Hattie Hamilton requested a private interview with Robert in her hotel bedroom. He somewhat reluctantly agreed and found her in uncontrollable hysterics, shaking and saying that she didn't feel accepted by Jesus as his child. He apparently sat beside her on her bed and put his arm around her, during which time he explained to her the unwise and unorthodox teaching that Dr Foster had shared with them during his recovery from breakdown in 1872. This was that 'Christ wanted us to feel thrills up and down our bodies because this would make us feel closer to Him.'[63] The following morning Miss Hamilton went to Mr Stevenson Blackwood, Robert's Brighton sponsor, and related what he had said and that he had tried to make love to her. Blackwood summoned Robert to his office and made it clear that he accepted Hamilton's version of events and recommended that he halt his ministry immediately.

In a letter written after the event to Lord Mount Temple Robert stated:

I blame myself greatly yet I can say before God, my intentions were as free from the wish for adultery as were it my own child, I put my arm about her .... I do not defend or extenuate these thoughtless things – I condemn them without limit. Nothing beyond this was laid to my charge in the course of my hearing – But it was in my room and my door was locked – and I did desire the dear heartbroken child should find full rest in the manifested love of her Lord. I do not think my intentions could have been more pure to my own daughter.[64]

---

63 Henry, *The Secret Life of Hannah Whitall Smith*, p. 81.
64 Robert Pearsall Smith to Lord Mount Temple, Mount Temple Collection, Hampshire Record Office.

Needless to say what had transpired was eagerly reported in the press. *The Brighton Weekly* headlined the events: 'Famous Evangelist Found in Bedroom of Adoring Female Follower'.[65]

The first Keswick Convention did go ahead from 29 June to 2 July with crowds up to a thousand filling the large tent for the evening meetings. Harford-Battersby reported that 'the loss of the presence of the beloved brother who was to have presided seemed ... at first a great misfortune' but very quickly they recognized in this disappointment a grand opportunity to exercise trust in God.[66] One thing which Keswick owed to the Revival of 1858–9 was its slogan 'All One in Christ Jesus'.[67]

Robert and Hannah in America 1875–89

Robert was deeply shocked over what had happened. He suffered nausea and lost 20 pounds in weight. When he was sufficiently recovered Hannah persuaded the family to return home. In consequence of what had happened, the Smiths now felt that God had released them from their former ministry though their friends in the American Holiness Movement took a longer time to be convinced. Robert returned to his work of travelling for the Whitall-Tatum Company. Hannah meantime involved herself in her family, writing and temperance work.

By this stage Mary, Alys and Logan were the only ones of her children still living and Hannah devoted herself to them completely. She also busied herself with many speaking engagements and writing commitments. In the summer of 1876, after repeated entreaties, both Robert and Hannah spoke together at the Framingham camp meeting. By the end of 1877, however, Robert came to have increasing intellectual doubts and eventually lost his faith altogether. Hannah's outlook also broadened considerably but she retained her trust in Christ to the end. She wrote on 8 August 1876 to Anna Shipley:

> I waiver about myself continually. Sometimes I feel sure I have progressed wonderfully, and that my present sphinx-like calm and indifference to everything whether inward or outward except the Will of God is very grand. And then again I think I am an utterly irreligious and lazy fatalist, with not a spark of the divine in me. I do wish I could find out which I am. But at all events my orthodoxy has fled to the winds. I am Broad, Broader, Broadest![68]

---

65 Henry, *Secret Life of Hannah Whitall Smith*, p. 82.
66 *The Christian's Pathway of Power*, 2 August 1875.
67 J.E. Orr, *The Light of the Nations* (Paternoster Press, 1965), p. 206.
68 Smith, *A Religious Rebel*, pp. 35–6.

In this period Hannah threw her energies into the temperance cause, speaking at their rallies and urging friends and neighbours to take the pledge. She also became the National Superintendent of evangelistic work for the Women's National Christian Temperance Union and prepared study leaflet and prayer guides for the organization's study groups. Among other radical causes Hannah supported was the right of girls to have a College or University education.[69]

Last Years in England 1888–1911

In 1884 a young Irish Catholic graduate of Balliol College visited Harvard University. It set in motion a chain of events which eventually caused the Smith family to return to England permanently. Frank Costelloe fell in love with their daughter Mary, who followed him back to England in 1885. Despite Hannah's letters of protestation they were married at Oxford that year with Dr Benjamin Jowett, the Master of Balliol, hosting the wedding reception for Frank and his American bride. In 1887 their first daughter Ray Conn Costelloe was born.

Their return to America after the wedding was particularly difficult for Hannah. By 1888 Mary and the new granddaughter had convinced Hannah and Robert to return. Their visit in 1885 had given them the opportunity to renew friendships which they had made during their revival work ten years before including the now Lord and Lady Mount-Temple of Broadlands and their Quaker friends, the Gurneys. They settled in 1888 and rented a house two doors from Mary at 44 Grosvenor Road. Their son, Logan, became a student at Oxford.

Robert Pearsall's closing years in England were a confused mixture. His days were filled with rounds of social activities and nursing his real and imagined illnesses. Hannah did her best to care for him, though a late-in-life liaison with a woman across the Thames from their house further destroyed the harmony of their family. He died in 1898. Walter Sloan wrote, 'In him the Convention lost one who was perhaps its most used instrument; as he was in a special way made the channel of God's blessing to Ministers, Missionaries and Christian workers, who again became the instruments through whom the blessing passed on to untold numbers.'[70]

In 1891 the Pearsall Smith's daughter, Mary, left Frank Costelloe and the two little girls and went to Italy with Bernard Berenson. Frank died of cancer of the ear in 1899. Mary and Bernard were married the following year. Their daughter, Alys, married the atheistic philosopher Bertrand Russell in 1894 in a Quaker wedding. The marriage was effectively broken by 1902, though they stayed together until 1911 when Russell finally forced her to agree to a separation. They divorced in 1920. Alys died in 1951.

---

69 H.W.S. to Anna Shipley 14 August 1873 cited Smith, *A Religious Rebel*, p. 18.
70 Sloan, *These Sixty Years*, p. 74.

Hannah cared for Mary's children until they reached adult age while her daughter lived away with Berenson. Mary had several affairs which made her husband angry but the marriage somehow survived. Hannah completed her autobiography *The Unselfishness of God* in 1903 and *The God of All Comfort* in 1906. She was 'safely gathered' on 1 May 1911.

Despite the fact that both Robert and Hannah drifted way from their biblical and holiness roots there can be no doubt that they were a major influence on the Victorian evangelical world. Their teachings impacted many clergy, Anglicans in particular, as well as a great many middle- and upper-class lay people. Their writings, and especially those of Hannah, were widely read in Britain. Their teaching at Broadlands, Oxford and Brighton clearly inspired Harford-Battersby and Robert Wilson to found the Keswick Convention which became the dominant force in Evangelical spirituality down to the First World War and beyond.

CHAPTER 11

The Impact of American Revivalism

John Kent in his study of Revivalism was generally speaking critical of the impact made by nineteenth-century American revivalists, particularly those who came before Moody and Sankey. Referring to the arrival of these two men he speaks of revivalism passing 'from comparative American failure to comparative American success'.[1] One of the main points of his contention was that Anglican Evangelical interest remained lukewarm prior to their arrival. Of that period Kent wrote similarly that 'without widespread Anglican ministerial support, revivalism could not become more than a marginal factor, and this support remained minimal in the 1860s'.[2] That said, it is all too easy to put down the work of nineteenth-century American revivalists on the ground that they failed to reach objectives which the revivalists themselves and those who invited their services neither planned or envisaged. Men such as Lorenzo Dow or James Caughey never anticipated reaching out beyond the local town or Methodist circuit in which they were operating. Moody and Sankey were in fact the only individuals with a vision for large numbers and campaign strategies to influence large towns and cities.

Individual Contributions

Lorenzo Dow undoubtedly made a significant contribution to the origin and development of Primitive Methodism. His strong social and religious rebellious streak certainly fired Hugh Bourne and his followers. It was Dow's demonstration of 'the great usefulness of Camp Meetings' which led to Bourne forming the Camp Meeting Methodists. This in turn resulted in Bourne and later William Clowes' expulsion from the Wesleyans for taking part in them, and their subsequent formation of the Primitive Methodist Church in 1811. American-style camp meetings became widely accepted and served to bring whole circuits together. They were a particularly useful means of bringing people together in circuits where there were very few chapels that could hold more than a thousand people. Camp meetings also had an important social function, uniting people together across a wide area and creating social solidarity in a countryside that was often dominated by the squire, clergyman

---

1 Kent, *Holding the Fort*, p. 132.
2 Kent, *Holding the Fort*, p. 126.

and farmers. The very act of a small group of revivalistic Primitive Methodists banding together to erect a chapel in a small village was often the first step towards undermining the spiritual authority of the Anglican clergyman and, by the same token, beginning to break the hold of the established church over village and parish life. Many Victorian trade-union leaders were born of a Primitive Methodist Sunday school education and chapel experience, and many early unions patterned their organization on Primitive Methodist structures.[3]

Charles Finney came twice to England, the first occasion being in 1849–51 just after his second marriage to Elizabeth Atkinson and the second between January 1859 and August 1860. His Birmingham meetings were packed and the results of his time in London where he preached at Whitefield's tabernacle were impressive. Kent is somewhat disparaging in assessing his time in the British Isles stating that despite the glowing account of his work which he gave in his *Memoirs,* 'he does not seem to have made a great impression, and in July 1860 the newspaper reports were finding excuses for him'.[4] A *The Wesleyan Times* report in January 1850 appears to add some weight to this view suggesting that though 'powerful in argument ... he is never quite so effective as Mr Caughey having little or no imagination – a quality in which Mr Caughey abounded'.[5] The same correspondent also noted that Finney 'generally preaches long, and seldom holds prayer meetings after his week-night services'. The article did however also state that 'the class of Mr R. Turner, of Birmingham, have presented him with a handsome copy of Burkitt's *Notes on the New Testament,* elegantly bound, in acknowledgement of his zeal in the promotion of Christian piety'.[6] Whilst his 'new' measures, so called, divided American Presbyterians most of whom also eschewed his doctrine of Christian perfection, the publication of his *Lectures* in England certainly did much to endear many evangelical Christian leaders to his teaching and evangelism. Finney has been described as 'pre-eminently the nineteenth century apostle of Revival'. It has been estimated that over two hundred and fifty thousand souls were converted as a result of his preaching.[7] Hambrick-Stowe's assessment of Finney's time and impact in England is somewhat more positive than Kent's. He reminds us that Finney clearly considered the English tour of 1849–51, and especially his revival at Whitefield's Tabernacle, one of the most satisfying campaigns of his career.[8] Finney's second visit to England brought many invitations, and his time in Southwark and at Bolton, where he spoke to Congregational and Methodist churches, was particularly effective.[9]

---

3 See N.A.D. Scotland, 'Trade Unionism', in J.A. Vickers, *Dictionary of Methodism in Britain and Ireland* (Epworth Press, 2000), pp. 356–7.
4 Scotland, 'Trade Unionism', p. 78.
5 *Wesleyan Times,* 7 January 1850, p. 14.
6 *Wesleyan Times,* 7 January 1850, p. 14.
7 E.E. Shelhamer, *Finney on Revival* (Dimension Books, 1974), preface.
8 Hambrick-Stowe, *Charles Finney,* p. 248.
9 Hambrick-Stowe, *Charles Finney,* pp. 254 and 260.

James Caughey was both an unusual and remarkable individual who was clearly greatly loved by the Wesleyans of Rochdale, Sheffield and other northern English towns, but eschewed by the Wesleyan Methodist Conference and the followers of Jabez Bunting. His style of revivalism was clearly in the spirit of John Wesley and he stressed the importance of the doctrine of the Spirit and of practical holiness. Of all the American revivalists who set foot on English soil in the nineteenth century, Caughey was certainly at the forefront when it came to devising means to persuade people to make a decision to follow Christ. There is no doubt that some of his revival techniques amounted to the manipulation of his congregations. For this and his seeming 'hot line to God' he was no doubt justly vilified by the Wesleyan authorities. That said, his presence in England in the 1840s undoubtedly helped to break the oppressive straight-jacketed conference dominated by Jabez Bunting and his circle. Caughey was indeed, in Kent's words, 'the hero of the Wesleyan Reformers' and their protest and secession undoubtedly helped to democratise the clerical autocracy of the parent body and pave the way for a more socially concerned outlook among the Wesleyans. Kent cites figures from Caughey's meetings up until 1847 which, even allowing for some duplication, indicate that his impact was considerable. Caughey's concern for holiness certainly fed into the movement that later generated the Keswick Convention and the Pentecostal outpourings at the turn of the century. His strong views and advocacy of temperance certainly found a ready hearing in Birmingham and Sheffield and other places where he campaigned.

The Palmers, who first came to England in 1859, shared Caughey's concern with holiness, and like him they published lists of the numbers who were sanctified during their various meetings. Theirs was possibly a more genteel and world-denying version of holiness than Caughey's rather more blunt in-your-face meetings. They did however both regard temperance as an integral aspect of holiness. Phoebe Palmer's particular contribution to British Christianity lay in her influence on William and Catherine Booth, the founders of the Salvation Army. They appear to have received 'entire sanctification' soon after meeting Mrs Palmer at Newcastle in 1859. The Army became a significant part of British religious life in the 1870s and 1880s, though its influence among the poor was declining in the 1890s.

The Pearsall Smiths were also a part of the holiness tradition, but theirs was a particularly intense version of the doctrine which required considerable mental and physical discipline. Their stress was on a holiness achieved both by faith and by self-discipline of a fairly austere and rigid kind. The ethos of their conventions at Oxford and Brighton was almost that of a Protestant asceticism, yet it had a profound effect on English Christianity since it led directly to the founding of the Keswick Convention in the Lake District with its strong emphasis on full surrender as the means of obtaining holiness. The movement and ethos which sprang from it impacted several generations of Church of England Evangelicals and indeed turned that section of the establishment in on itself. The last two decades of the nineteenth century in consequence saw a gradual withdrawal of Evangelicals in general from their earlier concern with politics and social action leaving the active concern to the later Christian Socialists and Slum ritualists.

William Payson Hammond's concern for revivalism among children was not only important in America, it had a major impact on children's work in the British Isles. Hammond had thought deeply about the doctrine of salvation and the ways in which children, who were said in the New Testament to be a part of God's kingdom, could be reached with the Christian message. Hammond's extended campaigns in London in particular led to the formation of the Children's Special Service Mission (CSSM). Its organization not only invigorated a large number of Sunday schools, it resulted in many beach missions being held in coastal towns and cities. In this aspect it was reaching the children of middle-class parents who were indulging in the Victorian fashion for seaside holidays which had been made affordable and possible by the rapid growth of the railways.

The active campaigns of Zilpha Elaw and Amanda Berry Smith were shorter compared with those of other American revivalists who set foot in England. Be that as it may their influence was widespread on account of both being black women. Both were radical in that they were strong opponents of slavery and advocates of temperance and women's rights. Nineteenth-century England was a period in which opportunities for women were only just beginning to open up. The proscribed wisdom was that evangelical women should remain in the home and fulfil a domestic and family calling. Women such as Zilpha and Amanda were setting a new precedent which was to inspire their British counterparts such as Catherine Booth and Josephine Butler.

Moody and Sankey: A Watershed in American Revivalism

Of all the nineteenth-century American revivalists Moody and Sankey made the most significant impact both in terms of their influence on the churches and the numbers who came and responded to their message. With their arrival in England in 1873 the whole apparatus of revivalism was poised to step up a gear. Long before their arrival in a town or city a highly organized machine moved into operation training helpers, organizing house-to-house visitations, and arranging for a widespread variety of publicity and leaflets to be posted and distributed. Moody would only go to those places where the clergy of all the denominations were united in extending the invitation to him to come. Thus for example, when he was first asked to Liverpool in November 1874, he received the request from 86 clergymen and ministers including Dissenters and those of the established church. In terms of venue Moody came increasingly to prefer buildings which belonged to no denomination for the reason that he was not then seen to be preferring one denomination to another and ordinary people would feel more comfortable in a non-church environment. Moody considered noon day prayer meetings to be a crucial reason for his effectiveness. These gatherings were frequently dominated by businessmen and others who could take time out for lunch from their work places. In Manchester they were attended by between two and three thousand and in Liverpool between four and five thousand.[10] Moody's campaigns were noted for his down-to-earth orthodox and straightforward preaching, massed choirs, the *Sacred Songs and Solos* of Ira Sankey and the Inquiry Meetings, where those who were concerned about their state before God could make a personal commitment of their lives to Christ.

Moody and Sankey were also a turning point for revivalism in nineteenth-century Britain in that the majority of those who crossed the Atlantic after them were lay men and lay women rather than ordained clergy. Amanda Berry Smith, Walter and Phoebe Palmer and the Pearsall Smiths were all unordained. The Civil War, as has been pointed out, had given opportunity for new expressions of popular music and song which spilled over into the churches. Sankey and later Charles Alexander[11] brought music from America which had far greater appeal than anything that had been used in the earlier years of the century. Moody and Sankey were also the first revivalists who worked on a national rather than a local scale. Additionally, they were the first who sought to work with the whole denominational spectrum including the established church. Their wider influence was also seen in their campaigns in the universities of Oxford and Cambridge.[12] Moody's meetings brought denominations into working relationships in such a way that it led on to the founding of interdenominational mission societies.

A Stimulus to British Revivalism

There had of course always been British revivalists and particularly so since the time of the Wesleys. Nevertheless the activities of American men and women in this country undoubtedly stimulated a quickening of interest in evangelism and a searching for new ways in which to convey the Christian message. Owen Chadwick wrote of the impact of revivalism on some Anglo-Catholic parishes as a 'remarkable new development of the sixties'[13] though it was probably not until after Moody's visits in the 1870s that a real quickening of interest and concern took place. One evidence of this was the growing number of parishes that began to organize weeks of special preaching with calls on the hearers to make personal commitments. Prominent among those who engaged in these kind of mission activities were Hay Aitken and Richard Twiss. Some bishops

---

10 *Narrative of Messrs Moody and Sankey's Labors in Great Britain and Ireland* (Supplementary Issue No. 4), pp. 97–8,
11 Charles Alexander assisted Reuben Torrey who preached to very large numbers in the British Isles in the Alexander Palace and later went on to work with Dr J. Wilbur Chapman who also held Moody style campaigns in Britain in 1905.
12 *The Record*, 24 November 1882.
13 O. Chadwick, *The Victorian Church* (Adam & Charles Black, 1970), Part 2, p. 287.

even took the initiative by using a canonry to free a man from all parochial responsibilities and give him the freedom to travel and engage in evangelistic preaching. One of the most celebrated among their number was George Body (1840–1911) who became 'canon missioner' of Durham in 1883 and who combined evangelical fervour with Tractarian principles and published many devotional works.[14]

There were other English revivalists of a more independent spirit, among them were Reginald Radcliffe (1825–95) and Richard Weaver. Radcliffe, who was the son of a Liverpool lawyer, began preaching in his home city in the 1850s and later worked with Baptist Noel in London where they ran midnight meetings for the reclamation of prostitutes at St James Restaurant in Piccadilly. In 1860, in the wake of Charles Finney's short visit to Edinburgh, Radcliffe and Weaver were unable to locate a large enough building for their meetings. On one day during their time in the city 1,800 people crowded into one of the city churches with thousands still outside the building. The two evangelists had to walk backwards and forwards over the shoulders of strong men as they changed over from ministry inside and outside the building.[15] In the summer of 1861 Radcliffe went to Liverpool, this time following the campaigns of Edward Payson Hammond who had brought hundreds to the inquiry rooms. Once again the meetings which he held in the Corn Hall were overflowing.[16] Weaver had a similar experience when he held a series of follow-up gatherings in Cardiff in 1862 shortly after Phoebe and Walter Palmer had led for 30 days what was described as 'a remarkable work of the Spirit'. Weaver had taken the Music Hall, the largest building in South Wales, which was crammed with 4,000 attending each night and hundreds turned away.[17] Weaver evoked both approbation and denunciation, *The Revivalist* defending his preaching style and *The Record* claiming that he 'vulgarised the apprehension of conversion'.[18] In fact it may have been *The Record*'s general lack of enthusiasm for revival which deprived British revivalists of the support, publicity and encouragement that they needed. In contrast, *Evangelical Christendom* rejoiced in the impact on London 'of the wave of celestial blessings' from the United States.

> And thus it has happened. The Bible-woman in the homes of the poor, the pulpit in the theatre, prayer meetings in the ragged schools, and lastly mid-night meetings, attest that the religious revival in this mighty heart of British civilisation is not simply a thing of sentiment, but a practical

---

14 Body remained in post at Durham until 1911 and also lectured in pastoral theology at Kings College, London in 1909.
15 Orr, *The Light of the Nations*, p. 137.
16 Orr, *The Light of the Nations*, p. 147.
17 Orr, *The Light of the Nations*, p. 142.
18 Kent, *Holding the Fort*, p. 121.

power – the hallowed flame of Heaven stimulating to the benevolent activities of earth.[19]

Greater Parochial Concern

Undoubtedly many incumbents of the established churches threw themselves wholeheartedly behind revival endeavours. Among their number were men such as William Haslam (1817–1905), a former ritualist who had himself been converted in his own Cornish parish during a Methodist revival. He related that when Moody and Sankey began their meetings in the Opera House in the Haymarket in the spring of 1875 he offered to obtain tickets for any who wanted to attend. The vestry was besieged and he was kept busy for an extended period distributing more than three hundred cards every week.[20] Evan Hopkins and Wilson Carlisle were impacted by William Booth's brand of military style revivalism and began to experiment with their own anglicanized versions of his organization. Evan Hopkins who was incumbent of Holy Trinity, Richmond, was dissatisfied with his home mission work. This led in 1881 to his visiting Booth at Whitechapel in consequence of which he started a similar work in his parish called *The Church Gospel Army* which emphasized consecration and held lively holiness meetings on Friday nights.[21] Two years later, in the autumn of 1883, Wilson Carlisle, another Evangelical Anglican, founded the Church Army.[22] During his time in London from May 1850 to April 1851 Charles Finney was greatly interested in a movement that sprang up among Church of England clergy, numbers of whom attended his meetings. He recalled that one of the rectors, Mr Allen, 'made up his mind that he would try to promote a revival in his own parish' and went round and established 20 prayer meetings at different points. According to Finney, 'the Lord greatly blessed his labours and more than fifteen hundred persons had been hopefully converted'.[23] Finney further stated that 'When I left, there were four or five Episcopal churches that were holding daily meetings and, and making efforts to promote a revival.'[24]

It is quite possible that the Anglo-Catholic 'Twelve Days Mission to London' was in part provoked by the successes of Protestant revivalism which had taken root in various parts of the country. Commencing on Sunday 14 November 1869 services were held at the same time in 122 different churches. Among the promoters was Canon Gregory who preached a mission sermon at St Paul's

---

19 *Evangelical Christendom*, 1 March 1860, pp. 158–9.
20 W. Haslam, *Yet Not I or More Years from My Ministry* (Jarrold & Sons, 1897), p. 266.
21 A. Smellie, *Evan Henry Hopkins A Memoir* (Marshall Brothers, 1920), pp. 40–4.
22 E. Rowan, *Wilson Carlisle and the Church Army* (Hodder & Stoughton, 1905), pp. 136–8. See also *The Record*, 13 October 1882.
23 Finney, *An Autobiography*, p. 341.
24 Finney, *An Autobiography*, p. 341.

Cathedral. It was unquestionably a High Church endeavour though, as *Evangelical Christendom* pointed out, 'some few Evangelicals appear to have felt led to take part'. Among the main features were frequent celebrations of communion, private confession, renewal of Baptismal vows and prayer meetings.[25]

Encouragement to Foreign Missions

Every revival of religion in a nation is felt within a decade on the foreign mission field and nineteenth-century England was no exception. Hudson Taylor who founded the China Inland Mission Society in 1865 wrote that

> Moody's first visit in 1873 had brought to the front again the supreme duty of soul-winning, preparing the way for many a forward movement, including the appeal for the Eighteen and the opening up of China; and now, when a fresh advance was to be made in missionary enterprise, the heart of Christian England was being stirred to its depths by a practical, overwhelming demonstration of the power of the Gospel. Who can say how much the world-wide work of foreign missions owes to these devoted evangelists.[26]

There can be no doubting that the labours of American revivalists made a significant contribution to the growth of missionary enterprise. The Keswick Convention which arose out of the Pearsall Smiths' teaching at the Brighton Conference was an interdenominational movement, and this in turn helped to promote both the founding and interest in interdenominational foreign missionary societies. The Taylors in their biography of Hudson were of the view that 'the conferences on the lines of Keswick, which indeed grew out of them, were drawing Christians of all denominations. Notable among these were the Brighton Convention of this summer (ten days in June, 1875) when audiences of two to three thousand filled the Corn Exchange, and rivers of blessing were opened in many hearts that were to flow to the ends of the earth'.[27] The last quarter of the nineteenth century saw recruitment to Evangelical missionary societies reach a peak. By the beginning of the twentieth century the Church Missionary Society had more than seven hundred missionaries in the foreign field. The interdenominational London Missionary Society had reached its high point 12 years earlier. At no time was the impact of American revivalism on British overseas missions more apparent than the time of Moody's visit to Cambridge for eight days in November 1882. Among the converts, some of

---

25 *Evangelical Christendom*, 1 December 1869, pp. 418–19.
26 H. Taylor, *Hudson Taylor and the China Inland Mission* (Marshall, Morgan and Scott, 1919), p. 379.
27 Taylor, *Hudson Taylor*, p. 265.

whom had been guilty of disruptive behaviour at the meetings, were Gerald Lander who became a missionary bishop and Charles Studd (1862–1931), the Cambridge and England cricket captain. A group who became known as 'the Cambridge Seven' toured British universities stirring students to faith and commitment. They held one final great meeting in London on 4 February 1885 before sailing to China.[28] According to John Pollock, the China Inland Mission itself was raised in consequence from comparative obscurity to an almost embarrassing prominence.'[29]

Stimulus to Radicalism

It is clear that American revivalists provided a stimulus to a number of radical movements on both sides of the Atlantic. Revivalism is in essence a form of protest against religion that is perceived to be cold and formal. Indeed it has been regarded by some historians as the most primitive form of protest. With the passage of time what began as a religious protest sometimes transfers, or develops into, social or political protest. As has already been noted, such was the case with Primitive Methodism which began as a reaction against the growing formalism of the Wesleyan parent connection but gradually emerged to become a protest against the social control and parochial dominance of the Anglican clergy, particularly in the English countryside. In particular researches have shown that many, indeed perhaps the majority of trade-union leaders in nineteenth-century Britain, were Primitive Methodist and to a lesser extent Wesleyans.[30]

This study has demonstrated that nineteenth-century American revivalists made a particular contribution to movements for women's rights, temperance and anti-slavery. On the matter of women's rights both Zilpha Elaw and Amanda Berry Smith were Black Americans and were vigorous anti-slavery campaigners. During their time in England both strongly asserted the right of women to preach and speak in the face of opposition from ministers of their own Methodist denomination. Even more outspoken was the contribution of Phoebe Palmer. Not only did she preach widely in Methodist circuits, her book *Promise of the Father* was a powerful and well-argued case for women's public ministry which provided cogent answers to the Pauline texts which up until that point had been considered as irrefutable.

The majority of American revivalists who set foot on Victorian soil were part of the holiness tradition. For them the human body was the temple of the Holy Spirit and anything that defiled it must of necessity be rejected. In this context it is not difficult to understand why they campaigned so strongly against the

---

28 See Pollock, *Moody without Sankey*, p. 208 and J.C. Pollock, *The Cambridge Seven* (John Murray, 1953), pp. 71–89.
29 Pollock, *The Cambridge Seven*, p. 87.
30 See for example, Scotland, 'Trade Unionism', pp. 356–7.

selling and consumption of alcoholic beverages. Indeed Phoebe Palmer could not consider the possibility of revival apart from the pledge to total abstinence. Since the Palmers' holiness teachings influenced William and Catherine Booth it is quite likely that it also carried over and impacted the Salvation Army's rejection of intoxicating drink. Significantly the nineteenth-century British temperance and teetotal cause was embraced by a number of radical movements including the Chartists and many trade unionists. They argued that if the working man and woman could be persuaded to give up their drink there would be more money for books and many more sober heads who could give their full attention to ordered protest against their unjust conditions. Additionally, it is not without significance that the founders of the revivalist Primitive Methodists were both strong teetotal advocates from the very beginning of their movement.

Enduring Legacy

American revivalists undoubtedly strengthened the teetotal and temperance cause. Taking the pledge particularly featured in the ministries of the holiness preachers such as Caughey and the Palmers, but it also became an increasing feature in D.L. Moody's revivals. As Kent observed 'revivalism played an important part in recruiting for the cause and in helping to make Nonconformist chapels in particular into a kind of teetotal closed-shop'.[31]

By the end of the nineteenth century, revivalism had clearly become an organized business enterprise that could be promoted and planned. That said, it was less appealing than had been the case in the 1860s and 1870s.[32] Biblical criticism was beginning to gain a hold in the universities and the middle classes were in consequence attracted to more liberal interpretations of the Old and New Testaments and the possibilities of a social gospel. Indeed William Booth was himself drawn into the social gospel, a fact which he made clear to the world in 1890, with the publication of his most celebrated book *In Darkest England and The Way Out.* That said, there can be no doubt that American revivalists were a major feature of the religious landscape of nineteenth-century Britain and a significant influence on its religious life and worship. Their endeavours undoubtedly increased the membership of evangelical churches and the impact of evangelical religion on British society.

---

31 Scotland, 'Trade Unionism', p. 89.
32 Revivalism was clearly not a total dead letter since in 1905 Reuben Torrey preached to crowds as great as those who had listened to Moody and Sankey.

Bibliography

Archive Sources

Children's Special Service Mission Collection, Scripture Union Archives.
Hammond Collection, Bodleian Library, Bodleian Library.
Keswick Collection, Wheaton College Archives, Wheaton, Illinois.
Lorenzo Dow Collection, Billy Graham Archives.
Methodist Collections, Wesley College, Bristol.
Mount Temple Collection, Hampshire Record Office.

Journals

Birmingham Gazette.
English Labourers' Chronicle.
Guide to Holiness.
National Reformer.
Sheffield Independent.
The Birmingham Daily Post.
The Birmingham Post.
The Christian Mirror.
The Christian.
The Christian's Pathway to Power.
The Dumfries Standard, 30 January 1861.
The Hampshire Telegraph and the Sussex Chronicle.
The Liverpool Mercury.
The Nonconformist.
The Record.
The Revival Advocate.
The Revivalist.
The Times.
The Way of Holiness.
Wesleyan Methodist Magazine.
Wesleyan Times.

Secondary Sources

Account of the Union Meeting for the Promotion of Scriptural Holiness, held at Oxford, August 29.
Anon., *The Eccentric Preacher: Or a Sketch of the Life of the Celebrated Lorenzo Dow* (E.A. Rice, 1841).
Anon., *The Life of Hugh Bourne Founder of the Primitive Methodist Connexion* (James B. Knapp, 1982).
Antliff, W., *The Life of the Venerable Hugh Bourne* (George Lamb, 1872).
Armstrong, J.H., *Reformation and Revival*, Volume 1, Number 2 (Spring 1992).
Asbury, H., *A Methodist Saint. The Life of Bishop Asbury* (Alfred A. Knopf, 1927).
Balleine, G.R., *A History of the Evangelical Party in the Church of England* (Longman, Green, 1933).
Baring, C., *A Charge Delivered to the Clergy of the Diocese of Gloucester and Bristol at His Primary Visitation of the Diocese in October 1857* (Seeley, Jackson and Halliday, 1857).
Bartlett, D.C, and McClellan, L.A., 'The Final Ministry of Amanda Berry Smith. An Orphanage in Harvey, Illinois 1895-1918', *Illinois Heritage*, Vol. 1, No. 2.
Bond, T.B., *T.B.B. of the C.S.S.M A Memoir of Tom Bond Bishop, for Fifty-three Years Honorary Secretary of the Children's Special Service Mission* (Children's Special Service Mission, 1923).
Booth-Tucker, F. De L., *The Life of Catherine Booth*, 2 volumes (Revell, 1892).
Briggs, F.W., *Bishop Asbury: A Biographical Study* (Wesleyan Conference Office, 1879).
Cartwright. P., *The Backwoods Preacher being the Autobiography of Peter Cartwright* (Charles H. Kelly, undated).
Carwardine, R., *Transatlantic Revivalism: Popular Evangelicalism in Britain and America 1790–1865* (Greenwood Press, 1878).
Caughey, J., *Methodism in Earnest being the History of a Great Revival in Great Britain* (Charles H. Pierce, 1850).
— *Helps to the Life of Holiness and Usefulness or Revival Miscellanies* (J.P. Magee, 1852).
— *Earnest Christianity Illustrated* (J.P. Magee, 1855).
— *Arrows from my Quiver* (W.C. Palmer Junior, 1868).
— *Showers of Blessing from Clouds of Mercy* (W.C. Palmer, 1868).
— *Glimpses of Life in Soul-saving* (W.C. Palmer Junior, 1868).
— *Letters on Various Subjects* (Simpkin, Marshall, 1846).
— *Revival Sermons and Addresses* (Richard D. Dickinson, 1891).
— *Revival Miscellanies* (Houlton and Stoneman, undated).
Chadwick, O., *The Victorian Church,* Parts 1 and 2 (Adam & Charles Black, 1970).
— *The Secularisation of the European Mind in the 19th Century* (Canto, 1990; original Cambridge University Press, 1975).
Church, T., *Popular Sketches of Primitive Methodism being a Link in the chain of British Ecclesiastical History* (Thomas Church, 1850).
Cleeveland, C.C., *The Great Revival in the West 1797–1805* (University of Chicago, 1916).
Coffee, J., 'Democracy and Popular Religion: Moody and Sankey's Mission to Britain 1873–1875' in E.F. Biagini (ed.), *Citizens in Community* (Cambridge University Press, 1996).
Collier, R., *The General Next to God* (Collins, 1966).

Colton, C., *History and Character of American Revivals of Religion* (1832).
Cross, W.R., *The Burned-Over District* (Harper and Row, 1965).
Dale, A.W., *The Life of R.W. Dale of Birmingham* (Hodder and Stoughton, 1898).
Daniels, W.H., *D.L. Moody and His Work* (American Publishing Company, 1875).
Davidson, R., and W. Benham, *Life of Archibald Cambell Tait*, 2 volumes (MacMillan, 1891).
Davis, G., *Dwight L. Moody The Man and His Mission* (K.T. Boland, 1900).
Dayton, L.S and D.W. Dayton, '"Your Daughters Shall Prophesy": Feminism in the Holiness Movement', *Methodist History*, Volume XIV, No. 2, January 1876.
Dimond, S.G., *The Psychology of the Methodist Revival* (Oxford University Press, 1926).
Dixon, L.E., 'The Importance of J.N. Darby and the Brethren Movement in the History of the Conservative Theology', *The Christian Brethren Review*, Volume 41, 1990.
Dorsett, L.W., *A Passion for Souls: The Life of D.L. Moody* (Moody Press, 1997).
Dow, L., *Travels, Providential Experience of Lorenzo Dow*, 2 volumes (self published, 1806).
— *Journal in the Dealings of God, Man and the Devil* (W.M. Faulkener, 1833).
— *History of Cosmopolite or the Writings of Lorenzo Dow* (Joshua Martin and Alex S. Robinson, 1849).
— *The Dealings of God, Man, and the Devil: as exemplified in the Life, Experience, and Travels of Lorenzo Dow* (1860).
— *On Camp Meetings* (1860).
— *Omnifaroius Law* (Applegate, 1860).
— *Nuggets of Golden Truth; or Reflections on the Love of God, on Predestination, Deism and Atheism and on Christian Experience* (R. Davies, 1863 edition).
Eddy, G.S., *A Spiritual Awakening Being Points and Directions from the Life and Lectures of Charles Finney* (Morgan and Scott, 1915; Eerdmans, 1996).
Edwards, J., *A Narrative of Many Surprising Conversions*, 1737 (Banner of Truth Trust, 1991).
— *The Distinguishing Marks of a Work of the Spirit of God*, 1741 (Banner of Truth Trust).
Elaw, Z., *Memoirs of the Religious Experience, Ministerial travels and Labours of Mrs Zilpha Elaw; Together with Some Account of the Great Religious Revivals in America* (first published by the authoress and sold by Mr T. Dudley and Mr B. Taylor, 1846; facsimile edition, Indiana University Press, 1986).
Engels, F., *Condition of the Working Classes in England* (1892 edition).
Ensor, R.C.K., *England 1870-1914* (Oxford University Press, 1936).
Figgis, J.B., *Keswick from Within* (Marshall Bros., 1914).
Findlay, J.F., *Dwight L. Moody American Evangelist 1837-1899* (Chicago Press, 1969).
Finney, C.G., *An Autobiography* (Hodder and Stoughton, 1832).
— *Revivals of Religion* (Marshall, Morgan and Scott, 1910).
— *Revivals of Religion Lectures by Charles Grandison Finney* (Marshall, Morgan and Scott, 1910; Oliphants, 1928).
Finney, C.H., *Lectures on Systematic Theology* (Oberlin, 1878; Eerdmans, 1953).
— *The Memoirs of Charles G. Finney: The Complete Restored Text*, edited by G.M. Rosell and R.A.G. Dupuis (Zondervan, 1989).
Foos, H.D., 'Moody, Dwight Lyman', in M. Couch (ed.), *Dictionary of Premillennial Theology* (Kregel, 1996).

Fullerton, W.Y., *F.B. Meyer A Biography* (Marshall, Morgan and Scott, second edition undated).
Garrison, S.O. (ed.), *Forty Witnesses. Covering the Whole Range of Christian Experience* (1888).
Gaskell, E., *North and South* (Penguin, 1970).
Gilbert, A.D., *Religion and Society in Industrial England: Church, Chapel and Social Change 1740–1914* (Longman, 1976).
Gilbert, J., *Perfect Cities: Chicago's Utopias of 1893* (University of Chicago Press, 1991).
Gill, R., *The Myth of the Empty Church* (SPCK, 1993).
Goodspeed, E.J., *A Full History of the Wonderful Career of Moody and Sankey in Great Britain and America* (Concord, 1876).
Goss., C.F., *Echoes from the Pulpit and Platform* (A.D. Worthington, 1900).
Gregory, B., *Side Lights on the Conflicts of Methodism* (Cassel, 1898).
Grubb, N., *C.T. Studd Cricketer and Pioneer* (Religious Tract Society, 1935).
Hambrick-Stowe, C.E., *Charles Finney and the Spirit of American Evangelicalism* (Eerdmans, 1996).
Hammond, E.P., *Early Conversion* (Paternoster and Alabaster, undated).
— *Gathered Lambs* (Marshall, Morgan and Scott, undated).
— *The Conversion of Children* (Marshall, Morgan and Scott, undated).
— *The Better Life and How to Find It* (Morgan and Chase, undated).
Harding, W.H., *Revivals of Religion Lectures by Charles Grandison Finney* (Marshall, Morgan and Scott, 1860).
Harding, W.H. (ed.) *Revivals of Religion* (Oliphants, 1928).
Harries, J., *Campbell Morgan* (Fleming H. Revell, 1930).
Harrison, B., *Drink and the Victorians 1815–1872* (Faber, 1972).
Haslam, W., *Yet Not I or More Years from My Ministry* (Jarrold & Sons, 1897).
Headley, P.C., *The Reaper and the Harvest: scenes in connection with the work of the Holy Spirit in the Life and Labours of the Rev E. Payson Hammond* (Marshall, Morgan and Scott, undated).
Henry, M., *The Secret Life of Hannah Whitall Smith* (Zondervan, 1984).
Hofstadter, R., *Anti-intellectualism in American Life* (Knopf, 1964).
Hudson, W.S., *Religion in America* (Charles Scribner's Sons, 1965).
Hughes, G., *The Beloved Physician: Walter C Palmer MD and His Sun-Lit Journey to the Celestial City* (Palmer and Hughes, 1884).
Inglis, K.S., *Churches and the Working Classes in Victorian England* (Routledge & Kegan Paul, 1963).
Ironside, H.A., *Historical Sketch of the Brethren Movement* (Zondervan, 1993).
Kendall, H.B., *The Origin and History of Primitive Methodist Church*, 2 volumes (Dalton, 1907).
Kent, J., *Holding the Fort* (Epworth, 1978).
Lander, J.K. *Itinerant Temples: Tent Methodism 1814–1832* (Paternoster Press, 2003).
Laqueur, T.W., *Religion and Respectability: Sunday Schools and Working Class Culture 1780–1850* (Yale University Press, 1976).
Lovelace, R.E., *Dynamics of Spiritual Life* (Paternoster Press, 1979).
MacPherson, J., *Henry Moorhouse the English Evangelist* (Morgan and Scott, undated).
Marsden, G., *Fundamentalism and American Culture* (Oxford University Press, 1980).
McGready, J., 'Narrative of the Revival in Logan County', *New York Missionary Magazine* (1803).

McLeod, H., *Religion and Society in England 1850–1914* (MacMillan, 1996).
McLoughlin, W.G., *Modern Revivalism: Charles Grandison Finney to Billy Graham* (Ronald Press, 1959).
— *Modern Revivalism; Charles Grandison Finney to Billy Graham* (Ronald Press, 1959).
— *Revivals, Awakenings, and Reform* (University of Chicago Press, 1980).
Moody, D.L., *Echoes from the Pulpit and Platform* (A.D. Worthington, 1900).
Moody, W.R., *The Life of Dwight L. Moody by His Son* (Fleming H. Revell, 1900).
Moore, C.E. (ed.), *Amanda Smith: An Autobiography* (Hodder and Stoughton, 1894).
Morgan, P.B., 'A Study of the Work of American Revivalists in Britain from 1874–1914' (B.Litt thesis, Oxford, 1961).
Murray, I.H., *Revival and Revivalism: The Making and the Marring of American Evangelicalism 1750–1858* (The Banner of Truth Trust, 1994).
Narrative of Messrs Moody and Sankey's Labors in Great Britain and Ireland (Supplementary Issue 4).
Noll, M., *A History of Christianity in the United States and Canada* (Eerdmans, 1992).
— *The Old Religion in a New World* (Eerdmans, 2002).
Nutall, G.F. and O. Chadwick (eds.), *From Uniformity to Unity 1662–1962* (SPCK, 1962).
Orr, J.E., *The Light of the Nations* (Paternoster Press, 1965).
— *The Re-study of Revival and Revivalism* (School of World Mission, 1981).
Palmer, P., *Four Years in the Old World* (Walter C. Palmer Jr, 1869).
— *Promise of the Father or A Neglected Speciality of the Last Days Addressed to the Clergy and Laity of all Christian Communities* (Henry V. Degen, 1859).
— *The Way of Holiness* (Lane & Scott, 1851; Palmer and Hughes, 1867).
— *Full Salvation* (Schmul Publishers, 1979 edition).
Parsons, G., *Religion in Victorian Britain* (Manchester University Press, 1988).
Pell, E.L., *Dwight L. Moody His Life, His Work, His Words* (B.F. Johnson, 1900).
Petty, J., *The History of the Primitive Methodist Connexion From its Origin to the Conference of 1860* (R. Davies, 1864).
Pollock, J.C., *Moody without Sankey: A New Biographical Portrait* (Hodder & Stoughton, 1863).
— *A Cambridge Movement* (John Murray, 1953).
— *The Cambridge Seven* (John Murray, 1953).
— *The Good Seed* (Hodder and Stoughton, 1959).
Price, C., and I. Randall, *Transforming Keswick* (OM Publishing, 2000).
Railton, G., *Twenty-One Years in the Salvation Army* (Salvation Army, 1891).
Rattenbury, J.E., *Wesley's Legacy to the World* (Epworth, 1928).
Reed, A., and J. Matheson, *A Narrative of the Visits to the American Churches by Deputies of the Congregational Union of England and Wales*, 2 volumes (1835).
Robertson, J.W., *The Day Before Yesterday: Memories of an Uneducated Man* (Methuen, 1951).
Rowan, E., *Wilson Carlisle and the Church Army* (Hodder & Stoughton, 1905).
Royle, E., *Radical Politics, Religion and Unbelief 1790–1900* (Longman, 1971).
Ruthven, M., *The Divine Supermarket* (Chatto and Windus, 1989).
Ryder, H., *Charge Addressed to the Clergy and People of Lichfield and Coventry at His Third Visitation* (A. Morgan, 1832).
Sandall, R., *The History of the Salvation Army*, 2 volumes (Thomas Nelson and Sons, 1947).

Sandeen, E.R., *The Roots of Fundamentalism* (University of Chicago, 1970).
Sankey, I.D., *Sacred Songs and Solos* (Marshall, Morgan and Scott, revised and enlarged edition, undated).
Scotland, N.A.D., *Methodism and the Revolt of the Field in East Anglia 1872–96* (Alan Sutton, 1981).
— 'Trade Unionism', in J.A. Vickers (ed.), *Dictionary of Methodism in Britain and Ireland* (Epworth Press, 2000).
— *Evangelicals in a Revolutionary Age* (Paternoster Press, 2004).
Sellers, C.C., *Lorenzo Dow The Bearer of the Word* (Minton, Balch, 1928).
Sellers, I., *Nineteenth-Century Nonconformity* (Edward Arnold, 1977).
Shelhamer, E.E., *Finney on Revival* (Dimension Books, 1974).
Simpkinson, C.H., *The Life and Work of Bishop Thorold* (Isbister, 1896).
Sizer, S., *Gospel Hymns and Social Religion* (Ark Publishing, 1979).
Sloan, W.B., *These Sixty Years: The Story of the Keswick Convention* (Pickering and Inglis, 1935).
Smellie, A., *Evan Hopkins Henry Hopkins A Memoir* (Marshall Brothers, 1920).
Smith, A., *Amanda Smith* (J.H. Brooks, 1977).
Smith, H.W., *The Record of a Happy Life* (J.B. Lippincott, 1873).
— *The Unselfishness of God and How I Discovered It: A Spiritual Autobiography* (Flemming H. Revell, 1903).
— *The Christian's Secret of a Happy Life* (Zondervan, 1984 edition).
Smith, L.P. (ed.), *A Religious Rebel The Letters of H.W.S.* (Nisbet, 1949).
Smith, P.L., *Unforgotten Years* (Little, Brown, 1939).
Smith, R., *Holiness Through Faith. Light on the Way to Holiness* (Marshall, Morgan and Scott, 1875).
Smith, T.L., *Revivalism and Social Reform* (Harper and Row, 1965).
Sprague, W., *Lectures on Revivals of Religion* (Banner of Truth, 1959).
Spring, G., *Personal Reminiscences of the Life and Times of Gardiner Spring*, 2 volumes (1866).
Stone, B.W., *A Short History of the Life of Barton Stone Written by Himself* (J.A. and U.P. Jones, 1847).
Stout, H., *The Divine Dramatist George Whitefield and the Rise of Modern Evangelicalism* (William B. Eerdmans, 1991).
Taylor, H., *Hudson Taylor and the China Inland Mission* (Marshall, Morgan and Scott, 1919).
Torrey, R.A., *Why God Used D.L. Moody* (Kessinger, 2006; first published 1923).
Underwood, A.C., *A History of the English Baptists* (Kingsgate Press, 1947).
Vidler, A.R., *The Church in an Age of Revolution* (Penguin, 1971).
Wheatley, R., *The Life and Letters of Mrs Phoebe Palmer* (W.C. Palmer, 1876).
— *The Life and Letters of Mrs Phoebe Palmer* (W.C. Palmer, 1876).
White, C.E., *The Beauty of Holiness: Phoebe Palmer as Theologian, Revivalist, Feminist and Humanitarian* (Ph.D. thesis: Francis Asbury Press, 1986).
Wickham, E.R., *Church and People in an Industrial City* (Lutterworth Press, 1969).
Wilson, B., *Religion in Secular Society* (Watts, 1966).
Wolffe, J., *The Expansion of Evangelicalism* (Inter-Varsity Press, 2006).
Wesleyan Methodist Conference Minutes.

Index

Abbott, Revd Lyman 162
Adventism 17
After Meetings 108
Aitken, Revd Hay 146, 194, 221
Aitken, Robert 146
Alabama 142
Albany 19, 34, 92
Aldersgate Street 12
All Day Meetings 159
Alstone, Fanny 118
altar calls 110
American Methodist Episcopal Church 197, 198
Anglo-Catholic 155, 221, 223
Annan 169
Annapolis 54, 63
anti-slavery 3, 15, 16, 76, 134, 136, 225
Antliff, William 48
Antwerp 69, 71
Anxious Rooms 86
anxious seat 8, 72, 85, 86
Asbury, Bishop Frances 3, 17, 44, 47
Atherton, Revd William 94, 110
Atkinson, Elizabeth 77, 218

Babb, Dr C.E. 186
Balliol College 215
Baltimore 34, 54, 127, 187, 188, 192
Banbury 131, 137
baptism xix, 20, 26, 68, 120, 128, 143, 146, 152, 202, 205, 208
Baptism in the Holy Ghost, the Holy Spirit, the Spirit 26, 68, 120, 126, 127, 128, 129, 143, 152, 204, 205, 208
Baptist Missionary Society xix
Baptists xix, 2, 3, 21, 46, 145, 147, 160, 170, 175, 202, 207
barking 2, 5

Bath (UK) 175, 176, 179
Bath (USA) 52, 179
Beecher, Revd Dr Lyman 12, 71
Beechman, Lady 194
Belfast 30, 128
Bentley, Todd 52
Berenson, Bernard 199, 215, 216
Berlin 211
Berry, Mariam 187
Berry, Samuel 187, 188
Bible Christians xxi, 160
Bible, the 8, 9, 23, 26, 44, 67, 83, 122, 131, 140, 145, 147, 148, 152, 154, 158, 159, 161, 171, 184, 187, 203, 207, 210, 222
biblical criticism 14, 154, 226
Bickersteth, Edward 157
Billing, Revd R.C. 160
Birmingham 22, 77, 94, 103, 138, 145, 149, 150, 154, 156, 157, 158, 218, 219
Bishop, Tom Bond 171, 172, 173
Blackwood, Mr Stevenson 213
Bliss, Philip 162
Boardman, Dr William 207
Boardman, Revd George 181
Body, George 222
Bolton 79, 80, 85, 218
Bonar, Horatius 155
Booth, Catherine 133, 136, 219, 220, 226
Booth, William 12, 97, 133, 136, 155, 186, 219, 223, 226
Borough Road Chapel 78, 79
Boston (UK) 94, 137, 179
Boston (USA) 9, 35, 54, 69, 71, 74, 86, 139, 173, 178
Bourne, Hugh xx, 27, 41, 42, 45, 46, 47, 217
Bow 65, 161

Boyle, James 84
Bradford 57
Bradlaugh, Charles 24
Bray, Billy xxi
Brethren, the 79, 80, 94, 132
Brighton 212, 213, 216
Brighton Conference 212, 224
Brighton Convention 212, 213, 219, 224
Bristol 38, 99, 145
Broadlands Conference 194, 195, 197, 198, 209, 210, 216
Broadway Tabernacle 75
Brown, Mr Potto 77, 78
Brunswick Chapel 57, 95, 97, 114
Bunting, Jabez 15, 21, 94, 98, 114, 219
Burton-on-Trent 99

Cairns, Lord 147, 150
California 175, 183, 186
Calvin xix, 6, 188
Calvinism, Calvinistic, Calvinists xix, xx, 2, 3, 4, 5, 35, 39, 48, 67, 85, 86, 88, 160, 203
Cambridge 150, 224
Cambridge Seven 225
Cambridge University 170, 221, 225
Campbell, Miss Etta 178
camp meetings xx, xxi, 9, 10, 11, 13, 16, 25, 31, 32, 39, 40, 41, 42, 43, 46, 48, 50, 53, 54, 61, 85, 118, 127, 129, 192, 193, 197, 198, 199, 204, 207, 214, 217
Canada 30, 40, 76, 92, 93, 117, 118, 124, 127, 169, 185
Cane Ridge 2, 3
Cardiff 138, 169, 222
Carey, William xix
Carlisle 137, 169
Carlisle, Wilson 223
Carr's Lane Chapel 78
Cartwright, Peter 10, 11, 17, 39, 45
Carver Street Chapel 97, 113
Carwardine, Richard xx, xxi, 91, 104, 113, 114, 115
Caughey, James 10, 14, 15, 17, 18, 26, 87, 91–115, 151, 162, 176, 217, 218, 219, 226
Cavan, Lord 169, 180
Chadbourne, Professor 165

Chadwick, Owen 23, 24, 221
Charismatics 13
Chartists 226
Chatham Garden Theatre 74
Chesterfield 94
Chicago 9, 139, 140, 142, 143, 144, 145, 148, 161, 162, 173, 182, 195
children 10, 27, 32, 42, 54, 74, 103, 118, 128, 134, 135, 139, 143, 165, 168, 169, 170, 171, 172, 173, 174, 178, 179, 180, 181, 182, 183, 184, 185, 186, 187, 188, 195, 198, 209, 214, 216, 220
Children's Special Service Mission (CSSM) 170, 172, 220
China Inland Mission 224, 225
Christian Perfection 118, 120, 121, 122, 218
Christopher, Revd Alfred 210, 211
Church Army 223
Church Gospel Army 223
Church Missionary Society 224
Church of England xix, xx, 14, 20, 21, 46, 126, 145, 146, 160, 170, 211, 219, 223
Civil War 141, 142, 155, 161, 189, 207, 221
Clarke, Dr Adam 91
Clifford E. 194
Clowes, William xx, 42, 217
Coffee, John 149, 153
Coke, Thomas 3, 30
Cole, Dr R.E. 183
Colton, Revd C.G. xxi, 6, 7, 8
Congleton 40, 46, 47
Congregational, Congregationalists xix, xx, 2, 21, 36, 71, 80, 113, 140, 160, 169, 218
Consecration Meetings 196, 209, 210, 211
Conventicle 41
Conversionism 13
Costelloe, Frank 199, 215
Covenant, the 182, 183
Cowper-Temple, W.F. 147, 155, 209
Cree, Thomas 159
Crosby, Fanny 157, 162
Cullis, Dr Charles 207
Currens, Revd J.B. 186

Index 235

Dale, R.W. 157, 158
dancing 2, 11, 45, 46, 48, 233
Daniels, W.H. 139, 143, 149, 159
Darby, John Nelson 18, 151
Davis, George 146
Davis, Revd Benjamin 171
Dean, Humphrey 27
decoy penitents 110, 115
Delamere Forest xxi
Delaware 7, 74
Derbyshire xxi, 16
Dispensationalism 18, 233
dock labourers 148, 149, 233
Dolbeare, Lucy 37
Doncaster 94, 195
doubts 9, 17, 23, 154, 167, 189, 214, 233
Dow, Lorenzo xx, 8, 9, 12, 13, 14, 16, 27–48, 151, 162, 183, 217
Dow, Tabitha 27
drink 17, 103, 130, 131, 189, 195, 226, 233
drunkenness 2, 153, 154, 233
Dublin 29, 30, 34, 38, 46, 93
Dumfries 169, 176, 177
Dwight, Revd Timothy 3

Edinburgh 79, 145, 147, 165, 169, 222
Edwards, Jonathan 1, 3, 6, 8, 87, 117
Elaw, Joseph 49
Elaw, Zilpha xxiii, 16, 49–65, 198, 220, 225
Elliott, Charlotte 14
emancipation of women 79, 233
emotionalism 12, 41, 111, 233
Engells, Frederick 22
Entire Salvation 123
Eton College 147
Europe 19, 36, 84, 92, 208, 209, 211, 212, 233
Evangelical Alliance 103, 174, 233
Evangelical/s 20, 21, 63, 79, 103, 145, 152, 162, 174, 210, 211, 216, 217, 219, 220, 222, 223, 224, 233
Evans Mills 69, 71

falling 2, 5, 10, 27, 39, 40, 45, 82, 102, 162, 233
Farwell Hall 141, 142, 145

Farwell, John V. 140
Female Anti-Slavery Society 76
female reform 15, 76, 233
Female Society of Oberlin for the Promotion of Health 76
feminists, feminism 15, 64, 76
Findlay, James 148
Finney, Charles 6, 7, 8, 9, 12, 14, 15, 16, 43, 67, 68, 69, 70, 71, 72, 73, 74, 75, 76, 77, 78, 79, 80, 81, 82, 83, 84, 85, 86, 87, 88, 89, 104, 117, 151, 157, 162, 218, 222, 223
Finney, Lydia 69, 76, 78, 79
First World War 216
Fishbourne, Admiral 147
Fiske, Revd J.O. 176, 179
Fletcher, J.W. 127
follow up 61, 112
Fox, George 40
Franklin, Benjamin 7
Freemasons, Freemasonry 38, 48, 160
Full Salvation 124, 196
full surrender 206, 210, 219
fundamentalism, fundamentalists 9, 10, 15, 154

Gale, George 67, 68, 69, 88
Gasper River xx
Gateshead 94, 133, 137
Gill, Robin 22
Gladstone, William 150
Gloucester 22
Gobat, Bishop Samuel 174
Gordon, Duchess of 168
Gouveneur 71
Great Awakening 1, 45, 87
Green, William 74
Gregory, Benjamin 110, 223
Grenfell, Wilfred T. 156
Grubb, George 194
Guide to Holiness 118, 119, 124, 128, 204

Hall, Newman 170
Hambrick-Stowe, Charles 77, 78, 80, 87, 89, 218
Hamline, Leonidas 119
Hammond, Edward Payson 165–186, 222
Hammond, William Payson 220

handbills 6, 38, 46, 47, 111, 159
hand raising 129
Hanley 98, 99, 103, 107, 113
Hanover Square 209
Harford-Battersby, Canon T.D. 193, 213, 214, 216
Harriseahead 47
Hartford 54, 60, 62
Haslam, William xxi, 223
Hastings, Thomas 87
Haswell, Revd John 114
Haymarket 147, 161, 223
healing 155, 198
heaven 9, 17, 27, 44, 45, 52, 54, 59, 63, 96, 98, 100, 103, 106, 125, 128, 136, 152, 153, 155, 184, 205, 223
Heber, Reginald 155
hell 6, 9, 17, 19, 27, 31, 44, 84, 105, 106, 115, 152, 153, 177
Herod, George 43, 45
higher criticism 14, 233
Higher Life 199, 205, 206, 208, 210, 213, 233
Holcomb, Peggy 32, 33
Holden, Betsy 139
holiness 5, 17, 25, 47, 62, 64, 76, 78, 81, 88, 101, 103, 117, 118, 120, 123, 124, 129, 130, 132, 135, 136, 145, 152, 167, 192, 196, 198, 204, 206, 207, 208, 216, 219, 223, 225, 226, 233
Holy Ghost 11, 56, 59, 60, 62, 68, 102, 120, 127, 128, 191, 208, 233
Holyoake, George Jacob 24
Holy Spirit 1, 12, 19, 26, 31, 52, 54, 60, 62, 68, 73, 74, 81, 83, 98, 99, 100, 101, 108, 109, 112, 114, 121, 127, 128, 129, 143, 152, 153, 168, 194, 195, 197, 204, 205, 206, 212, 225, 233
Hopkins, Canon Evan 194, 223
Houghton 77, 78
Howley, Dr William 20
Huddersfield 58, 64, 94, 110
Hughes, Thomas John 171
Hull 42, 57, 58, 94, 96, 97, 98, 111, 112, 115, 125
Hull West Circuit 96
Huntingdon, Countess of xx, 56, 160

hymns 9, 12, 43, 59, 87, 118, 149, 153, 154, 155, 157, 171, 175, 178, 181, 182, 233
Hymns and Spiritual Songs 12
Hymns of Salvation 171, 181

Impression, impressions 7, 37, 38, 47, 48, 107, 108, 143, 233
In Darkest England and The Way Out 226
In Memoriam 25
inquiry meeting 72, 172, 177, 233
inquiry room 13, 18, 157, 158, 162, 170, 178, 182, 233
intemperate, intemperance 59, 103, 169, 174

James, Revd John Angell 78
Janes, Edmund 119
Jennings, Revd S.K. 46
jerks, jerking 2, 5, 11, 30, 31, 32, 39, 45, 46, 48, 233
John Street 170, 181
Jowett, Dr Benjamin 215
judgement 10, 18, 41, 106, 108, 154, 233
justification 95, 96, 101, 102, 129, 176, 196, 202, 203, 204, 233

Kaiser Wilhelm 211
Kansas 108
Kendall, H.B. xxi, 44
Kent, John xxi, 6, 7, 8, 13, 14, 22, 23, 25, 42, 45, 146, 147, 151, 153, 155, 156, 217, 218, 219, 226
Kentucky 2, 3, 27, 30, 31, 142
Kessingland 166
Keswick 193, 194, 198, 213
Keswick Conference 198
Keswick Convention 119, 193, 197, 199, 209, 213, 214, 216, 219, 224
Keswick Higher Life Movement 120
Kimball, Edward 139
Knapp, Phoebe Palmer 118
Knox, John 166
Knoxville 30

Laicism 14
Lake District 219
Lander, Gerald 225

Index

Lane Presbyterian Seminary 75
Lankford, Sarah 117, 118, 119, 120, 121, 122, 134
Lankford, Thomas 117, 118, 119
La Prairie 92
Laqueur, T.W. 24
Latitudinarian 21
Lectures on Revival 9, 75, 80, 84, 86
Lectures on Revivals of Religion 4, 6, 26, 77
Leeds 22, 57, 93, 95, 96, 138
Leicester 42
Le Raysville 69
Lewiston 173, 179
Limerick 93
Lincoln 94, 99
Lincoln, Abraham 134, 140, 141, 143
Literalism 8, 9
Liverpool 12, 22, 41, 45, 47, 55, 56, 57, 78, 93, 95, 99, 103, 126, 127, 137, 145, 146, 149, 156, 159, 160, 169, 193, 194, 220, 221, 222
Logan, James 199
London xxi, 7, 20, 22, 47, 55, 56, 58, 59, 63, 65, 78, 79, 85, 102, 108, 126, 145, 146, 147, 148, 149, 150, 156, 159, 160, 161, 162, 169, 170, 171, 173, 179, 181, 182, 184, 185, 209, 212, 218, 220, 222, 223, 224, 225
London Docklands Conference 108
London Docks 56, 59
London Mission, 1875 146, 147, 160, 161
London Missionary Society 224
Lord's Day 56, 59, 166
Louth 98, 138
love feast 107, 192
Lowestoft 166
Luther, Martin 12, 155
Lynn 54

Macclesfield 40, 43, 94, 137
Magic Methodists xxi
Mahan, Asa 75, 80
Maine 52, 173, 178, 179
Manchester 57, 58, 80, 93, 98, 112, 130, 137, 138, 145, 156, 221
Mann, Horace 23
Market Rasen 99

Massachusetts 1, 28, 33, 54, 63, 151
Matheson, James 2
McGready, James 10, 45
McLouglin, William 12
Merritt, Revd Timothy 118
Methodism xx, xxi, 16, 21, 29, 35, 38, 42, 43, 48, 92, 94, 108, 113, 114, 150, 217, 225, 233
Methodist Episcopal Church 3, 10, 91, 135, 143, 197, 198, 233
Methodist Free Chapel 99, 233
Metropolitan Tabernacle 151, 171
Meyer, F.B. 145, 147
Mildmay Conference 145, 208
millennium 9, 18
Miller, William 19, 32
Millet, Sarah 133
mine workers 16
Mississippi 33, 40, 142
Mohawk Valley 19
Montreal 92, 93, 173
Moody and Sankey xxi, 146, 147, 148, 149, 150, 155, 161, 162, 217, 220, 221, 223, 226
Moody, Dwight Lyman xxi, 9, 14, 17, 18, 19, 26, 47, 87, 105, 139, 139–163, 173, 178, 185, 212, 217, 220, 221, 223, 224, 226
Moody, Edwin 139
Moorhouse, Henry 145, 147
Motherwell 168
Mount Temple, Lord 194, 198, 209, 213
mourners 31, 40, 43, 44, 110, 170, 233
Mow Hill 41
Muller, George 144, 170
music 6, 7, 14, 45, 67, 86, 87, 112, 118, 143, 144, 154, 155, 156, 157, 158, 162, 221, 233
Musselburgh 165, 179

Nebraska 186
Nettleton, Revd Asa 71, 88
Nevin, John W. 80
New Brunswick 184
Newcastle-under-Lyme 98
Newcastle-upon-Tyne 58, 59, 126, 129, 132, 145, 158, 159, 219
New Jersey 49, 92, 199, 201, 203

New School Presbyterians 88, 117
New York Anti-Slavery Society 83
New York Missionary Magazine 10
New York State 19, 40, 67, 69, 91, 180
Nicolite Quakers 30
Noel, Revd Baptist 170, 182, 185, 222
North Carolina 3
North Market Mission 139, 140
North Street Mission 140
Nottingham xix, 42, 94, 97, 99
Noyes, Humphrey 84

Oakington 192
Oakland 175, 183
Oberlin College 15, 75, 76, 77, 80, 89, 132
Oberlin Female Anti-Slavery Society 76
Oberlin Female Moral Reform Society 76
Oberlin First Congregational Church 80
Oberlin, Jean Frederick 75
Odd Fellows 190
Older Dissenters xx, 21
Old School Calvinists 85
Old School Congregationalism 88
Old School Presbyterians 75, 88
Origin of Species 23, 24
Oriskany Creek 73
Orr, J. Edwin 5
Oxford 210, 215
Oxford Conference 210, 211, 212, 216, 219
Oxford Place Chapel 95
Oxford University 150, 152, 199, 215, 221

Pakefield 166
Paley, Archdeacon William 21, 25
Palmer, Dr Walter 14, 17, 26, 87, 117–138, 221, 222, 226
Palmer, Phoebe 12, 14, 15, 16, 17, 26, 87, 103, 117–138, 196, 207, 219, 221, 222, 225, 226
parochial boundary 159
Patterson, James 72
Pearsall Smith, Hannah Whitall 196, 199–216
Pearsall Smith, Logan 199, 200, 201, 202, 209, 212, 214, 215

Pearsall Smith, Robert 196, 199–216
Pearsall Smith, Robert and Hannah 14, 87, 199, 200, 201, 202, 208, 209, 210, 211, 212, 213, 214, 215, 219, 221, 224
penitent form 5, 11, 13, 83, 109, 233
penitents 13, 43, 86, 105, 110, 157, 233
Pennefather, William 145, 172
Pennsylvania 32, 49, 143, 189, 199, 200, 202, 204
Penrith 129, 137
Pentecost 56, 100, 143
Pentecostal, Pentecostalism 114, 128, 129, 219
Perceval, Spencer 20
Philadelphia 34, 50, 54, 72, 74, 77, 143, 159, 191, 199, 200, 203, 211
Pittsfield Circuit 29
Plain Account of Christian Perfection 76
Plymouth Brethren 21, 160, 202, 203
Pontefract 56, 57
Poole 131, 137
Poor Law 20, 23
Portland, Maine 173, 178
post-millennial 18
Potteries 40, 42, 46, 98
prayer, prayer meetings 67, 70, 83, 85, 110, 112, 132, 156, 157, 218, 221, 222, 223, 224, 233
preacher, preaching 1, 4, 5, 6, 7, 8, 10, 11, 14, 15, 17, 19, 21, 27, 28, 29, 30, 31, 32, 33, 34, 36, 38, 39, 40, 44, 47, 53, 54, 55, 56, 58, 60, 61, 62, 63, 67, 69, 70, 71, 72, 74, 75, 77, 78, 79, 81, 82, 83, 84, 85, 88, 89, 91, 92, 93, 97, 98, 99, 100, 104, 105, 106, 111, 112, 114, 120, 131, 132, 133, 136, 143, 145, 146, 148, 150, 152, 153, 154, 157, 158, 161, 166, 169, 171, 174, 176, 178, 189, 190, 192, 195, 200, 208, 209, 211, 218, 221, 222, 233
Pre-Millennialism 151, 152
Presbyterian Church 3, 72, 73, 74, 88, 128, 169, 179, 186, 194, 233
Presbyterians 21, 31, 46, 75, 117, 160, 202, 205, 218, 233
Price, Charles 197
Primitive Methodism, Primitive Methodist xx, xxi, 15, 16, 27, 42, 43, 44, 48, 95, 217, 218, 225, 233

Index 239

Primitive Methodist Magazine 42, 233
Promise of the Father 132, 225
prophesying 1, 9, 56, 133, 145
prostitutes 140, 141, 222
Protracted Meeting 25, 85
Providence 35, 92, 115
publicity xxi, 6, 15, 46, 47, 83, 86, 111, 112, 159, 162, 220, 222, 233

Quaker/s, Quakerism 21, 30, 31, 46, 51, 55, 199, 200, 202, 213, 215, 233
Quebec 92, 93

racial equality 62
Radcliffe, Reginald 222
Radicalism 15, 225, 233
Radstock, Lord 147
Randall, Ian 197
Rayl, Rebecca 80
Red River xx
Reed, Andrew 2
Rees, Revd Arthur 145, 160
Reid, Revd William 169
Religious Census, 1851 23
Religious Exercises 45, 233
Religious impressions 233
Revell, Emma 142
Revival Hymnbook 12, 233
revivalism xx, xxi, 1, 3, 5, 6, 8, 12, 13, 15, 19, 21, 22, 26, 44, 45, 47, 60, 73, 80, 89, 94, 104, 113, 114, 155, 162, 180, 196, 202, 217, 219, 220, 221, 223, 224, 226, 233
revivalists xxi, xxiii, 3, 4, 5, 8, 9, 10, 12, 13, 14, 15, 16, 17, 18, 19, 21, 25, 26, 40, 52, 60, 89, 91, 103, 136, 147, 167, 199, 217, 219, 220, 221, 222, 224, 225, 226, 233
revival methods 71, 91, 233
Revival Miscellanies 106, 109, 110, 112, 233
Revival songs 233
Rhode Island 35, 38, 55, 115
Richardson, Revd Thomas 148
Rochdale 111, 219
Rochester 19, 35, 69, 72, 73, 85, 86, 150, 180, 181

Roman Catholic, Roman Catholicism 13, 14, 35, 48, 107
Rome 69, 70, 72, 82
Ryder, Henry (Bishop of Lichfield) 20

Sacred Songs and Solos 12, 18, 149, 156, 157, 162, 221
Salem 54, 56, 64, 191, 192
Salford 57
Salvation Army 97, 120, 133, 134, 186, 219, 226
San Francisco 174, 186
Sankey, Ira David xxi, 12, 14, 18, 143, 144, 145, 146, 147, 148, 149, 150, 153, 154, 155, 156, 157, 158, 161, 162, 217, 220, 221, 223, 226
Sankey's hymns 12, 149
Savannah 30, 46
Scarborough 94
Scioto Circuit 11
Scotland 126, 148, 150, 159, 167, 168, 169, 174, 175, 179, 194, 210
Second Coming 18, 19, 151
Second Great Awakening xix, xx, 1, 2, 3, 5, 10, 12, 17, 30, 31, 39, 45, 82, 85
Second World War 162
secularisation 22, 23, 25, 233
Sellers, C.C. 35, 48
sermons xx, 7, 20, 38, 44, 54, 58, 64, 71, 78, 83, 85, 89, 93, 97, 101, 104, 107, 111, 112, 113, 117, 143, 144, 145, 153, 154, 156, 160, 176, 177, 209, 233
Shaftesbury, Seventh Earl of 20, 147, 152
shaking 5, 30, 47, 213, 233
Sheffield 20, 22, 94, 97, 98, 99, 100, 107, 113, 114, 145, 149, 160, 219
Sheffield West Circuit 114
Shum, Mr Ralph Bressey 65
singing xxi, 11, 12, 14, 16, 43, 45, 49, 51, 59, 61, 99, 112, 130, 145, 155, 156, 166, 174, 178, 181, 182, 192, 197, 233
Sing Sing Camp Ground 192, 197
slave, slavery 3, 15, 16, 17, 39, 62, 63, 76, 83, 89, 134, 135, 136, 141, 187, 188, 194, 220, 225, 233
Smith, Amanda Berry 14, 15, 16, 187–198, 220, 221, 225
Smith, Mazie 191, 192

Snethen, Nicholas 28, 44
songs 12, 18, 45, 49, 130, 144, 149, 155, 156, 157, 158, 162, 198, 233
South Carolina 3, 141
South Wales 222
Southwold 166
speaking with tongues 128, 129, 145
Spiers, Samuel 171, 172, 173
Spitalfields 59
Sprague, William 4, 5, 26
Spring, Gardiner 5
Spurgeon, Charles 144, 161, 171
Staffordshire xxi, 27, 42, 46, 98
Staffordshire Potteries 98
status of women 1, 5, 7, 10, 14, 15, 16, 21, 22, 24, 25, 26, 37, 42, 55, 56, 57, 64, 76, 77, 79, 89, 117, 120, 122, 128, 132, 133, 136, 140, 142, 147, 155, 156, 157, 168, 170, 177, 178, 185, 186, 192, 194, 195, 196, 198, 210, 220, 221, 225, 233
St George's Circuit 65
St Ives 78, 83
St Lawrence 68, 69
St Louis 174
St Marylebone 20
Stockport 58
Stone, Barton 2, 16, 45
Stone, Lucy 15, 76
Stout, Harry 7
Stroud 126, 137
Studd, Charles 151, 225
Sunday School 24, 141, 143, 153, 162, 172, 173, 220
Sunderland 12, 48, 59, 94, 126, 137, 145, 150
supernaturalism 10, 11
Surrey Chapel 170, 182
Switzerland 208, 210, 213

Tait, Archbishop 150
Tappan, Arthur 75
Tappan, Lewis 74
Taylor, Dan xix, 21
temperance 3, 17, 26, 89, 93, 95, 103, 120, 130, 131, 132, 136, 153, 161, 196, 198, 214, 215, 219, 220, 225, 226
temperance movement 130, 136

Tennessee 2, 10, 11, 27, 30, 31, 142
Tennyson 25
Tent Methodists xxi
The Covenant Book 182
The Female Missionary Society of the Western District the State of New York 69
Thoburn, James 187, 198
Thorold, Anthony, Bishop of Rochester 149, 150
Three Rivers 93
Tillicoultry 168
Tonnon Street Chapel 57
Toronto 92
Torrey, Reuben 87, 143, 221, 226
tracts 26, 41, 42, 47, 134, 142, 184
trade unionism, trade unionists 149, 155, 218, 225, 226
Troy 35, 70, 71, 72, 73, 91, 106
Tunstall 27, 42
Twelve Days Mission to London 223
Twiss, Richard 221
Tyler, Samuel 171

Under Ground Railroad 16, 188
union meetings 16, 155, 175, 213
Union Theological Seminary 165
Unitarians 6, 21
United Methodist Free churches 113
United Methodists 99, 150, 160
United Presbyterian Church 169
Upham, Phoebe L. 122, 134
Utica 19, 73, 87, 186

Vermont 31, 34, 92, 165
visiting prisoners 134, 135, 186

Wakefield 94
Walker, Revd R.G. 169, 180
Walsall 99, 138
Wandsworth 161
Ward, Mrs Humphry 23
Warfield, Benjamin 209
War of Independence 2
Warren Circuit 28
Warrington 34, 40
Washington 34, 35, 54, 61, 174
Waterloo 19

Index

Weaver, Richard 222
Wesleyan Methodism, Methodist 21, 27, 40, 42, 94, 95, 97, 98, 110, 113, 114, 125, 126, 133, 136, 219
Wesleyan Methodist Magazine 40, 125, 126
Wesleyan/s xx, xxi, 15, 16, 21, 27, 29, 40, 41, 42, 55, 56, 57, 58, 59, 65, 93, 94, 95, 97, 98, 100, 101, 110, 113, 114, 115, 125, 126, 129, 131, 133, 136, 150, 160, 217, 218, 219, 225
Wesleyan Times 100, 218
Wesley, Charles xix, xx, 12, 155, 157
Wesley Grove camp meetings 192
Wesley, John xix, xx, 12, 21, 31, 39, 40, 76, 97, 100, 101, 102, 105, 108, 127, 133, 135, 192, 219
Westminster Confession 88
Weston-Super-Mare 169, 180
Westwall, R. 171
Wheatley, Richard 124, 136
Whitall, Hannah Tatum 199, 200, 201, 214
White, Charles 120
Whitefield, George xx, 1, 3, 6, 7, 31, 40, 47, 78, 89, 218
Whitefield's Tabernacle 78, 218

Whitehall circuit 91
Willard, Frances 132
Williams College 165
Wilson, Robert 213, 216
Wimber, John 108
Winslow, Miss M.E. 182
Wise, Revd Daniel 95, 111, 113
Wishaw 168
Wolverhampton 20, 99, 103, 138
Woman Preacher 134
Women's Christian Temperance Union 196
Women's National Christian Temperance Union 215
women's rights 15, 76, 136, 220, 225
Woodworth-Etter, Maria 52
Worrall, Henry and Dorothea 117, 118
Wright, Benjamin 67, 68

Yale 3, 67
Yates, Reverend Richard 20
York 94, 145, 147, 159
Yorkshire 56, 57, 65
Young, Ebenezer 168, 175
Young Men's Christian Association (YMCA) 140, 141, 142, 144, 145

www.ingramcontent.com/pod-product-compliance
Lightning Source LLC
Chambersburg PA
CBHW050437240426
43661CB00055B/2420